TEACHING PLATO IN ITALIAN RENAISSANCE UNIVERSITIES

STUDIA ARTISTARUM
ÉTUDES SUR LA FACULTÉ DES ARTS DANS LES UNIVERSITÉS MÉDIÉVALES

VOLUME 51

Directeurs honoraires
Louis Holtz
Olga Weijers

Sous la direction de
Luca Bianchi, *Università degli Studi di Milano*
Dominique Poirel, *Institut de Recherche et d'Histoire des Textes*

Secrétaire de rédaction
Emmanuelle Kuhry, *Paris*

Henk Braakhuis, *Nijmegen*
Charles Burnett, *London*
Dragos Calma, *Dublin*
Anne Grondeux, *Paris*
Jean-Pierre Rothschild, *Paris*
Cecilia Trifogli, *Oxford*

Teaching Plato in Italian Renaissance Universities

Edited by
EVA DEL SOLDATO AND MAUDE VANHAELEN

BREPOLS

© 2024, Brepols Publishers n.v., Turnhout, Belgium.

All rights reserved. No part of this publication may be reproduced, stored in a retrieval system, or transmitted, in any form or by any means, electronic, mechanical, photocopying, recording, or otherwise without the prior permission of the publisher.

D/2024/0095/47
ISBN 978-2-503-60785-6
eISBN 978-2-503-60786-3
DOI 10.1484/M.SA-EB.5.135221
ISSN 2032-1252
eISSN 2294-8376

Printed in the EU on acid-free paper.

Contents

Introduction   7

Teaching Plato in Sixteenth-Century Italy
Maude VANHAELEN   21

Teaching Plato in Sixteenth- and Seventeenth-Century Florence and Pisa. From Francesco Cattani da Diacceto to Girolamo Bardi
Simone FELLINA   59

Shifting Away from Aristotelianism towards Platonism. Paolo Beni's Project
Barbara BARTOCCI   91

Plato between Pavia and Milan in the Sixteenth Century
Eva DEL SOLDATO   119

Bibliography   149

Index   169

Introduction

The chapters collected in this volume evolved out of two research events, a conference panel organized by Maude Vanhaelen at the Renaissance Society of America (RSA) Annual Meeting held in Toronto in March 2019, followed by a workshop organized by Eva Del Soldato, at the Dipartimento "Piero Martinetti" di Filosofia at the Università Statale of Milan in June 2019. The purpose of these events was twofold: first, to examine the extent to which Renaissance university professors engaged directly with Plato's dialogues in their teaching, and second, to reflect on why modern scholars have neglected this important chapter in the history of the Platonic tradition. Several studies have already shown that Plato made some limited incursion into university teaching from the middle of the fifteenth century onwards, culminating with the creation of a chair of Platonic philosophy at the University of Pisa in 1576[1]. But the general consensus is that those who taught Plato were "Platonists", who either proposed, like Francesco de' Vieri (Verino Secondo, 1524-1591), a watered-down version of Ficino's Platonism that could be easily accommodated with Aristotle and the Christian ideals of the Counter-Reformation, or made vain attempts, like Francesco Patrizi da Cherso (1529-1597), to propose a radical overhaul of university teaching and replace Aristotle with Plato and the Pre-Socratic tradition. It is generally assumed that, in

---

1 P. O. KRISTELLER, "Francesco da Diacceto and Florentine Platonism in the Sixteenth Century", in Id., *Studies in Renaissance Thought and Letters. I*, Rome, Edizioni di Storia e Letteratura, 1956, pp. 287-336: 291-93; C. B. SCHMITT, "Platon et Aristote dans les universités et les collèges du XVIe siècle. L'introduction de la philosophie platonicienne dans l'enseignement des universités à la Renaissance", in M. DE GANDILLAC and J.-C. MARGOLIN (eds), *Platon et Aristote à la Renaissance*. XVIe colloque international de Tours, Paris, Vrin, 1976, pp. 93-104; M. MUCCILLO, "Il platonismo all'Università di Roma: Francesco Patrizi", in P. CHERUBINI (ed.), *Roma e lo Studium Urbis. Spazio urbano e cultura dal Quattro al Seicento*. Atti del convegno (Roma, 7-10 giugno 1989), Rome, Ministero per i beni culturali e ambientali, 1992, pp. 200-247; P. GRENDLER, *The Universities of the Italian Renaissance*, Baltimore, Johns Hopkins University Press, 2002, pp. 297-309; C. VASOLI, "Platone allo Studio Fiorentino-Pisano", in *Rinascimento*, 41, 2nd s., 2001, pp. 39-69; S. FELLINA, "Platone a scuola: l'insegnamento di Francesco de' Vieri detto il Verino secondo", in *Noctua*, 2/1-2 (2015), pp. 97-181 and Id., *Platone allo Studium Fiorentino-Pisano (1576-1635)*, Verona, Scripta, 2019.

contrast, professors of Aristotelian philosophy never ventured to lecture on Plato; when they did mention Plato in their courses, it was only to pay lip service to a philosophical movement that developed mainly outside the university walls[2].

Indeed, if one is to evaluate the presence of Plato in Italian universities uniquely on superficial quantitative elements, one would be disappointed by the scarce number of university chairs of Platonism and their relatively short-lived success. And yet, by the second half of the sixteenth century, Plato was playing an important role in university teaching, not necessarily in courses focused on his philosophy, but rather in courses devoted to the standard texts of Aristotelian teaching. In fact, a relevant number of university lectures and commentaries on Plato were offered by prominent intellectuals who are today considered "Aristotelians". These works are far from being the result of a nebulous or indirect engagement with Platonic ideas; rather they provide unmistakable evidence that, especially after the 1540s, Aristotelians devoted much time and effort to read and interpret in great detail Plato's dialogues, sometimes in the context of their teaching[3]. The story of the Zimara family, father and son, is particularly instructive in this sense and revealing of a "Platonic" turn among Aristotelians: the father, Marcantonio (c. 1470-1532 or 1537) was a professor in Padua and regarded Plato's philosophy with contempt. In contrast, his son Teofilo (1515-1589), a physician in Lecce, published a commentary on *De anima* (1584), in which he stated that it was impossible to understand Aristotle without an adequate knowledge of Plato's philosophy[4]. And in some cases these "Aristotelians" like the younger Zimara were interested in Plato not simply to gain a better understanding of the *corpus Aristotelicum*[5], but out of sheer interest in Platonic philosophy. Moreover, in spite of the ephemeral existence of the chair of Platonism, a more careful study of the Platonic philosophy taught at the University of Pisa by *magistri* like Francesco de' Vieri, suggests that, far from being simply a diluted version of Ficino's Platonism, it was the result of varied and complex exegetical strategies, which in turn led to significant and often new interpretations of Plato's dialogues. Conversely, Patrizi's

---

2 See e.g. GRENDLER, *The Universities of the Italian Renaissance*, p. 298.
3 On the reception of Plato in sixteenth-century Italy, see M. VANHAELEN, "Éclectisme, aristotélisme et platonisme dans la pensée italienne du XVIe siècle", in D. DUMOUCHEL et C. LEDUC (eds), *Les -ismes et catégories historiographiques: Formation et usage à l'époque moderne*, Quebec City, Les Presses de l'Université Laval, 2021, pp. 95-112, and her forthcoming monograph *Plato in the Place of Aristotle. The Reception of Plato's Dialogues in Sixteenth-Century Italy*.
4 See T. ZIMARA, *In tres Aristotelis libros De anima*, Venice, Giunta, 1584, f. 305v. See also B. NARDI, *Saggi sull'aristotelismo padovano dal secolo XIV al XVI*, Florence, Sansoni, 1958, pp. 321-363; C. BLACKWELL, "Neo-Platonic Modes of Concordism Versus Definitions of Difference", in S. CLUCAS, P.J. FORSHAW, V. REES (eds), *Laus Platonici Philosophi*, Leiden, Brill, 2011, pp. 321-432.
5 In some cases, reading Plato helped to expose Aristotle's mystifications. See, e.g., C. MARTIN, "Interpreting Plato's Geometrical Elements in Renaissance Aristotle Commentaries", in A. CORRIAS and E. DEL SOLDATO (eds), *Harmony and Contrast: Plato and Aristotle in the Early Modern Period*, Oxford, Oxford University Press, 2022, pp. 149-171.

project to replace Aristotle with Plato did not develop out of nothing, but was one of several attempts to respond to the religious and cultural crisis of the time, which can be traced back to the very early years of the sixteenth century, if not to the mid-fifteenth century.

Another assumption that has led modern scholars to downplay the presence of Plato in university teaching is the idea that, unlike Aristotle's treatises, Plato's dialogues could hardly be accommodated to the university curriculum: in the Middle Ages, the majority of the dialogues were unavailable in Latin translation; their unsystematic, cross-disciplinary character did not fit the strict disciplinary boundaries of medieval university teaching; and the attention Plato paid to the dramatic setting of the dialogues was deemed foreign to the study of philosophy[6]. However, as already shown by Luca Bianchi, it is difficult to understand why Plato, who was held in such high esteem by the Church Fathers and ancient *auctoritates* like Cicero, became a marginal author in the universities of the thirteenth century. After all, Platonic manuscripts were available in the Middle Ages, the dialogues were not more difficult to translate than Aristotle's treatises, and there existed an exegetical tradition (i.e. Neoplatonism) that could have allowed the West to familiarize itself more fully with Plato[7]. In fact, one of the points of the present book is to explore the extent to which Renaissance commentators reconnected with the tradition of teaching Plato and Aristotle in the Neoplatonic schools of Late Antiquity, in Rome, Athens and Alexandria, between the third and the sixth centuries AD. The specifically pedagogical elements of the Neoplatonic tradition include the establishment of a proper school curriculum determining the order in which to study Plato's dialogues and the way to integrate Aristotle, as well as numerous commentaries written by the professors teaching in those schools (from Plotinus to Olympiodorus). In the context of their teaching, these professors progressively re-organized the dialogues into systematic analyses of Plato's philosophy, established detailed comparison with Aristotle, re-casted Plato's arguments into Aristotelian syllogisms, and even sometimes attempted to make them compatible with Christianity — all aspects that could appeal to students in pre-modern and early modern universities[8]. In other words, this

---

[6] The same assumption is made in relation to Renaissance teaching: see e.g. GRENDLER, *The Universities of the Italian Renaissance*, p. 308.

[7] L. BIANCHI, "L'acculturazione filosofica dell'Occidente", in *Id.* (ed.), *La filosofia delle università. Secoli XIII-XIV*, Florence, La nuova Italia, 1997, pp. 17-21.

[8] On the Neoplatonic curriculum, see A.-J. FESTUGIÈRE, "L'ordre de lecture des dialogues de Platon aux ve/vi^e siècles", in *Museum Helveticum*, 26, 1969, pp. 281-296; I. HADOT, "The Role of the Commentaries on Aristotle in the Teaching of Philosophy According to the Prefaces of the Neoplatonic Commentaries on the *Categories*", in H. BLUMENTHAL and H. ROBINSON (eds), *Aristotle and the Later Tradition*, Oxford, Oxford University Press, 1991, pp. 175-189; *Ead.*, "Aristote dans l'enseignement philosophique néoplatonicien. Les préfaces des commentaires sur les *Catégories*", in *Revue de Théologie et de Philosophie*, 124, 1992, pp. 407-425; P. HOFFMANN, "La fonction des prologues exégétiques dans la pensée pédagogique néoplatonicienne", in B. ROUSSEL and J.-D. DUBOIS (eds), *Entrer en matière*, Paris, Cerf, 1998, pp. 209-245; *Id.*, "What

tradition, which was progressively recovered in the Renaissance, not only reveals that Plato had been taught alongside Aristotle in an institutionalized setting for several centuries, but also, and more importantly, that he could be taught within a pedagogical context that could be adapted, at least in part, to the university curriculum. Renaissance specialists have often neglected the didactic elements of the Neoplatonic tradition, in part because Marsilio Ficino, who was the first to recover the Neoplatonic commentaries in a comprehensive way, favoured the allegorical, theological and mystical dimensions of Neoplatonism. But the revival of Neoplatonic texts did not stop with Ficino, and evidence suggests that the sixteenth century witnessed a renewed interest in commentators like Olympiodorus, whose extant lecture notes on Plato provide a pedagogical interpretative framework (lemmatic structure, use of syllogisms, etc.) that significantly overlap with some of the exegetical techniques used by Renaissance professors of Aristotelian philosophy[9]. Moreover, even ancient biographical sources could conjure to the eyes of Renaissance philosophers the image of Plato as an effective teacher. The passage in which Diogenes Laertius claimed that Aristotle "attached himself to Plato and resided with him for twenty years", became almost proverbial among those who were eager to prove Plato's merits and claimed that Aristotle would have not accepted to follow an incompetent and confusing teacher for so many years[10].

The questions that arise from these preliminary findings are, therefore, three: first, why have modern scholars systematically ignored a vast array of philosophical works on Plato produced in sixteenth-century Italy? Second, how and why did some Aristotelians turn to the interpretation of Plato in their teaching? And, third, could the format and content of Plato's dialogues, generally considered as

---

was Commentary in Late Antiquity? The Example of the Neoplatonic Commentators", in M. L. GILL and P. PELLEGRIN (eds), *A Companion to Ancient Philosophy*, Oxford, Blackwell, 2006, pp. 597-622.

9 On sixteenth-century copies of Olympiodorus' and Damascius' Platonic commentaries (all attributed to Olympiodorus in the Renaissance), see W. NORVIN (ed.), *Olympiodori in Platonis Phaedonem commentaria*, Leipzig, Teubner, 1913, pp. v-x; L. G. WESTERINK (ed.), *Olympiodorus. Commentary on the First Alcibiades of Plato. Critical Text and Indices*, Amsterdam, North-Holland Publishing Company, 1956, p. VII, and C. B. SCHMITT, "Olympiodorus Alexandrinus philosophus", in P. O. KRISTELLER et al. (eds), *Catalogus translationum et commentariorum*, Washington, Catholic University of America, vol. II, 1971, pp. 199-204.

10 DIOGENES LAERTIUS, *Lives of Eminent Philosophers* 5.1.9. Diogenes Laertius' *Lives* were translated into Latin by Ambrogio Traversari (1433). The trend of celebrating Plato as a revered teacher of Aristotle was likely launched — relying on Laertius — by Cardinal Bessarion in his *In calumniatorem Platonis*, a work that widely circulated in the university milieu for at least two centuries after its publication in 1469. See C.B. SCHMITT, *Aristotle and the Renaissance*, Cambridge, MA, Harvard University Press, 1983, p. 41; E. DEL SOLDATO, "Bessarion as an Aristotelian, Bessarion among the Aristotelians", in S. MARIEV (ed.), *Bessarion's Treasure. Editing, Translating and Interpreting Bessarion's Literary Heritage*, Berlin-Boston, De Gruyter, 2021, pp. 169-184.

ill-suited to university teaching, be actually adapted to Renaissance curricula, and in what context?

Maude Vanhaelen tackles these questions in Chapter I, by arguing that the limited attention modern scholars have paid so far to Plato's incursion in fields traditionally reserved to Aristotle is borne out, first, of misconceived ideas about university teaching practices. University statutes, which since 1255 imposed upon the Arts Faculty the obligation to teach from the Aristotelian corpus, do not necessarily provide the final word on the teaching material that was covered in the classroom[11]: the continuous circulation of glossed *Timaeus* manuscripts between the Middle Ages and the Renaissance, as outlined among others by James Hankins[12], suggests that the practice of reading the *Timaeus* at pre-university and university level survived despite the prohibition by University authorities to read other authors than Aristotle. Similarly, extant university lectures presented in this chapter show that professors could easily deviate from the prescribed syllabus and discuss Platonic philosophy, either in the private setting of their homes, or in public lectures. Second, she argues that the increasing success of Plato in contexts dominated by Aristotle has often been mislabelled as a form of "eclecticism", with little attention being actually paid to *how* and *why* Renaissance interpreters felt the need to either integrate Platonic material in commentaries on Aristotle, or interrupt their study of Aristotle altogether and devote their teaching to Plato's dialogues[13]. Her main argument, which is in part borrowed from the conclusions of John Dillon and others in relation to eclecticism in Late ancient philosophy[14], is that the "eclectic" attitude of sixteenth-century Renaissance philosophers was motivated by a need to put some order in a philosophical tradition that had become diffuse and multiform, and to establish a clearer distinction between, on the one hand, the authors and their commentators, and on the other, Aristotle's arguably biased representation of Plato, and Plato's actual thought. Through close examination of hitherto unstudied commentaries and university lectures written

---

11 On this important point in relation to medieval university curricula, see D. BUZZETTI, "La Faculté des arts dans les universités de l'Europe méridionale. Quelques problèmes de recherches", in O. WEIJERS and L. HOLTZ (eds), *L'enseignement des disciplines à la Faculté des arts (Paris et Oxford, XIIIe-XVe siècles)*, Turnhout, Brepols, 1997, pp. 457-466: 465: "on a ainsi constaté que non seulement la diffusion des doctrines est le résultat de la production des textes, mais aussi que l'évolution et l'élaboration finale des textes sont elles-mêmes le résultat de la diffusion des doctrines et de la persistance de leur enseignement. C'est l'utilisation continue dans la pratique d'enseignement qui fixe, après un processus qui dure parfois plusieurs générations, la forme finale des ouvrages qui nous sont parvenus".

12 J. HANKINS, "The Study of the *Timaeus* in Early Renaissance Italy", in A. GRAFTON and N. SIRAISI (eds), *Natural Particulars: Nature and the Disciplines in Renaissance Europe*, Cambridge, MA, MIT University Press, 1999, pp. 77-119.

13 On Aristotelian eclecticism, see C.B. SCHMITT, *Aristotle and the Renaissance*, Cambridge, MA, Harvard University Press, 1983.

14 J. M. DILLON and A. A. LONG (eds), *The Question of "Eclecticism". Studies in Later Greek Philosophy*, Berkeley-Los Angeles-London, University of California Press, 1988.

by prestigious university professors in Padua, Bologna, Rome, and Venice, she argues that some sixteenth-century interpreters like Francesco Piccolomini, for instance, turned towards Plato precisely because they wished to verify the veracity of what both ancient commentators and Aristotle himself had written about Plato, and offer a more "balanced" account of the *comparatio* between Plato and Aristotle[15]. She also shows that the format of Plato's dialogues was carefully adapted for the purpose of teaching, their structure reorganized in the form of thematic treatises and their arguments recast in the form of syllogisms, such as in the case of Chrysostomus Javelli's monumental Platonic commentaries; that commentators progressively distanced themselves from Ficino's interpretation by renouncing, at least in part, the mystical aspects of Neoplatonism and by placing instead greater emphasis on Plato's moral and natural philosophy and rhetoric; and how, in this context, some interpreters came to privilege the didactic and philological aspects of the Neoplatonic tradition, by either turning towards lesser known ancient commentators like Olympiodorus, or exploiting the pedagogical aspects of better known commentaries such as Proclus' lectures on Plato's *Republic*. In that respect, therefore, one can argue that these Renaissance professors appropriated key elements of the pedagogical framework inherited from the Platonic schools of Late Antiquity, to propose a new Plato that could be taught in the universities.

Paradoxically, perhaps, these new perspectives on Plato developed primarily in Aristotelian circles, because they were often closely linked to the new exegetical and philological advances of what Luca Bianchi has called "scholastic humanism"[16]. But they were also to a great extent related to the cultural and religious crises of the time: as all four chapters show, both the Pomponazzi affair and the Counter-Reformation played a crucial role in the reassessment of the place Plato could take in philosophical curricula. More specifically, reading Plato sometimes allowed university professors to solve the tensions between philosophy and faith that the Averroist interpretations of Aristotle had considerably contributed to worsen, and offer what was perceived as a more spiritual form of thought. Of course, by the sixteenth century the notion that Plato was more compatible with Christianity than Aristotle was a commonplace: it had roots in patristic literature, had been central to Cardinal Bessarion's defence of Plato and had been taken up by Marsilio Ficino to justify his *renovatio platonica* against the impious commentators of Aristotle. But what has not been sufficiently appreciated, perhaps,

---

15 On this trend see also E. DEL SOLDATO, "Between Past and Present: Paganino Gaudenzi (1595-1649) and the *comparatio* Tradition", in CORRIAS and DEL SOLDATO, *Harmony and Contrast: Plato and Aristotle in the Early Modern Period*, pp. 172-188.
16 L. BIANCHI, "Una caduta senza declino? Considerazioni sulla crisi dell'aristotelismo fra rinascimento ed età moderna", in F. DOMINGUEZ, R. IMBACH, T. PINDL and P. WALTER (eds), *Aristotelica et Lulliana magistro doctissimo Charles H. Lohr septuagesimum annum feliciter agenti dedicata*, Turnhout, Brepols, 1995, pp. 181-222 and *Id.*, "Interpréter Aristote par Aristote. Parcours de l'herméneutique philosophique à la Renaissance", in *Methodos*, 2 (2002) [https://journals.openedition.org/methodos/98?lang = fr, last accessed December 7, 2021].

is the length to which some sixteenth-century commentators went to offer new interpretations of Plato to serve Christianity, and — even more importantly — the fact that they often did so independently from Ficino's Neoplatonic heritage, that is to say, they moved away from Ficino's theological and mystical interpretation and provided instead a more "philological" reading of Plato's dialogues. By comparison, commentators reflecting on the relation between Aristotle and Christianity reacted mostly in two ways: either they embraced the incompatibility of Aristotle with Christianity and focused their efforts on studying Aristotle's natural philosophy in order to free themselves from the theological issues arising from some of his doctrines (an approach they paradoxically recovered from Bessarion)[17]; or they attempted in their turn to Christianize the Philosopher, in continuity with a trend established in the Middle Ages[18].

Taking into consideration this context, the Florentine Platonism of the late sixteenth century, best exemplified by Francesco de' Vieri, no longer appears as a marginal phenomenon or a vague repetition of Ficinian ideas. As Simone Fellina's chapter shows, the practice of teaching Plato *diebus festivis* at the University of Pisa during the sixteenth and the seventeenth centuries was never easy or straightforward: rather than being embedded permanently in the very structure of the University, it always depended on the willingness of keen politicians and the availability of Platonically oriented intellectuals. However, it was not simply an isolated occurrence destined to honour the politics of the Medici regime: it appears as a coherent philosophical movement, which drew partly on exegetical strategies that had been implemented by contemporary Aristotelian authors; used Plato's arguments to engage with the main philosophical debates of the time; and sometimes even followed interpretative trends that were typical of scholastic humanism. In other words, this tradition sought to provide answers to the very philosophical issues that defined sixteenth-century philosophy as a whole, including the question of method and order, the relationship between Plato and Christianity, and the Plato-Aristotle controversy. More specifically, these professors of Platonic philosophy appear to have exploited the various philosophical debates of the time precisely to justify the introduction of Plato in the university curricula: thus, their priority was to come up with exegetical strategies that allowed them to underline Plato's compatibility with Christianity, his agreement with Aristotle and his scientific and pedagogic merits. More importantly, Fellina shows how in this context Ficino's legacy progressively lost its importance. If in the early sixteenth century Francesco Cattani da Diacceto, Ficino's favorite pupil, had already renounced comparing paganism and Christianity, in the hands of these Platonic professors, Ficino's ideals of *prisca theologia* and *pia philosophia*, which formed the core of his revival of Plato, became mere commonplaces; the Neoplatonic authors that sustained Ficino's project of spiritual renovation progressively disappeared

---

17 See DEL SOLDATO, "Bessarion as an Aristotelian, Bessarion among the Aristotelians".
18 On the Christianisation of Aristotle, see L. BIANCHI (ed.), *Christian Readings of Aristotle from the Middle Ages to the Renaissance*, Turnhout, Brepols, 2011.

from the corpus of *auctoritates*, often to be replaced by ancient and modern Aristotelian sources. However, the very fact that clear trends can be identified when discussing this lineage of Platonic professors, from de' Vieri to Bardi, passing through Mazzoni, proves that all of them — collectively and individually — had a well-defined philosophical program. Even if they were not able to achieve their goal, namely, to grant Plato a more secure institutionalized presence within the university, they nonetheless represented a vibrant, original page in the history of early modern Platonism, alternative not only to Ficino, but also to Jean De Serres[19].

Towards the end of the century, around the time de' Vieri was teaching Plato in Pisa, another important figure — Paolo Beni (d. 1625) — offered an altogether different perspective on Plato's dialogues, which in part echoed Patrizi's position and in part developed independently. Paolo Beni was already known as the author of the longest and most detailed commentary on the *Timaeus* ever written, only parts of which are available in print. What was not known is that Beni developed his interpretation of Plato in the context of his teaching. As shown by Barbara Bartocci in Chapter III, it was initially as a professor in various Jesuit schools that Beni lectured on Plato's dialogues and started to defend the superiority of Plato over Aristotle on the grounds that the former was closer to Christianity than the latter, an idea that was a far cry from the Jesuits' project of teaching a new form of Christian Aristotelianism to the world. Similarly, as a lecturer of natural philosophy at the Roman *studio*, Beni drew on the ideas of his friend Patrizi to argue that the compatibility of Plato with Christianity made him a more suitable author to study philosophy. Among the mass of documents pertaining to Beni's life and work, now in the Archivio Segreto Vaticano, several lecture notes taken by Beni's students (*reportationes*) show that in his courses on Aristotle Beni introduced long digressions where he compared Aristotle unfavourably with Plato. But Beni's defence of Plato went well beyond that: like many authors before him, he was aware that Plato's dialogues were deemed confusing and disorderly and, as a result, he took on the task of transforming Plato's dialogues to make them teachable. In a striking echo to what Javelli had done in Bologna fifty years earlier, Beni set out to demonstrate the systematic and coherent character of Plato's philosophy by choosing to interpret it in a scholastic commentary. Even more importantly, perhaps, Bartocci demonstrates that Beni's purpose was above all motivated by the political and religious climate of his time: like Patrizi he considered that "Platonism was a body of common knowledge on which there could be universal consensus, offering therefore the perfect ground for rebuilding Christian unity".[20] Rejecting the Neoplatonic prism used by Ficino to read Plato's dialogues, and being ready to expose the occasional limits of Platonism in matters of religion, Beni presented Plato's thought as a philosophy that could provide a

---

19 On Jean de Serres see E. N. TIGERSTEDT, *The Decline and Fall of the Neoplatonic Interpretation of Plato: An Outline and Some Observations*, Helsinki, Societas Scientiarum Fennica, 1974.
20 See p. 103.

better foundation to natural philosophy, especially astronomy, without undermining the prerogatives of Christian faith.

In Chapter IV, we come full circle with Eva Del Soldato's study of Platonic influences in the context of the university of Pavia (in public and private teaching, and in local academies), and the *Scuole Cannobiane* in Milan. In contrast with the other chapters of the volume, the focus here is very much on Platonic incursions within various Aristotelian frameworks — what would be traditionally described as forms of "eclectic Aristotelianism" — rather than on instances of exclusive engagement with Plato's dialogues. Yet as Del Soldato's detailed research shows, the study of the historical and cultural context in which Aristotelians integrated Platonic material in their lectures or commentaries on Aristotle, not only allows us to explain how and why these examples of philosophical selection took place, but also to link these to a well-established trend — that of lecturing on Plato or at least including considerable Platonic sections in university courses — which developed over a period of several decades throughout the sixteenth century. More specifically, she shows how the creation of a Platonic chair (again *diebus festivis*) at the University of Pavia in 1606 is in fact the result of a long history of varied Platonic presences within the walls of the *Studium Ticinense*. If in the first decades of the sixteenth century Plato in Pavia was mostly associated with metaphysical and theological discussions, he then became for several "Aristotelians" in the *Studium* (and its surroundings) an inescapable reference for understanding the Philosopher. Exegetical needs were the main, but not exclusive, reasons that led authors like Francesco Vimercato, Ottaviano Ferrari and Flaminio Papazzoni to engage with Platonic philosophy. Vimercato, in particular, had the merit to systematically re-introduce the pedagogical use of the *comparationes* in the university *milieu*, yet his attitude toward Plato had a particularly complex evolution dictated by the polemical needs of his times[21]. These *magistri*, Del Soldato shows, frequently engaged with Plato because of Aristotle's frequent criticisms of his teacher's doctrines. These criticisms, as seen also in the first essay in this volume, represented a welcome opportunity to delve into Platonic doctrines when commenting the corpus *Aristotelicum*. But even if Vimercato, Ferrari and Papazzoni generally embraced wholeheartedly Aristotle's rejection of Plato, their teaching practice allowed them to display an impressive familiarity with Platonic works, a familiarity that in the case of Papazzoni made of him a credible candidate for an ill-fated chair of Platonism in Bologna. Papazzoni's case is a definitive proof of the blurred divide, in terms of professors's expertise and in spite of their philosophical preferences, between Plato and Aristotle in the universities. On the basis of *reportationes*, curricula, and other documents, and by taking into consideration different aspects of the intellectual life of the university (public and private teaching at different levels, and the connections with local academies), Del Soldato shows

---

21 On Vimercato and Plato, see E. DEL SOLDATO, *Early Modern Aristotle. On the Making and Unmaking of Authority*, Philadelphia, University of Pennsylvania Press, 2020, pp. 55-61.

how in the second half of the sixteenth century introducing Plato in "traditional" courses was a given. This is demonstrated both by the double label of "Platonic" and "Aristotelian" attributed to some of the most celebrated university *magistri* of that time, and — conversely— by recommendations aimed at reducing the unofficial presence of Plato in the curriculum, which was evidently perceived at times as rambunctious and useless. Yet, a careful study of the various protagonists at play shows that there existed a philo-Platonic alliance of prominent intellectuals and theologians — some of whom, like Agostino Valier, had taught Plato at the university — who sought to push, often in vain, for university authorities to officially recognize the importance of teaching Plato alongside Aristotle.

One major centre of Platonic teaching that is not covered in this volume is Ferrara. Together with Rome, Pisa and Pavia, it is the only Italian university to have established a chair of Platonic philosophy, which was held by Francesco Patrizi between 1578 and 1592; Patrizi was subsequently invited by Pope Clement VIII to hold the newly created Platonic chair in the university of Rome (1592-1596 or 1597). The circumstances surrounding Patrizi's teaching are well-known[22], and given that his actual university lectures are no longer extant, we have decided not to include a specific study devoted to him in the present volume, and concentrate instead on lesser studied contexts and material. Suffice it to say here that the university of Ferrara had already witnessed the introduction of Platonic teaching in the fifteenth century: the Greek émigré Theodore Gaza lectured on Plato's *Gorgias* in 1446, whereas a professor of natural philosophy named Sebastiano Aquila (c. 1440-c. 1510) appears to have taught the *Timaeus* on holidays in 1497[23]. Similarly, Platonic studies in Ferrara do not seem to have stopped with Patrizi. In 1587, Tommaso Giannini (1556-1638), who taught dialectics, medical botany

---

22 See GRENDLER, *The Universities of the Italian Renaissance*, pp. 300-307 and, more specifically on Patrizi's teaching in Ferrara, see A. FRANCESCHINI, *Nuovi documenti relativi ai docenti dello Studio di Ferrara nel sec. XVI*, Ferrara, SATE, 1970, pp. 153, 157, 159, 164, 169, 174, 179, 185, 190, 195, 265; F. RASPADORI, *I maestri di medicina ed arti dell'Università di Ferrara (1391-1950)*, Florence, Olschki, 1991, p. 261; on his teaching in Rome, see MUCCILLO, "Il platonismo all'Università di Roma: Francesco Patrizi"; Ead., *Platonismo, ermetismo e 'prisca theologia'. Ricerche di storiografia filosofica rinascimentale*, Florence, Olschki, 1996.

23 On Theodore Gaza's teaching, see J. MONFASANI, "The Byzantine Rhetorical Tradition and the Renaissance", in J. J. MURPHY (ed.), *Renaissance Eloquence. Studies in the Theory and Practice of Renaissance Rhetoric*, Berkeley, University of California Press, 1983, pp. 174-87: 180; Id., "L'insegnamento universitario e la cultura bizantina in Italia nel Quattrocento", in L. AVELLINI (ed.), *Sapere e/è potere. Discipline, Dispute e Professioni nell'Università Medievale e Moderna: Il caso bolognese a confronto*, 3 vols, Bologna, Istituto per la Storia di Bologna, 1990, I, pp. 43-65: 48. The text of Gaza's course is preserved in MS V a 123 in the Folger Shakespeare Library in Washington. On Sebastiano Aquila, see P. O. KRISTELLER, *Supplementum Ficinianum Marsilii Ficini Florentini Philosophi platonici opuscula inedita et dispersa*, 2 vols, Florence, Olschki, 1937, II, p. 211 and Id., "Marsilio Ficino e Venezia", in *Studies in Renaissance Thought and Letters IV*, Rome, Edizioni di Storia e Letteratura, 1996, pp. 245-263: 260-261. The source is a letter Ariosto sent Aldo Manuzio in 1498 (L. ARIOSTO, *Lettere*, ed. A. STELLA, Milan, Mondadori, 1965, p. 3).

and natural philosophy at the Ferrarese *Studium*[24], published a work entitled *De providentia ad sententiam Platonis et Platonicorum liber unus*, which put together an impressive array of Platonic sources on the theme of providence[25]. Then, in 1594, another prominent figure, Antonio Montecatini (1537-1599), who was a close friend of Patrizi and the master of Giannini, and who taught astrology, moral and natural philosophy between 1560 and 1594[26], wrote commentaries on Aristotle's and Plato's political philosophy, printed in a two-volume edition: it includes a translation of, and commentary on Aristotle's *Politics*, Plato's *Republic*, *Laws* and *Epinomis*, as well as ancient excerpts on the five constitutions criticized by Aristotle in Book II of the *Politics*, all of which are presented in a highly didactic format (together with diagrams, analytical tables and annotations presenting the philosophical arguments as a list of bullet points) that is reminiscent of the philosophical textbooks *en vogue* at the time[27]. He also composed the draft of a *concordia* between Plato and Aristotle, now lost[28].

Through the studies presented in this book, we see that Plato was not only present in the universities that established Platonic chairs (Pisa, Ferrara, Rome, Pavia), but that he also made — in different ways, but according to well-identifiable patterns — significant incursions into all the major teaching centres of Italy (Venice, Bologna, Padua, Milan). Further research would possibly allow us to extend our conclusion to other universities, such as Naples or Salerno, for instance, and it is to be hoped that future studies will allow us to get a fuller picture of the influence of Plato in Italian universities as a whole. What this book reveals, however, is that sixteenth-century Italy represents a particularly important turning-point in the history of the Platonic tradition: it is precisely in that context that new aspects of (Neo)Platonism came into light and were fully exploited in academic settings, and that prominent intellectuals started to

---

24 He taught dialectics (1584-1587), medical botany (1588-1592) and natural philosophy (1587-1596). See FRANCESCHINI, *Nuovi documenti relativi ai docenti dello Studio di Ferrara*, pp. 248, 255-256 and 260.
25 See S. FELLINA, "Platone a Ferrara: il *De providentia ad sententiam Platonis et Platonicorum liber unus* di Tommaso Giannini", in *Noctua*, 5, 2019, pp. 466-553.
26 Montecatini is registered in the university rolls as professor of moral philosophy (1560-1561), astrology (1563-1564), philosophy (1563-1564) and natural philosophy (1567-1569): see FRANCESCHINI, *Nuovi documenti relativi ai docenti dello studio di Ferrara*, pp. 253-255, 262, 265, 266; RASPADORI, *I maestri di medicina ed arti dell'Università di Ferrara (1391-1950)*, p. 252 and S. CHIELLINI, "Contributo per la storia degli insegnamenti umanistici", in P. CASTELLI (ed.), *La rinascita del sapere. Libri e maestri dello Studio ferrarese*, Ferrara, Marsilio, 1991, pp. 210-245: 236-237. For a detailed analysis of Montecatini's Platonic commentaries, see VANHAELEN, *Plato in the Place of Aristotle. The Reception of Plato's Dialogues in Sixteenth-Century Italy*.
27 On diagrams and synoptic tables in Renaissance philosophical commentaries and textbooks, see C. B. SCHMITT, "The Rise of the Philosophical Textbook", in C. B. SCHMITT and Q. SKINNER (eds), *The Cambridge History of Renaissance Philosophy*, Cambridge, Cambridge University Press, 1988, pp. 792-804; R. OOSTERHOFF, *Making Mathematical Culture: University and Print in the Circle of Lefèvre d'Étaples*, Oxford, Oxford University Press, 2018, pp. 110-121.
28 DEL SOLDATO, *Early Modern Aristotle*, p. 68.

challenge the Ficinian heritage and favour the elements of Plato's philosophy that could be accommodated to the university curriculum. In that respect, we can argue that the case studies presented in this volume anticipate to a great extent the small "revolution" in the history of the Platonic tradition that has been too hastily ascribed to philosophers like Leibniz or Brucker, who both attempted to "rationalize" Plato and set him apart from the Neoplatonic tradition[29]. Moreover, these case studies show how the approach to the study of Aristotle himself became more refined: *magistri* increasingly developed an awareness of the necessity of being familiar with Plato in order to interpret and understand the Aristotelian *corpus*, often in spite of their own philosophical preferences. The fact that in the second half of the seventeenth century the practice of the *comparatio* will become a merely didactic exercise *sine ira ac studio* aptly proves how the dialogue between Plato and Aristotle had grown into a typical pedagogical exercise in the previous decades[30]. Finally, these outcomes were not the result of a few isolated attempts, as has often been assumed: the studies presented in this book allow us to identify several networks of like-minded intellectuals, who all contributed to the introduction of Plato in university teaching. Thus, Federico Borromeo, who was the addressee of several works by Francesco Patrizi, intensely studied Platonic texts, including with his teacher at Pavia, Flaminio Papazzoni, before unsuccessfully lobbying with Agostino Valier to create a Platonic chair in Bologna; Valier, as mentioned above, lectured on Plato at the Rialto school and briefly encountered Marc-Antoine Muret in Venice, who then went on to teach Plato's *Republic* in Rome[31]; Muret himself was in close contact with Giovanni Battista Camozzi, who was, like Federico Pendasio, a student of Lodovico Boccadiferro, whose known Platonic sympathies appear to have spurred his students to incorporate (albeit in completely different ways) Plato's dialogues into their teaching; both Andrea Camuzio and Paolo Beni were protected by Cardinal Cristoforo Madruzzo, a key-actor in the Counter-Reformation, and Beni was also a friend of Francesco Patrizi and a member of the *Academia Aldobrandini*, whose founder

---

29 On this context, see J.-L. VIEILLARD-BARON, *Platon et l'idéalisme allemand (1770-1830)*, Paris, Beauchesne, 1979, pp. 29-40 and 57-62; M.-N. RIBAS, "S'affilier. Le Platon de Leibniz", in D. ANTOINE-MAHUT and S. LÉZÉ (eds), *Les classiques à l'épreuve: Actualité de l'histoire de la philosophie*, Paris, Éditions des archives contemporaines, 2018, pp. 23-34; L. CATANA, *The Historiographical Concept 'System of Philosophy'. Its Origin, Nature, Influence*, Leiden, Brill, 2008.

30 See F. PURNELL JR., *Jacopo Mazzoni and His Comparison of Plato and Aristotle*, Ph.D. dissertation, Columbia University, 1971, p. 81 and DEL SOLDATO, *Early Modern Aristotle*, pp. 77-78.

31 In 1568, Muret sent from Rome a letter to Agostino Valier, then Bishop of Verona, where he recalls the time they spent together in Venice (*Epistola* I, 84, in M. A. MURET, *Epistolae*, Paris, Michel Clopeiau and Robert Coulombel, 1580, f. 89r-v: "soleo libenter, quoties incidit occasio, de summis virtutibus tuis loqui, et commemorare in omni sermone eum usum, qui mihi tecum olim Venetiis maximus ac suavissimus intercessit, cum et ego te propter tantam doctrinae copiam tantamque morum sanctitatem, quantam in homine adolescente numquam videram, colerem atque adfectarer, et tu mecum, quae tua est humanitas, tua omnia familiarissime communicares".

campaigned, without success, for the permanent introduction of Plato into the university curricula to serve the new ideals of the Church.

And it was certainly not the case that these intellectuals were merely making superficial, mechanical references to a philosophical movement that they had little sympathy for; rather their efforts were linked to the realisation that, by the end of the sixteenth century, Plato was an *incontournable* in the philosophical landscape of the universities. And here lies the paradox that this volume seeks to illustrate: whereas Aristotle never ceased to exert a monopoly of some sort in university teaching, it became increasingly difficult for university professors of philosophy to ignore the importance of Plato. Even in spite of the virulent opposition in certain religious milieux, which especially in the wake of the Patrizi affair cast a dark shadow on Plato's piety and usefulness for Christianity[32], Platonism found many ways to prosper — officially and unofficially — within university halls.

The editors wish to express their gratitude to Luca Bianchi and Dominique Poirel for agreeing to publish this volume in the series as well as the anonymous reviewers for their precious comments. We also thank Emmanuelle Khury for her assistance during the editorial process, Marina Donikian and Alexander Sterkens for their editorial work, and Giuseppe Bruno-Chomin for revising the English of some of the contributions.

Eva Del Soldato and Maude Vanhaelen

---

[32] One of the most famous anecdotes in this context, which illustrates the Jesuits' attitude towards both Plato and Aristotle, is reported by G. FULIGATTI in his *Vita del cardinale Roberto Bellarmino della Compagnia di Giesù*, Rome, Herede di Bartolomeo Zannetti, 1624, pp. 116-117: "[Pope Clement VIII] volle consultare con esso lui [Bellarmino], se fosse bene il legger nella Sapienza di Roma publicamente la filosofia di Platone; alla qual lezione, se bene vidde il papa molto inclinato, non lasciò, egli pertanto di dirgli liberamente il suo pensiero, discorrendo che assai più pericoloso era su le scuole Platone di quello che fosse Aristotele, per essere quello più vicino a' nostri dogmi, in quella guisa che tutto dì s'esperimenta maggior danno dalla lezione de' libri eretici che di quelli de' Gentili".

MAUDE VANHAELEN

Teaching Plato in Sixteenth-Century Italy[*]

Introduction

Although the Arts curriculum was officially based on Aristotle, we know that professors occasionally taught Plato at European universities throughout the fifteenth and the sixteenth centuries. In a seminal article published in 1946, Paul Oskar Kristeller provided a preliminary overview of the introduction of Platonic courses in Italian universities. This was subsequently complemented in 1976 by Charles B. Schmitt, who provided a more general examination of Platonic teaching activities in European universities[1]. One of the first to teach Plato in a European university was the Greek émigré Theodore Gaza, who lectured on Plato's *Gorgias* in his course of rhetoric in Ferrara in 1446[2]; similarly, in Leipzig Paulus Niavis (1460-1514), a school master of rhetoric and humanities, lectured on Plato's *Lovers* and *Letters* in 1489 to teach his students the necessity to unite eloquence and philosophy[3]. In the field of natural philosophy Sebastiano Aquila

---

[*] Research conducted for this chapter was funded by a Leverhulme Research Fellowship. I wish to express my gratitude to Dario Brancato, Jean-Eudes Girot, Alessio Marziali Peretti, Eva Del Soldato as well as the two anonymous reviewers for their helpful comments and suggestions.

[1] P. O. KRISTELLER, "Francesco da Diacceto and Florentine Platonism in the Sixteenth Century", in *Id., Studies in Renaissance Thought and Letters*, I, Rome, Edizioni di Storia e Letteratura, 1956, pp. 287-336: 291-293; C. B. SCHMITT, "Platon et Aristote dans les universités et les collèges du XVIe siècle. L'introduction de la philosophie platonicienne dans l'enseignement des universités à la Renaissance", in M. DE GANDILLAC and J.-C. MARGOLIN (eds), *Platon et Aristote à la Renaissance. XVIe colloque international de Tours*, Paris, Vrin, 1976, pp. 93-104. See also P. F. GRENDLER, *The Universities of the Italian Renaissance*, Baltimore, Johns Hopkins University Press, 2002, pp. 297-309.

[2] J. MONFASANI, "The Byzantine Rhetorical Tradition and the Renaissance", in J. J. MURPHY (ed.), *Renaissance Eloquence. Studies in the Theory and Practice of Renaissance Rhetoric*, Berkeley, University of California Press, 1983, pp. 174-187: 180. The text of this course is preserved in MS V a 123 in the Folger Shakespeare Library in Washington.

[3] P. NIAVIS, *Liber de philosophia Platonis*, Leipzig, Moritz Brandis, 1490 and *Divi Platonis epistolae*, Leipzig, Conrad Kachelofen, 1490. See SCHMITT, "Platon et Aristote dans les universités

---

Maude Vanhaelen • UQAM

Teaching Plato in Italian Renaissance Universities, ed. by Eva Del Soldato and Maude Vanhaelen, Studia Artistarum, 51 (Turnhout: Brepols, 2024), pp. 21–58

(c. 1440-c. 1510) taught Plato's *Timaeus* on holidays in 1497 at Ferrara[4], whereas Niccolò Leonico Tomeo (1456-1531) probably taught Plato in Greek at Padua in 1500, and translated a section of Plato's *Timaeus* along with Proclus's commentary[5]. In the 1550s Pier Vettori (1499-1585) taught Plato's *Lysis* in his course of moral philosophy at the University of Florence and viewed the dialogue as complementary to Aristotle's discussion of friendship in *Nicomachean Ethics*[6]. As the fourth chapter in this volume will show, other vain or short-lived attempts were made to introduce Plato into the official curriculum at Bologna and Pavia[7]. And as the second chapter will explore in detail, this effort culminated with the creation of the first official chair of Platonic philosophy in 1576 by Grand Duke Francesco I de' Medici at the University of Pisa, which eventually allowed the appointed professor to teach Plato on holidays. Already at the very beginning of the sixteenth century, Francesco Cattani da Diacceto, who was Ficino's most faithful disciple, introduced a Platonized version of Aristotle in Pisan teaching, and did not hesitate to openly favour Plato over Aristotle when there was disagreement between the two. In contrast, at the end of the century, Verino il Secondo, who was appointed professor of both Aristotelian and Platonic philosophy, taught Plato in a perspective that underlined complementarity and harmony with Aristotle and Christianity[8]. A more radicalized, anti-Aristotelian Platonism was taught by Francesco Patrizi who, after holding the chair of Platonic philosophy at the University of Ferrara (1578-1582), lectured on Plato at the University of Rome (1592-1597), with the explicit intention of substituting Plato and other ancient thinkers to Aristotle in the university curriculum, in order to purge philosophy from the un-Christian doctrines disseminated through Averroes; Patrizi's mission,

---

et les collèges du XVIe siècle", p. 95 and G. MCDONALD, *Marsilio Ficino in Germany from Renaissance to Enlightenment. A Reception History*, Geneva, Droz, 2022, pp. 397-399.

4 See P. O. KRISTELLER, *Supplementum Ficinianum Marsilii Ficini Florentini Philosophi platonici opuscula inedita et dispersa*, 2 vols, Florence, Olschki, 1937, II, p. 211 and Id., "Marsilio Ficino e Venezia", in Id., *Studies in Renaissance Thought and Letters IV*, Rome, Edizioni di Storia e Letteratura, 1996, pp. 245-263: 260-261. The source is a letter Ariosto sent Aldo Manuzio in 1498 (L. ARIOSTO, *Lettere*, ed. A. STELLA, Milan, Mondadori, 1965, p. 3).

5 N. LEONICO TOMEO, *Platonis ex Timaeo De animorum generatione, cum explicatione et digressione Procli Lytii traductio*, in *Opuscula nuper in lucem aedita quorum nomina proxima*, Venice, Bernardinus Vitalis, 1525, f. LXXVr-CXXXIXv. The translation covers *Timaeus* 36a-36e and PROCLUS, *In Timaeum*, ed. E. DIEHL, Leipzig, Teubner, 1906, II, pp. 119-292.

6 See S. MARTINELLI TEMPESTA, "La versione latina di Pier Vettori del *Liside* platonico", in *Atti e memorie dell'Academia Toscana di scienze e lettere La Colombaria*, 65 [51 n.s.] (2000), pp. 112-171.

7 E. COSTA, *Ulisse Aldrovandi e lo Studio bolognese nella seconda metà del secolo XVI*, Bologna, Stabilimento Poligrafico Emiliano, 1907, p. 90 (already cited in KRISTELLER, "Francesco da Diacceto and Florentine Platonism in the Sixteenth Century", p. 292).

8 On Diacceto and Verino see, in addition to Simone Fellina's chapter in this volume, S. FELLINA, "Platone a scuola: l'insegnamento di Francesco de' Vieri detto il Verino secondo", in *Noctua*, 2/1-2 (2015), pp. 97-181 and Id., *Platone allo Studium Fiorentino-Pisano (1576-1635)*, Verona, Scripta, 2019.

which was initially supported by the Pope, failed after rival factions in the Vatican managed to put his work to the Index *donec corrigatur*[9]. Modern scholars generally consider these attempts as isolated cases; it is assumed that the dissemination of Plato was mostly a phenomenon that occurred outside the university and that professors of Aristotelian philosophy were only indirectly influenced by the revival of Plato through the availability of Greek Neoplatonic commentators on Aristotle (such as Simplicius, who defended the concord between Plato and Aristotle): according to this view, they often integrated in their commentaries on Aristotle Platonic doctrines when they found Aristotle's solution to be questionable, but they never ventured to lecture on Platonic texts[10].

Contrary to this, this chapter suggests that the practice of lecturing on Plato on the part of university professors was much more widespread than has been acknowledged by modern scholars. This is not to say that Platonic texts formed the official basis of the curriculum: university statutes prescribed that the teaching of philosophy be based on Aristotelian texts, and Aristotle continued to enjoy a quasi-monopoly in university curriculum well into the seventeenth century. However, a detailed census of Platonic works produced in sixteenth-century Italy shows that several university professors, some of whom were hired specifically to teach Aristotle, not only wrote commentaries on Plato, but also intentionally deviated from the official curriculum and taught Plato's dialogues into their courses.

There are three reasons that explain why modern scholars have neglected this important aspect in the history of the Platonic tradition. First, sixteenth-century Platonism is often seen as a vague and nebulous repetition of fifteenth-century Platonism, as it was revived by Marsilio Ficino. Ficino's theological and mystical perspective on Plato's dialogues, it is often argued, could hardly be accommodated to the university curriculum. Yet, as we will see, in the sixteenth century several university professors of philosophy and humanities read Plato's dialogues in their courses; in this context, they often adopted a reading of Plato that was markedly different from Ficino's theological interpretation, focusing on what in Plato's dialogues pertained to natural philosophy and ethics rather than theology or mysticism.

Secondly, it is generally assumed that university statutes, which prescribe which texts should be part of the curriculum, are the final word on teaching practices in medieval and Renaissance universities. It is true that university curricula changed in the middle of the thirteenth century: for instance, before 1255 the teaching of moral philosophy was based on three texts: Aristotle's *Nicomachean*

---

9 See M. MUCCILLO, "Il platonismo all'Università di Roma: Francesco Patrizi", in P. CHERUBINI (ed.), *Roma e lo* Studium Urbis. *Spazio urbano e cultura dal Quattro al Seicento*. Atti del convegno (Roma, 7-10 giugno 1989), Rome, Ministero dei beni culturali e ambientali, 1992, pp. 200-247.
10 See GRENDLER, *The Universities of the Italian Renaissance*, p. 298.

Ethics, Boethius' *Consolation of Philosophy*, and Plato's *Timaeus*[11]; after 1255 the university of Paris statutes prescribed that the teaching be based exclusively on Aristotle, at which point the texts of Boethius and Plato ceased to be part of university examinations. And yet the uninterrupted transmission of glosses on the *Timaeus* during a period that spans from the ninth to the fifteenth centuries seems to suggest that despite the new university regulations there was a sustained interest in that particular dialogue, and that this interest continued to take place, at least in part, in a teaching context[12]. Some of these medieval interpreters of the *Timaeus* belonged to the famous Chartres school, but we also find marginal annotations in the hand of grammar teachers as well as arts masters, which indicates that the *Timaeus* was more generally taught at pre-university and university level. A good example of this tradition is a thirteenth-century manuscript now in Pisa, which contains tables on texts by Aristotle, Boethius (including the *Consolatio*) and Plato's *Timaeus*[13]. In the fifteenth century, we know of one instance of the medieval *Timaeus* being annotated by a Paduan arts master, together with Bruni's Plato translations, thus suggesting that Plato might have been reintroduced in a university context, albeit unofficially[14]. Even more importantly, evidence indicates that, like their medieval predecessors, sixteenth-century university professors could deviate from the prescribed syllabus, not only in the private lectures they

---

11 See C. LAFLEUR and J. CARRIER, "L'enseignement philosophique à la Faculté des arts de l'Université de Paris en la première moitié du XIIIe siècle dans le miroir des textes didascaliques", in *Laval philosophique et théologique*, 60 (2004), pp. 409-448.
12 On the *Timaeus* in the Middle Ages, see R. KLIBANSKY, *The Continuity of the Platonic Tradition*, London, The Warburg Institute, 1939; T. GREGORY, *Platonismo medievale. Studi e ricerche*, Rome, Istituto storico italiano per il Medio Evo, 1958; M. GIBSON, "The Study of the *Timaeus* in the Eleventh and Twelfth Centuries", in *Pensamiento*, 25 (1969), pp. 183-194; É. JEAUNEAU, '*Lectio philosophorum*': *Recherches sur l'École de Chartres*, Amsterdam, A. M. Hakkert, 1973, pp. 193-264; *Id*., "Extraits des *Glosae super Platonem* de Guillaume de Conches dans un manuscrit de Londres", in *Journal of the Warburg and Courtauld Institutes*, 60 (1977), pp. 212-222; S. GERSH, *Middle Platonism and Neoplatonism: The Latin Tradition*, 2 vols, Notre Dame, Notre Dame University Press, 1986, II, pp. 421-492; P. E. DUTTON, "Material Remains of the Study of the *Timaeus* in the later Middle Ages", in C. LAFLEUR (ed.), *L'enseignement de la philosophie au XIIIe siècle*, Turnhout, Brepols, 1996, pp. 203-230; *Id*., "Medieval Approaches to Calcidius", in G. REYDAMS-SCHILS (ed.), *Plato's Timaeus as Cultural Icon*, Notre Dame, University of Notre Dame Press, 2003, pp. 183-295; A. SOMFAI, "The Eleventh-Century Shift in the Reception of Plato's *Timaeus* and Calcidius' *Commentary*", in *Journal of the Warburg and Courtauld Institutes*, 65 (2002), pp. 1-21.
13 BSAP, MS 124: see L. STURLESE and M. R. PAGNONI STURLESE, *Catalogo di manoscritti filosofici nelle biblioteche italiane I*, Florence, Olschki, 1980, pp. 39-49.
14 J. HANKINS, "The Study of the *Timaeus* in Early Renaissance Italy", in A. GRAFTON and N. SIRAISI (eds), *Natural Particulars: Nature and the Disciplines in Renaissance Europe*, Cambridge, MA, MIT University Press, 1999, pp. 77-119, who mentions the existence of at least twenty-eight manuscripts of Calcidius' translation of or commentary on the *Timaeus* produced in Italy in the fourteenth and fifteenth centuries and twenty-three further earlier manuscripts (before 1350) that were present in Italian collections or were studied by Italian scholars in the fifteenth century.

gave in their home, but also in their official teaching. As we will see, some of them, like Marc-Antoine Muret, were quickly reprimanded by the university authorities, but others, like Agostino Valier, seemed to have had ample flexibility to teach pretty much any author they wished.

The third, and perhaps most important reason that explains why modern scholars have neglected the role of Plato in universities is that the interest in non-Aristotelian philosophies that occurred among Renaissance commentators is often described as a form of "eclecticism". To put it simply, modern scholars tend to reduce any interest in Plato on the part of so-called Renaissance Aristotelians to an "eclectic" attitude, without further elucidating the conditions of its development. To be sure, the way Aristotle was interpreted in the universities changed dramatically with the development of humanism: university philosophy (what we refer to as scholastic philosophy) envisaged the Aristotelian corpus in new ways, using humanistic methodology, which included philology and historical criticism, to interpret and teach the texts. This led to a reassessment of the Aristotelian corpus, tending towards a clearer distinction between authentic and spurious texts, an engagement with more accurate Latin translations of the Greek original, the use of ancient commentaries that were not known in the Middle Ages, and, most importantly, the development of a new interpretative method that consisted of interpreting "Aristotle through Aristotle" (as Aristarchus had done in the Hellenistic period with Homer), whilst at the same time looking more critically at what ancient and medieval commentators had said about him[15]. Given that these ancient commentators were themselves influenced by Neoplatonism, Scepticism, and other philosophical schools, scholastic philosophy effectively absorbed ideas and doctrines from non-Aristotelian philosophies and adapted their interpretation of Aristotle accordingly. Because the framework remained Aristotelian, that is to say, the introduction of non-Aristotelian ideas occurred within the context of explaining and interpreting Aristotelian texts, modern scholars have described this phenomenon as "Aristotelian eclecticism"[16]. And yet, as numerous specialists of ancient philosophy have shown, the label "eclecticism", as a historiographical category inherited from Eduard Zeller, is, at worst, a negatively connotated appellation that tends to oppose the "original" philosophical systems of the great philosophers of Antiquity to the derivative syntheses of their successors, and, at best, a category that is void of any real meaning, a convenient label that gives a name to a great variety of philosophical attitudes, but fails to explain or contextualize them[17]. Similarly, the expression "Aristotelian eclecticism" to describe Renaissance philosophical attitudes does not have the capacity to explain

---

15 L. BIANCHI, "Interpréter Aristote par Aristote. Parcours de l'herméneutique philosophique à la Renaissance", in *Methodos*, 2 (2002), permanent link at https://journals.openedition.org/methodos/98?lang=fr, [last accessed December 7, 2021].
16 C. B. SCHMITT, *Aristotle and the Renaissance*, Cambridge, MA, Harvard University Press, 1983.
17 J. M. DILLON and A. A. LONG (eds), *The Question of "Eclecticism". Studies in Later Greek Philosophy*, Berkeley-Los Angeles-London, University of California Press, 1988; I. HADOT, "Du bon

much: it refers to an attitude of selecting non-Aristotelian sources, but it does not give any clear indication of how and why this process of selection occurred[18]. It is often used to describe (and sometimes dismiss) any form of deviation from the norm (such as, in the present context, the scholastic interpretation of Aristotle) leading to the unfortunate neglect of important texts (such as university lectures and commentaries on Plato); more specifically, it prevents us from exploring how and why sixteenth-century Aristotelian philosophers showed a sustained interest in non-Aristotelian authors like Plato.

Context

In what follows, the chapter will present a selection of Platonic commentaries and university lectures written by university professors and show how these texts developed new perspectives on Plato's dialogues. Most of these works were written in a specific religious context, spanning from Luther's scathing attacks against the impiety of university teaching in the first decade of the sixteenth century[19] to the Counter-Reformation (i.e. the Council of Trent, 1545-1563), at a time when ecclesiastical authorities were still hoping that a reform of the Church from the inside would be sufficient to contain the rise of what was to become Protestantism. Another important event was the papal decree *Apostolici regiminis* promulgated in 1513 at the Fifth Lateran Council, which mandated that the teaching of philosophical doctrines that were contradicting Christian dogmas should be countered by the perspective of faith; the main target was the Paduan Aristotelians who were teaching Averroes' doctrines, which denied the Christian dogma of the immortality of the soul. This opened up a crisis in universities regarding the relationship between philosophy and theology; more specifically, it raised the question as to whether it was acceptable for professors of philosophy to prove or disprove philosophical doctrines that were incompatible with Christian dogmas. The most famous example of this tension between philosophy and

---

et mauvais usage du terme 'éclectisme' dans l'histoire de la philosophie antique", in R. Brague and J.-F. Courtine (eds), *Herméneutique et ontologie. Mélanges en hommage à P. Aubenque*, Paris, Presses universitaires de France, 1990, pp. 147-162.

18 On a reappraisal of the notion of eclecticism in relation to Renaissance philosophy, see L. Catana, *Late Ancient Platonism in Eighteenth-Century German Thought*, Cham, Springer, 2019, pp. 65-94 and M. Vanhaelen, "Éclectisme, aristotélisme et platonisme dans la pensée italienne du xvie siècle", in D. Dumouchel and C. Leduc (eds), *Les -ismes et catégories historiographiques: Formation et usage à l'époque moderne*, Quebec City, Les Presses de l'Université Laval, 2021, pp. 95-112.

19 On the role of Aristotelian Ethics in Reformation and Counter-Reformation, see R. Saarinen, "Renaissance Ethics and the European Reformations", in D. A. Lines and S. Ebbersmeyer (eds), *Rethinking Virtue, Reforming Society. New Directions in Renaissance Ethics, c. 1350-c. 1650*, Turnhout, Brepols, 2013, pp. 81-106. On Luther's relationship towards Aristotle and Plato, see McDonald, *Marsilio Ficino in Germany from Renaissance to Enlightenment*, pp. 537-538.

theology was the Pomponazzi affair (1516), when Pomponazzi argued that the Christian dogma of the immortality of soul could not be philosophically proven by relying on Aristotle, prompting several theologians to condemn his views or seek to attenuate them[20]. However, these two events — the rise of Protestantism and the realization that university philosophy was not always able to support the dogmas of Christianity — also led some philosophers and theologians to consider whether Plato could offer a more suitable alternative to Aristotle, and whether Platonic doctrines were more compatible with Christianity.

Of course, by the sixteenth century the question of the compatibility of Plato with Christianity, which had roots in patristic literature, was a commonplace: after having been revived in the fifteenth century by Cardinal Bessarion, it had been adopted by Marsilio Ficino to justify his *renovatio platonica* against the Averroist commentators of Aristotle; in the early days of the struggle between Catholics and Protestants, several theologians like Giles of Viterbo quietly drew on Ficino's heritage to develop a new form of Christian spirituality; and at the end of the century Patrizi and his papal allies would invoke the same idea to purge philosophy from Aristotelian impieties. But what is not sufficiently appreciated, perhaps, is that some sixteenth-century interpreters took up this idea independently from Ficino's heritage, that is to say, they moved away from Ficino's mystical and theological interpretation and developed instead new modes of reading Plato. More specifically, they did so by applying to Plato's dialogues the same philological and historicist attitude (typical of "scholastic humanism") that was generally used to comment on Aristotle: just as Renaissance interpreters were inclined to question the standard translations and interpretations of Aristotle's treatises, so too they started to envisage more critically some of the main commonplaces of the Plato-Aristotle controversy, including Aristotle's main criticisms against Plato, and this often led them to reassess the suitability of teaching Plato in a university context. The most important of these commonplaces were two: the first was that, unlike Aristotle who had expressed his philosophy in a clear and orderly fashion, Plato's philosophy was unclear and difficult for students to understand, because matters pertaining to the fields of university disciplines (moral philosophy, rhetoric, politics, physics and metaphysics) were scattered in various dialogues rather than being treated in separate thematic treatises. The second was the idea that Aristotle was a natural philosopher, who talked about earthly matters, whereas Plato was a spiritual philosopher mostly preoccupied with theological matters and the afterlife, which were not appropriate to study in a course of philosophy[21]. As we will see, some Renaissance intellectuals tried to

---

20 For a detailed overview of the Pomponazzi affair and relevant bibliography, see L. BIANCHI, *Pour une histoire de la "double vérité"*, Paris, Vrin, 2008, pp. 117-156.
21 See L. BIANCHI, "L'acculturazione filosofica dell'Occidente", in L. BIANCHI (ed.), *La filosofia delle università. Secoli XIII-XIV*, Florence, La nuova Italia, 1997, pp. 17-21. On the shift from Plato to Aristotle in the Middle Ages, see J. HANKINS, "Antiplatonism in the Renaissance and the Middle Ages", in *Classica et mediaevalia*, 47 (1996), pp. 359-376.

respond to these two ideas by transforming Plato's philosophy. More specifically, they used their best philological and critical skills to rearrange Plato's dialogues into thematic or lemmatic treatises that followed a traditional scholastic format, thus making them more accessible to readers familiar with the material and structure of university textbooks. In addition, these interpreters distanced themselves from Ficino's heritage and the Neoplatonic tradition, which presented Plato as a mystical philosopher, and envisaged Plato as a thinker who had important things to say in the fields of natural and moral philosophy.

Platonic Commentaries by University Professors

Among the numerous Platonic works that appeared in the sixteenth century — Latin and vernacular translations, commentaries, lectures — a new, discernible trend appears: that of transforming Plato's dialogues into scholastic treatises that could be better apprehended by readers familiar with Aristotelian commentaries. This trend finds its clearest expression in two monumental Platonic commentaries written by Chrysostomus Javelli (1470/2-1542)[22]. Before being appointed the inquisitor of Piacenza in 1523, Javelli held prestigious academic positions at the Domenican *studio* of Bologna, where he taught for several years before becoming regent master (1518-1521), and at the faculty of theology of the University, where he was incorporated as a full professor in 1516[23]. In addition to his Platonic

---

22 On Javelli's life and works, see C. H. LOHR, *Latin Aristotle Commentaries. II. Renaissance Authors*, Florence, Olschki, 1988, pp. 202-204; M. TAVUZZI, "Chrysostomus Javelli O. P. (*c*. 1470-1538). A Biobibliographical Essay. Part I: Biography", in *Angelicum*, 67 (1990), pp. 457-482 and *Id.*, "Chrysostomus Javelli O. P. (*c*. 1470-1538). A Biobibliographical Essay. Part II: Bibliography", in *Angelicum*, 68 (1991), pp. 109-121; M. BEUCHOT, "Chrysostom Javellus (b. 1472; d. 1538) and Francis Sylvester Ferrara (b. 1474; d. 1526)", in J. J. E. GRACIA (ed.), *Individuation in Scholasticism: The Later Middle Ages and the Counter-Reformation, 1150-1650*, Albany, NY, State University of New York Press, 1994, pp. 457-472; D. VON WILLE, "Javelli, Giovanni Crisostomo", in *Dizionario Biografico degli Italiani*, 62 (2004), permanent link at https://www.treccani.it/enciclopedia/giovanni-crisostomo-javelli_(Dizionario-Biografico), [last accessed December 3, 2023]; M. TAVUZZI, *Renaissance Inquisitors: Dominican Inquisitors and Inquisitorial Districts in Northern Italy, 1474-1527*, Leiden-Boston, Brill, 2007, pp. 222-223 and M. TAVUZZI, "Chrysostomus Javelli O. P. (c. 1470–1540): A Biographical Introduction", in T. DE ROBERTIS and L. BURZELLI (eds), *Chrysostomus Javelli. Pagan Philosophy and Christian Thought in the Renaissance*, Cham, Springer, 2023, pp. 3-28.
23 Archival documents show that in 1516, during his second year as *baccalaureus* in the *studium* of the convent of San Domenico in Bologna, Javelli graduated as *magister* of the faculty of theology of the University of Bologna and was incorporated (*incorporatus*) as a member of its *Collegium Doctorum*, that is, as a full professor in that Faculty. See C. PIANA, "La Facoltà teologica dell'Università di Bologna nella prima metà del Cinquecento", in *Archivum historicum franciscanum*, 62 (1969), pp. 196-266: 216 and 258; TAVUZZI, "Chrysostomus Javelli O. P. (*c*. 1470-1538). A Biobibliographical Essay. Part I: Biography", p. 469. Given that the faculty of theology was not a separate faculty within the university but consisted of the city's various

works, he wrote numerous commentaries on Aristotle and Thomas Aquinas[24]. He is famous for the important role he played in the Pomponazzi affair, but his Platonic works have fallen into near complete oblivion to this day. Dedicated to Catalano Trivulzio (then bishop of Piacenza), Javelli's Platonic commentaries were completed in 1535 and appeared in 1536 in Venice through the press of Aurelio Pinzi[25]. These texts constitute the second part of a triptych, which included similar compendia on Aristotle's moral and political philosophy, both of which were completed in 1535 and published separately in 1536 in Venice, as well as a monumental treatise on Christian ethics, which was published in different stages between 1536 and 1540. The complete Platonic, Aristotelian and Christian works were posthumously reprinted in a single compendium in Lyon in 1568[26]. Javelli's compendium constitutes one of the most important attempts to develop a form of Erasmian Christian philosophy centred upon the Scriptures alone, in answer to Luther's attacks against the philosophical practices of universities[27]. Javelli's aim is to substitute to pagan philosophy a truly Christian philosophy based on the interpretation of Scripture rather than on human reasoning. In this context, Javelli's commentaries on Aristotle and Plato appear to have served as preliminary studies on ethics and politics, in order to project onto the Scriptures the format and structure of pagan ethics as it was envisaged in philosophy, and thus in universities.

By the time the two Plato commentaries were published, Javelli had retired from his teaching position in Bologna, but he is still described as "philosophiae et theologiae professorem" in the colophons. This is significant, because, as we will see, Javelli's intention is to present Plato's philosophy as a systematic and

---

convent *studia*, this means that Javelli was teaching in his Dominican *studium* but could examine candidates and confer degrees that were recognized by the University: see GRENDLER, *The Universities of the Italian Renaissance*, pp. 357-384. Occasionally, the university also offered a course of theology (*ad metaphysicam*), but Javelli's name does not appear in the list of professors teaching this course.

24 A list is provided in TAVUZZI, "Chrysostomus Javelli O. P. (*c.* 1470-1538). A Biobibliographical Essay. Part II: Bibliography".

25 C. JAVELLI, *Moralis philosophie platonice dispositio*, Venice, in officina Aurelii Pincii Veneti, 1536.

26 C. JAVELLI, *In universam moralem Aristotelis, Platonis et Christianam philosophiam epitomes in certas partes distinctae*, Lyon, apud haeredes Jacobi Juntae, 1568.

27 Javelli's *Christiana philosophia* is briefly analysed in M.-D. CHENU, "Note pour l'histoire de la notion de philosophie chrétienne", in *Revue des Sciences philosophiques et théologiques*, 21/2 (1932), pp. 231-235. On Erasmus praised in Catholic circles (especially among the Domenican and the Augustinian orders) as a promoter of Catholic reform, see S. SEIDEL MENCHI, *Erasmo in Italia 1520-1580*, Turin, Bollati Boringhieri, 1987, pp. 270-285. On Erasmus' Christian philosophy, see J. D. TRACY, *Erasmus of the Low Countries*, Berkeley, University of California Press, 1996; A. W. STEENBEEK, "The Christologies of Erasmus and Lefèvre", in ERASMUS, *Opera omnia.* vol. IX/3. *Apologia ad Iacobum Fabrum Stapulensem*, Amsterdam, Elsevier, 1996, pp. 22-45; on his sympathy for Plato, whom he judges more compatible with Christianity than Aristotle, see MCDONALD, *Marsilio Ficino in Germany from Renaissance to Enlightenment*, pp. 169-171.

coherent doctrine, in answer to the general assumption that Plato's philosophy was disorderly, unclear and ill-suited to teaching. The division of Christian philosophy into *philosophia christiana moralis, civilis* and *oeconomica*, and that of Plato into *moralis* and *politica* evoke the traditional division of moral philosophy since the Middle Ages, and in doing so Javelli effectively adapts both Plato's dialogues and the Scriptures to a philosophical framework and format that was traditionally used for the teaching of Aristotle's moral philosophy.

Javelli's interpretation of Plato is particularly interesting, therefore, because it shows how scholastic humanism was applied to a non-Aristotelian author. For Javelli provides an interpretation of Plato that is in great part independent from Ficino's exegesis: to be sure, he quotes Plato in Ficino's translation, and even reproduces, without aknowledgement, entire sections from Ficino's commentaries. However, he never adopts Ficino's theological, mystical and allegorical interpretation, and he does not make a single reference to the Neoplatonic interpreters (such as Plotinus or Proclus) that were central to Ficino's interpretation. For instance, he strongly rebuts those who use Plato to convince people that God can be honoured by sacrifices and invocations — a clear allusion to the Neoplatonic theurgy that was strongly favoured by Ficino and his disciple Diacceto[28]. Instead he provides an interpretation of Plato that is based on a close reading of all his dialogues. As such, his commentary constitutes the first known attempt to interpret Plato through Plato and not through the ancient commentators. Equally importantly, Javelli presents Plato as a moral philosopher who talked about the same themes as Aristotle, but did so in a disorderly way. To put some order into Plato's dialogues, Javelli explains in the preface that he has decided to painstakingly reorganize Plato's dialogues into a set of thematic treatises, thus using a format typical of the traditional Aristotelian commentaries on moral and political philosophy[29]. Each treatise is divided into several chapters, which provide a detailed analysis of Plato's texts on a given theme through a complex system of cross-referencing between the various dialogues. In each chapter Javelli systematically summarizes Aristotle's views for the reader before analysing Plato's views. The aim here is to adopt a format that will suit an audience more familiar with Aristotle and provide a comparative perspective that allows Javelli to show that, when it comes to moral matters, Plato is closer to Christianity than Aristotle. As he states in the introduction to the epitomes, Plato's moral philosophy is superior to Aristotle's ethics, because it is closer to Christian philosophy and facilitates access to Christian religion[30]. A detailed *summa contentorum* appended at the end of the treatise provides a detailed and systematic synopsis of Plato's

---

28 JAVELLI, *Moralis philosophie platonice dispositio*, f. 6v. For a detailed overview of Javelli's independence from Ficino's interpretation, see M. VANHAELEN, "Chrysostomus Javelli's Commentaries on Plato's Moral Philosophy", in DE ROBERTIS and BURZELLI (eds), *Chrysostomus Javelli*, pp.171-194.
29 *Ibid.*, f. 3v.
30 *Ibid.*, f. Aiiv.

moral philosophy and is evidently designed as a study aid. The selection of themes shows that Javelli was not interested in the mystical possibilities that a Neoplatonic reading of Plato could offer, but in the philosophical questions that were addressed in the Aristotelian literature. It is important to note here that Javelli is not "aristotelizing" Plato or trying to make Plato and Aristotle compatible. Instead his aim is, first, to transform the structure and the format of Plato's dialogues into a coherent and well-structured philosophical system that follows the format of scholastic philosophy, and second, to use the new method of scholastic humanism to interpret Plato through a detailed and comprehensive study of his dialogues. His most central argument is that Plato's ethics is not only spiritual, but also practical, against the well-established idea according to which Plato had only talked about the divine Good and happiness after death. Javelli devotes several sections to what Plato had said about human moral values, which are systematically compared with Aristotle's ethics. According to him, Plato considered that earthly happiness is possible to a few and described human virtues in as much as they prepared for the afterlife. Javelli is therefore giving Plato's philosophy the status of a practical as well as contemplative philosophy, which gives him the opportunity to study the human aspects of Plato's ethics[31]. Interestingly he argues that, contrary to what previous scholars have stated, the fundamental difference between Aristotle and Plato does not lie in the fact that Plato has not talked about happiness on earth, but in the fact that Aristotle never talked about happiness in the afterlife: Aristotle does not envisage any other form of happiness for mankind than the one on earth, whereas Plato considers that man can reach an imperfect form of happiness on earth and a perfect one in the afterlife; in that respect, Javelli argues, Plato's doctrine is closer to truth than Aristotle's (*consona veritati*)[32].

A second important trend that develops in the sixteenth century is the tendency to read Plato as a literary as well as philosophical author. In this context, some interpreters move away from the metaphysical commentaries by Proclus or Damascius, which had been priviledged by Ficino, and focus instead on lesser known ancient Neoplatonic authors such as Olympiodorus, whose extant lecture notes provides a more didactic and philological version of Neoplatonism. Thus, in the second half of the sixteenth century, the humanist Giovanni Battista Camozzi (1515-81) wrote a commentary on the *First Alcibiades* of Plato, which bypasses the metaphysical and mystical Neoplatonic tradition revived by Ficino and is based instead on a more philological reading of Plato that derives mainly from the ancient Neoplatonist Olympiodorus[33].

---

31 *Ibid.*, f. 32r.
32 *Ibid.*, f. 71v.
33 On Camozzi, see P. Schreiner, "Camozzi, Giovanni Battista", in *Dizionario Biografico degli Italiani*, 17 (1974), permanent link at https://www.treccani.it/enciclopedia/giovanni-battista-camozzi_%28Dizionario-Biografico%29/, [last accessed December 3, 2023].

Camozzi was a student of Lodovico Boccadiferro, who taught philosophy in Bologna between 1527 and 1545 and also used Olympiodorus (and more specifically his commentary on the *Meteorology*) in his lectures on Aristotle; upon Boccadiferro's death Camozzi wrote a funeral oration in his honour[34]. In Bologna he was also a member of the Accademia Bocchiana, an academy with strong interests in the Platonic and Cabbalistic traditions[35]. The *rotuli* of the University of Bologna indicate that Camozzi held the student lectureship (*lectura universitatis*) of rhetoric in the academic year 1549-50, which means that he was still doing his doctorate[36]. He also seems to have held a teaching position in Padua, after which time he was appointed professor of philosophy at the University of Macerata, where he taught natural philosophy, Greek and the humanities (1554-64)[37]. He was subsequently called to Rome to serve under Pope Pius IV, and from 1574 to 1580 he was professor of rhetoric at the Roman *studium*, where he taught, among other texts, Cicero's *Philippics* and Aristotle's *Rhetoric*[38]. There he shared for several years the chair of rhetoric with the prominent humanist Marc-Antoine Muret, who, as we will see below, gave lectures on Plato on two consecutive years

---

34 G. B. Camozzi, *Oratio in funere Ludovici Buccaferreae clarissimi philosophi Bononiensis*, Bologna, in officina Bartholomaei Bonardi et Marci Antonij Groscii, 1545.

35 On Bocchi's Academy (first known reference in 1526), see E. S. Watson, *Achille Bocchi and the Emblem Book as Symbolic Form*, Cambridge and New York, Cambridge University Press, 1993, pp. 26-63, with a list of members at pp. 153-154; A. Rolet, "L'*Hermathena Bocchiana* ou l'idée de la parfaite académie", in M. Deramaix, P. Galan-Hallyn and G. Vagenheim (eds), *Les Académies dans l'Europe humaniste: idéaux et pratiques*, Geneva, Droz, 2008, pp. 295-323.

36 U. Dallari, *I Rotuli dei lettori legisti e artisti dello Studio bolognese dal 1384 al 1799*, 2 vols, Bologna, Merlani, 1888, II, p. 120.

37 See university rolls in A. Marongiu, "L'Università di Macerata nel periodo delle origini", in *Id., Stato e scuola. Esperienze della scuola occidentale*, Milan, A. Giuffrè, 1974, pp. 149-218: 198 [1554, "ad lectionem philosophiae humanarum Graecarumque litterarum"]; 199 [1556, "ad lectionem philosophiae humanarum Graecarumque litterarum"]; 200 [1557, "ad lectionem philosophiae"]; 201 [1561, "ad lectionem phisicae ordinariam"]; [rolls for 1562 and 1563 are missing]. He is twice described as *lector physicae* in the University's *atti* of 1565-66: see S. Serangeli, *Atti dello Studium Generale Maceratense dal 1551 al 1579*, Turin, Giappichelli, 1999, pp. 61 and 82; in his published translation of Alexander of Aphrodisias' commentary on *Meteorology* published in 1556, he is described as a professor of philosophy at the University of Macerata (*in urbe Macerata totius agri Piceni metropoli philosophiam publice profitente*). In the preface to the same work, he alludes to his teaching in Bologna and Padua: *Alexandri Aphrodisiensis in libros Aristotelis Meteorologicos commentarii, Ioanne Baptista Camotio interprete*, f. + iiir: "Ego enim cum superioribus annis a Patavina Bononiensique iuventute litterarum philosophicae studiosissima efflagitari et misere quasi vocibus omnium deposci viderem Alexandrum Aphrodisiensem in *Meteora* Aristotelis...".

38 E. Conte, *I maestri della Sapienza di Roma dal 1514 al 1787: i rotuli e altre fonti*, Rome, Istituto storico italiano per il Medioevo, 1991, I, p. 89 [1574-5; taught "primam Philippicam Ciceronis"], p. 101 [1575-6; taught "Philippicas Ciceronis"], p. 111 [1576, teaching material not indicated], [1577-8 missing], p. 116 [1579-90; taught "in primum Rhetoricae Arist."].

(1573-74 and 1574-75)[39]. An excellent Hellenist, Camozzi curated the six-volume edition of Aristotle's *opera omnia* published by the Aldine press in 1551-52[40]; he also edited and translated several Greek commentaries on Aristotle[41]. But he also wrote two important works that were never printed: a commentary on Aristotle's *Metaphysics* in Greek[42], and the Plato commentary under investigation here.

Camozzi's Plato commentary, extant in two manuscripts now in the Vatican Library[43], was written in the 1570s: we can work out this date from a passage at the end of the commentary, where Camozzi indicates that it was written twenty years after his commentary on Theophrastus' *Metaphysics*, which was published in 1551[44]. This date is confirmed by the dedication to Cardinal Filippo Boncompagni (1548-1586), a nephew of Pope Gregory XIII, who became cardinal in 1572. This means that the commentary was written, together with the preface, between 1572 and Camozzi's death in 1581, that is, at the time he was teaching rhetoric at the Roman *studium*.

It is impossible to determine whether he actually taught the *Alcibiades* or integrated some Platonic material in his course. It is interesting to note, however, that some twenty years earlier Camozzi expressed the possibility of reading some Platonic material (more specifically Olympiodorus' commentary on Plato's *Gorgias*) for the course on Aristotle's *Rhetoric* he gave at the University of Bologna, as indicated by a letter the Venetian philosopher Sebastiano Erizzo wrote to him in 1549[45]. More importantly, the very format and content of the

---

39 CONTE, *I maestri della Sapienza di Roma dal 1514 al 1787*, I, pp. 89-92 [1574-75], p. 111 ["Anno 1576: In Rhetorica, de mane: D. Ioannes Baptista Camotius: scuta 100. D. Thomas Correa: scuta 100. In Rhetorica, de sero: D. Marcus Antonius Muretus: scuta 500"], pp. 116-118 [1579-80]. On Muret, see below.
40 *Aristotelis omnem logicam, rhetoricam, et poeticam disciplinam continens*, Venice, apud Aldi filios, 1551-53.
41 *Ioannis Baptistae Camotii Commentarium in primum Metaphysices Theophrasti libri tres*, Venice, apud Federicum Turrisanum, 1551; *Olympiodorou philosophou Alexandreos Eis ta Meteora tou Aristotelous ypomnemata. Ioannou Grammatikou tou Philoponou Scholia eis to a ton Meteoron tou Aristotelous. Olympiodori philosophi Alexandrini In Meteora Aristotelis commentarii. Ioannis Grammatici Philoponi Scholia in primum Meteorum Aristotelis*, Venice, apud Aldi filios, 1551; *Pselli philosophi sapientissimi In Physicen Aristotelis commentarij, Ioanne Baptista Camotio philosopho interprete*, Venice, apud Federicum Turrisanum, 1554; *Alexandri Aphrodisiensis in libros Aristotelis Meteorologicos commentarii, Ioanne Baptista Camotio interprete, in urbe Macerata totius agri Piceni metropoli philosophiam publice profitente*, Venice, Ioannes Gryphius, 1556.
42 Paris, BNF, gr. 1940, f. 1-61 and BNF suppl. gr. 682, f. 43-81.
43 Città del Vaticano, BAV, Boncompagni K 27 and BAV, Barb. lat. 344. See P. O. KRISTELLER, *Marsilio Ficino and His Work After Five Hundred Years*, Florence, Olschki, 1987, pp. 138 and 171; Id., *Iter Italicum: A Finding List of Uncatalogued or Incompletely Catalogued Humanistic Manuscripts of the Renaissance in Italian and Other Libraries*, 6 vols, London, The Warburg Institute, 1990, III, p. 157.
44 Città del Vaticano, BAV, Barb. lat. 344, f. 125v.
45 See Erizzo's letter to Giovanni Battista Camozzi dated 31 December 1549, in BBV, MS G 3 8 7 (277), f. 159r-v, reprinted in *Lettere di XIII uomini illustri*, Venice, Comin da Trino, 1560,

Alcibiades commentary, as well as the didactic nature of the translation, suggest that Camozzi's work was primarily addressed to students.

At first sight Camozzi's *Alcibiades* commentary adopts a scholastic structure comparable to contemporary Aristotelian commentaries: it is structured in a succession of ten *dictiones*, i.e. large sections of the dialogue for which Camozzi provides his own translation (which is different from that of Ficino) followed by a commentary, itself divided into lemmas. On closer examination, however, it appears that Camozzi's commentary is actually modelled on the Neoplatonist Olympiodorus' commentary on Plato's *First Alcibiades*. Olympiodorus' commentary is a set of lecture notes and adopts a scholastic, lemmatic format typical of the courses of philosophy given in the Platonic schools of Late Antiquity. The term *dictio* Camozzi uses as heading for the ten sections of the commentary is an idiosynchratic translation of the Greek term *lexis* ("textual explanation"), the traditional heading used in Neoplatonic school lectures. In addition, the new Latin translation Camozzi provides of the *Alcibiades* is itself highly didactic: it contains numerous explanatory glosses, additions and etymological explanations, which suggests — given that Camozzi was an expert in Greek — that it was a working translation for the benefit of students[46].

Olympiodorus' Platonic commentaries were never translated into Latin and, although Ficino quoted his commentary on the *Phaedo*, we have no evidence that he used his commentary on the *Alcibiades*[47]. However, the relatively high number of copies made in the sixteenth century, most of which derive from one of Bessarion's two exemplars, indicates that Olympiodorus' commentaries enjoyed some success among Renaissance hellenists[48]. Camozzi probably got hold of a copy of Olympiodorus' *Alcibiades* commentary when he was in Venice,

---

pp. 636-637: "se vostra signoria sarà contenta in iscambio dell'Alessandro mandarmi il Proclo, l'accomoderò volentieri del mio Olimpiodoro sopra 'l *Gorgia*, il quale ho da quello esemplare antico, che ella vide nel mio studio, fatto trascrivere. Et il libro a punto è di nuovo scontrato correttissimo, del quale ancora ella potrà servirsi quanto le piacerà alla lettione della *Retorica* d'Aristotele, come mi scrive".

46 e.g. 103b ἔσχες] *te haberes animatusque esses* Camozzi (*te gereres* Ficino); 104d ὅτι ποτ' ἐστὶ τὸ σὸν πρᾶγμα] *quid tibi vis et quid istuc negotii est* Camozzi (*quid sit consilium tuum* Ficino) ; 104d ἐπιθυμεῖς εἰδέναι τί διανοοῦμαι] *tibi cordi ac studio est id scire et conoscere quae mihi mens et quod consilium sit hoc meum* Camozzi (*nosse et audire desideras quid cogitem* Ficino) ; 107e ὁ παιδοτρίβης] *is magister qui pueris exercendis praeest sive paedotriba vel gymnasii magister* Camozzi (*magister gymnasii* Ficino). In that respect, this translation is very similar to Vettori's Latin version of the *Lysis*, which was made for the purpose of teaching : see MARTINELLI TEMPESTA, "La versione latina di Pier Vettori del *Liside* platonico", p. 123.

47 L. G. WESTERINK, "Ficino's Marginal Notes on Olympiodorus in Riccardi Greek MS 37", in *Traditio*, 24 (1968), pp. 351-378: 352.

48 See L. G. WESTERINK, *Olympiodorus. Commentary on the First Alcibiades of Plato. Critical Text and Indices*, Amsterdam, North-Holland Publishing Company, 1956, p. VII for a detailed description of the manuscript tradition. Bessarion owned two independent copies of Olympiodorus' commentary, now BMV, Marcianus gr. 196, f. 118r-206r and Marcianus gr. 197, f. 114r-204v.

either through access to Bessarion's library, or through his friend Sebastiano Erizzo, who possessed two copies of the text[49]. More generally, Camozzi's choice of Olympiodorus as his main source (rather than Proclus or Damascius) is not innocent: Olympiodorus' commentary features aspects of late Alexandrian Neoplatonism that must have greatly appealed to Camozzi and his readers[50]. First, Olympiodorus' commentary is in the form of lecture notes. Since the *First Alcibiades* was the first set text to be read in the Neoplatonic curriculum, it is primarily addressed to students who were familiar with the school canon of Greek literature as well as with Aristotle, but were not yet initiated into the intrincacies of Neoplatonic metaphysics. In addition, Olympiodorus' commentary transmits a version of Neoplatonism that is strikingly less complex and theological than the one we find in the commentaries of his predecessors Proclus and Damascius. It provides an accessible explanation of Neoplatonic metaphysics, elucidates basic vocabulary and syntax, recasts Plato's arguments in the form of Aristotelian syllogisms, and focuses on the rhetorical aspects of the dialogue, making frequent references to a vast range of Greek literary, medical and historical sources that formed part of his audience's basic education. Finally, Olympiodorus, whose students were for the most part Christians, tones down and even Christianizes many of the Neoplatonic doctrines that were incompatible with Christianity[51]. All these aspects — the emphasis on rhetoric, the Christian interpretation of Neoplatonic doctrines, and the pedagogic nature of the commentary — are fully exploited by Camozzi: like Olympiodorus he makes frequent references to a vast body of literary and historical authors (in his case both Greek and Latin) to illustrate Platonic passages; similarly, he emphasizes the rhetorical aspects of the dialogue and the moral and spiritual dimension of Socrates' teaching rather than dwelling on Neoplatonic metaphysics; finally, he adopts Olympiodorus' Christianization of some of the more delicate Neoplatonic doctrines. For instance, when it comes to talking about Socrates' demon (briefly mentioned in *Alc. I* 305a), Camozzi paraphrases a passage from Olympiodorus where Socrates' demon is described in Christian terms as an angel and as the "conscience" of Socrates (τὸ συνειδός,

---

49 See again Erizzo's letter to Camozzi in BBV, MS G 3 8 7 (277), f. 159r-v, reprinted in *Lettere di XIII uomini illustri*, pp. 636-637, where Erizzo proposes to give him his copy of Olympiodorus' *Gorgias* commentary in exchange of Proclus' *Parmenides* Commentary.

50 On Olympiodorus' commentaries, see F. RENAUD, "Tradition et critiques: lecture jumelée de Platon et Aristote chez Olympiodore", in *Le commentaire philosophique dans l'Antiquité et ses prolongements: méthodes exégétiques (I)*, Laval théologique et philosophique, 64/1 (2008), pp. 89-104; on his *Alcibiades I* commentary, see F. RENAUD and H. TARRANT, *The Platonic Alcibiades I. The Dialogue and Its Ancient Reception*, Cambridge, Cambridge University Press, 2015, pp. 190-244; a complete English translation and detailed introduction is in M. GRIFFIN, *Olympiodorus: Life of Plato and On Plato First Alcibiades 1-9*, London, Bloomsbury, 2015 and Id., *Olympiodorus: On Plato First Alcibiades 10-28*, London, Bloomsbury, 2016.

51 M. GRIFFIN, "Introduction", in *Olympiodorus: Life of Plato and On Plato First Alcibiades 1-9*, pp. 3-7.

a central concept in patristic literature)[52]. What is important to note here is that, by following very closely Olympiodorus' interpretation, Camozzi is not only appropriating the pedagogic framework of the Platonic schools of Late Antiquity, but he also bypasses the entire tradition revived by Ficino and based on Neoplatonic commentators preceding Olympiodorus (Plotinus, Iamblichus and Proclus). For instance, Ficino endorsed much more fully and boldly Neoplatonic demonology, and effectively contradicted the negative judgement about pagan demons formulated by the Church Fathers[53]. In fact, although we have evidence that Camozzi was familiar with Ficino's translation of Plato's *First Alcibiades*[54], he makes no allusion to his interpretation of the text, nor does he mention any other Neoplatonic authors than the ones alluded to by Olympiodorus himself; he does not seem to have used Ficino's translations of Neoplatonic demonological texts, or to have firsthand knowledge of Proclus' commentary on the *First Alcibiades*. Apart from Aristotle, whom he cites on numerous occasions to underline the agreement between the Platonic and the Aristotelian traditions, he does not allude to any other philosophical source. Instead he cites (in addition to the sources mentioned in Olympiodorus' commentary) literary and historical authors, both Latin and Greek, who are used as *auctoritates* to elucidate or illustrate Plato's moral teaching. The distinctly literary flavour of the commentary is also apparent in the frequent instances where Camozzi appears to apologize for using technical philosophical terms[55].

Camozzi also emphasizes the profound significance of the dialogue for Christianity; he often adds passages from the Scriptures to illustrate some aspects of the *Alcibiades*: in the preface, he establishes a clear distinction between the medical and natural philosophy of Hippocrates and Aristotle on the one hand, and Plato's spiritual philosophy on the other. In the introduction to the dialogue, Camozzi explains that Plato's treatment of the dialogue's topic (man's nature) differs from that of both Hippocrates and Aristotle because he is the only philosopher to have envisaged the question from a spiritual point of view[56]. For, he argues,

---

52 BAV, Barb. lat. 344, f. 38r. Cf. OLYMPIODORUS, *In Alcibiadem* I, ed. WESTERINK, Amsterdam, North Holland Publishing Company, 1956, pp. 22,14-23,1.
53 On Ficino's views on Neoplatonic demonology vs. Augustine, see M. VANHAELEN, "L'entreprise de traduction et d'exégèse de Ficin dans les années 1486-89: Démons et prophétie à l'aube de l'ère savonarolienne", in *Humanistica*, 4/1 (2010), pp. 125-136.
54 BAV, Barb. lat. 344, f. 145r-v.
55 For instance, when using *ratiocinativa et imaginativa* to describe the parts of the soul, Camozzi adds *his verbis in philosophia utamur iamlicet* (BAV, Barb. lat. 344, f. 17r); or, when using the term "beings" (*entes*), he adds *hoc autem verbum iam in philosophiam usitatum est* (*ibid.*, f. 18r); conversely, when referring to Olympiorus' tripartite division of the dialogue into refutation, exhortation, and midwifery (*redargutorium, adhortatorium and obstetricarium*), he adds *liceat iam uti iis vocabulis in scholis philosophiae* (*Ibid.*, f. 30v) or *ad res specificatas ut hoc vocabulo uti liceat* (*Ibid.*, f. 125v).
56 *Ibid.*, f. 8v.

Plato considers that only the soul is what makes us human (*Alc. I* 130c)[57]. By encouraging us to neglect human affairs and elevate our soul to the divine, Camozzi concludes, Plato is closer than any other philosopher to Christian faith[58]. Here Camozzi uses the central tenet of the *First Alcibiades*, according to which one must ascend to God through the ladder of virtues, to defend the notion that Plato is closer to Christianity than any other philosopher. More specifically, he presents the *Alcibiades* as a text that teaches the way in which mankind can gain happiness on earth and in the afterlife. In this context, after paraphrasing Olympiodorus' account of the different interpretations of the dialogue's *skopos* (by Proclus, Damascius and Olympiodorus himself), he departs from Olympiodorus' commentary and devotes several pages to what, in his view, the dialogue is about: to show Alcibiades what true happiness is, which consists of leaving aside political and earthly matters and embrace the contemplative life, a thesis that, according to Camozzi, is supported by Aristotle and Isocrates[59]. Socrates' teaching ultimately aims at using the knowledge of oneself to lead a happy and contemplative life, in order to gain a likeness to God on earth[60].

A third important trend that one can observe in sixteenth-century Platonic works is the attempt to question constructively the ancient *comparatio* between Plato and Aristotle and reassess the extent to which both philosophers are (or not) compatible. It is fittingly illustrated by two works we will examine in tandem: Stefano Tiepolo's *Academicarum contemplationum libri decem*, a treatise on Plato's philosophy, which was published in 1576; and Francesco Piccolomini's *Universa philosophia de moribus*, a monumental treatise on moral philosophy published in 1583. Tiepolo was a prominent Venetian patrician and a student of Piccolomini, who was himself one of the most famous and successful university professors of the time and published towards the end of this career the very popular *Universa philosophia de moribus*, a treatise on Aristotelian moral philosophy[61].

---

57 *Ibid.*, f. 9r.
58 *Ibid.*, f. 46r.
59 *Ibid.*, f. 12r-16r.
60 *Ibid.*, f. 13r.
61 On Piccolomini, see A. POPPI, "Il problema della filosofia morale nella scuola padovana del Rinascimento: Platonismo e Aristotelismo nella definizione del metodo dell'etica", in DE GANDILLAC and MARGOLIN (eds), *Platon et Aristote à la Renaissance*, pp. 105-146: 119-122 and 124-132; A. E. BALDINI, "La politica 'etica' di Francesco Piccolomini", in *Il pensiero politico*, 13/2 (1980), pp. 161-185; A. E. BALDINI, "Per la biografia di Francesco Piccolomini", in *Rinascimento*, 20, 2nd s., (1980), pp. 389-420; N. JARDINE, "Keeping Order in the School of Padua: Jacopo Zabarella and Francesco Piccolomini on the Offices of Philosophy", in D. A. DI LISCIA, E. KESSLER and C. METHUEN (eds), *Method and Order in Renaissance Philosophy of Nature: The Aristotle Commentary Tradition*, Aldershot, Ashgate, 1997, pp. 183-209; D. A. LINES, *Aristotle's Ethics in the Italian Renaissance (c. 1300-1600): The Universities and the Problem of Moral Education*, Leiden, Brill, 2002, pp. 264-288; S. PLASTINA, "*Concordia discors*: Aristotelismus und Platonismus in der Philosophie des Francesco Piccolomini", in M. MULSOW (ed.), *Das Ende des Hermetismus: Historische Kritik und neue Naturphilosophie in der Spätrenaissance*, Tübingen,

Despite being a professor of Aristotelian philosophy, Piccolomini was well-known for his Platonic interests. In his biography of Piccolomini, for instance, Tomasini states that Piccolomini attempted to revive Platonic philosophy by both lecturing and commenting on it[62]. In addition, several sixteenth-century accounts state that Piccolomini was the author of Tiepolo's Platonic work. Piccolomini's own pupil and biographer Luigi Lollino recalls that Piccolomini held private lectures in his home on Aristotle and other authors and gave his favourite students the opportunity to publish under their own name works he had written himself. One of such instances was Stefano Tiepolo's *Academicarum contemplationum libri decem* (Venice, 1576), which, Lollino says, was in all but its title the work of Piccolomini[63]. The stratagem came into light, Lollino continues, when Piccolomini decided to publish several years later under his own name the *Philosophia universalis de moribus* (1583), thus revealing the extent to which Tiepolo had "plagiarized" Piccolomini and potentially ruining his reputation[64]. Lollino's account is well-known, and modern scholars have been divided regarding its accuracy: is Piccolomini the real author of these two works, or did his pupils make a liberal use of the method and material he taught in his lectures[65]?

At first sight, Piccolomini's *De moribus* and Tiepolo's *Academicarum* differ widely in scope: one is a treatise on moral philosophy primarily based on Aristotle; the other is a treatise on what Plato and the "Academics" have said about divine contemplation. However, a closer look reveals striking similarities between the two treatises. To start with, the two works use the same scholastic method of presenting various ancient opinions on a given question, followed by a "solutio" to philosophical problems. They share the same concern with reassessing the ancient, medieval and Renaissance interpretations of Plato and Aristotle, offering an allegedly more objective and accurate reading of the texts, and underlining the points of agreement and disagreement between the two. They are both very critical of the Neoplatonic attempts to reconcile Plato and Aristotle (in particular by Simplicius); they also distance themselves from Ficino's interpretation. Both treatises point to the need to refute the Aristotelian philosophers who reject Plato

---

Mohr Siebeck, 2002, pp. 213-234; J. KRAYE, "Eclectic Aristotelianism in the Moral Philosophy of Francesco Piccolomini", in G. PIAIA (ed.), *La presenza dell'aristotelismo padovano nella filosofia della prima modernità*. Atti del colloquio internazionale in memoria di Charles B. Schmitt (Padova, 4-6 settembre 2000), Rome-Padua, Antenore, 2002, pp. 57-82; A. POPPI, "Happiness", in LINES and EBBERSMEYER (eds), *Rethinking Virtue, Reforming Society*, pp. 243-275, part. pp. 267-269; D. A. LINES, "Latin and the Vernacular in Francesco Piccolomini's Moral Philosophy", in D. A. LINES and E. REFINI (eds), *'Aristotele fatto volgare'. Tradizione aristotelica e cultura volgare nel Rinascimento*, Pisa, ETS, 2014, pp. 169-199.

62 G. F. TOMASINI, *Elogia virorum literis et sapientia illustrium ad vivum expressis imaginibus exornata*, Padua, ex Typographia Sebastiani Sardi, 1644, p. 209.
63 See L. LOLLINO, *Francisci Piccolominei, Iacobique Zabarellae praestantium nostrorum temporum philosophorum vitae*, in *In Patavinorum professorum decadem*, in BCB, MS 505, f. 34v-35r.
64 *Ibid.*, f. 35r.
65 See BALDINI, "Per la biografia", pp. 399-402.

altogether, and to nuance the views of the commentators who exaggerate the similarities between the two. They reach the same conclusion that there are some points of doctrine on which Aristotle and Plato cannot be reconciled, and some on which they only disagree in words. Both treatises use similar expressions such as "verum lis haec potius in verbis quam in sententia est posita" and "lis eorum in solis verbis posita est". They also share the same interest in Stoicism's contribution to philosophy, which they generally reject in favour of Plato and/or Aristotle.

More importantly, there are significant overlaps between the two works: in many places Piccolomini's work reproduces, word for word, entire passages from Tiepolo's work; in others, Piccolomini reworks and reorganizes ideas that were already expressed in Tiepolo, thus suggesting that Piccolomini used Tiepolo's work as preparatory material for a more developed reflection on how to integrate Platonic and Aristotelian doctrines[66]. It is difficult to state with certainty that the two works were written by the same author, because there are slight variations in style and the overlaps are never completely exact and, above all, the scope of the two works is very different. What is certain, however, is that Piccolomini appropriated a vast amount of Platonic material from Tiepolo's *Academicarum contemplationum*, which he reelaborated and developed in the context of a reassessment of the relationship between Plato and Aristotle. Conversely, it is safe to assume that Tiepolo's work stems directly from lectures Piccolomini devoted to Plato: in the introduction to the *Academicarum contemplationum*, Tiepolo states that he wrote the work with the help of his two Paduan professors, Tommaso Pellegrini and Francesco Piccolomini, who are described as specialists of both Plato and Aristotle; Tiepolo also says that he made a well-informed use of both their public (i.e. university) and private lectures[67].

With this specific example, we touch upon an important point made in the introduction to this chapter, which is the issue of eclecticism: when we know that Piccolomini studied in detail Plato's dialogues, that he probably taught some of them, and that he appropriated entire sections from a Platonic commentary in his own published work, the label "eclecticism" that is often applied to his approach is no longer sufficient to describe his attitude towards Plato; it is rather the case that Piccolomini explored in great detail Plato's original texts to provide a more accurate picture of the Plato-Aristotle controversy and put some order in the various philosophical traditions that had been inherited in the Renaissance. More importantly, this approach is based on a direct engagement with Plato's dialogues; it is motivated by a need to consider the ancient commentary tradition more

---

66 e.g. F. PICCOLOMINI, *Universa philosophia de moribus*, Venice, apud Franciscum de Franciscis Senensem, 1583 (hereafter *DM*), Gradus IX, 22, p. 502 = S. TIEPOLO, *Academicarum contemplationum libri decem*, Venice, apud Petrum Dehuchinum, 1576 (hereafter *AC*), I, 4, p. 8; *DM*, p. 433 = *AC* I,6, pp. 12-13; *DM*, pp. 328-329 = *AC* VI, 5, pp. 108-110; *DM* IX, 7, p. 476 = *AC* IX, 6, pp. 177-179.

67 TIEPOLO, *Academicarum contemplationum libri decem*, Epistola dedicatoria, f. [*iii]r.

critically, and ultimately leads to a significant reappraisal of the role Plato could play in discussions pertaining to moral philosophy.

These three works illustrate how Plato's dialogues came to be envisaged in some sixteenth-century circles, often independently from Ficino's interpretation. They were written by philosophers who are generally described as Aristotelians, wrote commentaries on Aristotle, and held a university position. Although most of these works seem to have a didactic purpose, we cannot say with absolute certainty that the material they contained were actual university lectures. There are, however, several extant lectures on Plato by university professors, of which I will now present four examples.

Platonic Lectures by University Professors

The first is a set of university lectures on Plato's *Gorgias* and *Apology of Socrates* delivered by Agostino Valier (1531-1606)[68]. Before becoming cardinal and bishop of Verona, Valier taught moral philosophy between 1558 and 1565 at the Rialto school, a major teaching centre of logic and philosophy in Venice[69]. It is during that time that he wrote a work entitled *De recta philosophandi ratione*, a didactic treatise that sums up his ideas about how to teach philosophy. The book was only published in 1577 by Valier's friend Agostino Nani, when Valier had already left Venice to take up his responsabilities as bishop of Verona. In its printed version, the book includes ten *praefationes*, which are Valier's introductory lectures to his courses on Aristotle. However, a manuscript version of the same *De recta philosophandi ratione*, now in the Biblioteca Ambrosiana in Milan, does not include the *praefationes* to the Aristotle lectures, but contains instead two introductory lectures on Plato's *Apology* and *Gorgias*, as well as teaching notes (*annotationes*) on

---

68 On Valier, see S. NEGRUZZO, "Le Cardinal Auguste Valier, un humaniste au service de la Contre-Réforme", in *Seizième siècle*, 11 (2015), pp. 259-273. See also A. L. PULIAFITO, "Filosofia aristotelica e modi dell'apprendimento. Un intervento di Agostino Valier su *Qua ratione versandum sit in Aristotele*", in *Rinascimento*, 30, 2nd s. (1990), pp. 153-172; G. CIPRIANI, *La mente di un inquisitore. Agostino Valier e l'Opusculum* De cautione adhibenda in edendis libris *(1589-1604)*, Florence, Nicomp, 2009; and F. LUCIOLI (ed.), *Agostino Valier, Instituzione d'ogni stato lodevole delle donne cristiane*, Cambridge, Modern Humanities Research Association, 2015, pp. 5-11.

69 On the Rialto School, see B. NARDI, "La scuola di Rialto e l'umanesimo veneziano", in V. BRANCA (ed.), *Umanesimo europeo e umanesimo veneziano*, Florence, Sansoni, 1963, pp. 93-139; J. B. ROSS, "Venetian Schools and Teachers, Fourteenth to Early Sixteenth Century: A Survey and a Study of Giovanni Battista Egnazio", in *Renaissance Quarterly*, 29 (1976), pp. 521-566; F. LEPORI, "La scuola di Rialto dalla fondazione alla metà del Cinquecento", in G. ALADI and M. PASTORE STOCCHI (eds), *Storia della cultura veneta. III/2. Dal primo Quattrocento al Concilio di Trento*, Vicenza, Neri Pozza, 1980, pp. 539-605. On Valier's lectures at the Rialto school, see G. SANTINELLO, "Politica e filosofia alla Scuola di Rialto: Agostino Valier (1531-1606)", in *Quaderni del Centro tedesco di studi veneziani*, 24 (1983), pp. 1-24 [reprinted in his *Traduzione e dissenso nella filosofia veneta*, Padua, Antenore, 1991, pp. 116-139].

the same two dialogues[70]. In one of these lectures, we find the first explicit recognition that a professor of Aristotelian philosophy deliberately took the liberty to teach on Plato. Valier states that, although necessity and duty require him to teach Aristotle, he has nonetheless decided to devote some lectures to Plato, not only because Aristotle was Plato's pupil for twenty years (a well-known topos in ancient and Renaissance literature, as noted in this volume's introduction), but also because of the intrinsic value of his doctrines[71]. In the same passage, Valier criticizes the Aristotelians who condemn the practice of studying both Plato and Aristotle, consider Plato's thought to be airy and metaphorical, and treat Plato as an orator rather than a philosopher: according to him they have this opinion because they have not read or properly understood his dialogues; and by criticising Plato they unwillingly attack Aristotle, since the philosopher, indeed, benefitted from the teachings of Plato for twenty years. Valier also distances himself from the "radical" Platonists (*nimium Platonici*) who seek to interpret allegorically every word of Plato's dialogues; and he underlines the importance of Plato's philosophy in various fields, including natural, moral and political philosophy[72].

Valier's decision to teach the *Apology of Socrates* and the *Gorgias* as part of a course on moral philosophy could be surprising at first; it becomes less so when one considers that moral philosophy was often taught by professors of rhetoric rather than natural philosophers, leading to a greater emphasis on the literary and stylistic aspects of philosophical texts[73]. After all, as we have mentioned above, one of the first to teach Plato in a European university, Paulus Niavis, was a professor of rhetoric and humanities at Leipzig, and used Plato's dialogues precisely to teach his students the necessity to unite eloquence and philosophy. In addition, the *Gorgias* and the *Apology* were often perceived as belonging to the field of ethics: Leonardo Bruni considered that the *Gorgias* was concerned

---

70 BAM, D447 inf., f. 47r-48v (*Praefatio Augustini Valerii in Gorgiam Platonis*); f. 48v-58v (*Prima interpretatio in Gorgiam Platonis*); f. 60r-62v (*Praefatio in Apologiam Platonis*); f. 63r-65r (*Annotationes quam brevissimae in Socratis Apologia a Platone eius discipulo scripta*). A partial version of these texts is in Udine, Biblioteca communale, Manin 1308 (157).

71 A. VALIER, *Praefatio in Apologiam Platonis*, in BAM, D447 inf., f. 60r-v: "Multiplex variarum et pulcherrimarum rerum scientia, admirabilis ordo, verborum proprietas, quae omnia insunt in Aristotelicis scriptis, alliciunt homines ad ea studiose legenda. Sed certe gravissimas et maxime salutares sententias quas eximia eloquentia explicatas reliquit Plato, nemo sine iactura iudicii et eruditionis potest negligere. Quamobrem quamvis meum potissimum studium versetur et debet versari in explicandis Aristotelicis libris, statui tamen omnino non esse negligenda scripta hominis illius quo ille quem non immerito admiramur viginti annos usus est magistro. [...] Percipi meo iudicio multa possunt, ex illius dialogis de corporibus naturalibus, eorum principiis, atque accidentibus, de immortalitate animorum, de providentia Dei, de virtute amplectenda, de voluptate, vitiisque omnibus fugiendis, de republica recte instituenda, et gubernanda, quae omnes sunt maxime utiles, et salutares sententias, nec Themistium, Simplicium, Philoponum optimos Aristotelis explicatores Platonem contempsisse aut non diligenter legisse".

72 Ibid., f. 60r-v.

73 On the change of classification of moral philosophy in the sixteenth century, see LINES, *Aristotle's Ethics in the Italian Renaissance*, pp. 243-245.

with political virtue, on the grounds that the premise of Plato's exploration of rhetoric in the *Gorgias* is how one should live well (*Gorg.* 500c)[74]. Similarly, the *Apology of Socrates* was classified as pertaining to moral philosophy in Antiquity, with Socrates being presented as a model of moral and civic virtue.

Valier's lectures on the *Apology of Socrates* concern mostly the definition and the nature of Plato's rhetoric. For him Socrates is the model of civic and moral virtue par excellence, and Plato's eloquence is a philosophical rhetoric at the service of truth that can best serve the ideology of the Venetian state. There are clear civic and political undertones here: Valier describes Socrates' virtues in terms that echo the Christian virtues (truth, poverty, contempt for wealth, sobriety and continence), and after lamenting the little respect men have for these values, he states that any city would benefit from them, since one single Socratic man could purge a city from the vices of flattery and arrogance and teach the youth how to neglect exterior wealth and learn true virtues[75]. Imagine, Valier tells his audience, that Socrates were to resuscitate in our era: he would probably not be condemned to death in Venice, a city that is moderated by excellent laws, but he would be attacked and hated for his philosophical acumen, his freedom of speech and his contempt for ingenious and ambitious men, for truth begets hatred[76].

In the lectures on the *Gorgias*, Valier focuses again on Socrates' definition of rhetoric and compares it with that of Aristotle. In the first lecture, he discusses the different definitions of rhetoric, underlining the points of similarity between Cicero, Aristotle and Plato. In the second lecture, he discusses the different types of rhetoric with reference to Cicero. Valier also presents useful *documenta* on Plato in the form of edifying proverbs and sayings that recall university textbooks and florilegia[77]. Finally, he makes an interesting statement on the respective value of Aristotle and Plato, drawing on a topos that humanists had variously used to oppose Aristotle to Cicero or counter the attacks that Plato's philosophy was disorderly and unsystematic: Aristotle excelled at expressing philosophy with order, whereas Plato should be praised because he not only taught philosophy, but also inspired men to be virtuous and moderate[78]. Valier's teaching of Plato, with its emphasis on the literary as well as the ethical aspects of the dialogues, illustrates the way in which Plato was progressively dissociated from the realm of metaphysics in some teaching contexts, and came to be studied as a literary author comparable to Cicero, that is, as a model of moral virtue and eloquence. We

---

74 M. VENIER, "Note su due traduzioni umanistiche del *Gorgia*", in C. GRIGGIO and F. VENDRUSCOLO (eds), *Suave mari magno... Studi offerti dai colleghi udinesi a Ernesto Berti*, Udine, Forum, 2008, pp. 232-236.
75 BAM, D447 inf., f. 61r-v.
76 *Ibid.*, f. 62 r-v.
77 *Ibid.*, f. 48v.
78 *Ibid.*, f. 57r.

encountered earlier a similar approach in Camozzi, who often illustrated Plato's arguments with quotations from Greek and Latin literary authors.

This is not to say that Plato was not envisaged as a philosophical author: we have several examples of lectures on the *Timaeus* given by professors of natural philosophy. One of them is a set of three lectures on Plato's *Timaeus*, which are preserved in two copies, now in the Biblioteca Universitaria of Bologna and in the Biblioteca Comunale of Fermo respectively[79]. In both versions the text has the appearance of lecture notes taken by students (*reportationes*): it contains numerous misspellings, repetitions as well as gaps in places where the students appear to have lost track of what the professor was saying. They have been tentatively attributed to Ludovico Boccadiferro, one of the most influential professors of natural philosophy in the sixteenth century, because in the Fermo manuscript they are part of a collection of lectures, some of which (but not all) are by Boccadiferro[80]. The text preserved in the Bologna manuscript is undated; the one in the Fermo manuscript is part of a collection of lectures copied by one single hand and dated January 1554, that is, nine years after Boccadiferro's death; as the copist's note indicates, it is a copy (*descriptus*) of an original text[81]. There are clear overlaps between the *Timaeus* lectures and Boccadiferro's lectures. First, the content of the anonymous lectures indicates that it was part of a course on natural philosophy: at the end of the text, the author explicitly states that he wishes to interpret various questions "according to the principles of natural philosophy"[82]. The author also discusses a number of physical phenomena such as the comet Phaeton, the periodic rising of the Nile and the deluge, all of

---

79 BUB, MS Aldrov. 56, vol. 2, f. 270r-274v and BCF, MS 80 [4 CA 2/80], f. 99r-102v. For a full description of the Fermo manuscript, see S. PRETE, *I codici della Biblioteca Comunale di Fermo. Catalogo*, Florence, Olschki, 1960, pp. 108-110. For a description of the Bologna manuscript, see L. FRATI, with the collaboration of A. CHIGI and A. SORBELLI, *Catalogo dei manoscritti di Ulisse Aldrovandi*, Bologna, Zanichelli, 1907, pp. 59-62: 61, where Frati wrongly describes the text as "Expositio in Platonem *De republica*" and gives the wrong foliation (f. 270-277). The two manuscripts are mentioned in HANKINS, "The Study of the *Timaeus* in Early Renaissance Italy", pp. 89 and 118-119.

80 Among these, however, anonymous lectures on the *Ethics* have been identified as being authored by Antonio Bernardi: see LINES, *Aristotle's Ethics in the Italian Renaissance*, pp. 500-501. The *Timaeus* lecture is unlikely to be by this author, because it does not rely on the Greek text as in the case of the *Ethics* lectures. On Boccadiferro's teaching at the university of Bologna, see DALLARI, *I Rotuli dei lettori legisti e artisti dello Studio bolognese dal 1384 al 1799*, II, pp. 12-18, 21-35, 38, 52-105. On his teaching at the Roman *Studium*, see G. FANTUZZI, *Notizie degli scrittori bolognesi*, Bologna, San Tommaso d'Aquino, 1781, I, p. 212.

81 Both the Fermo and the Bologna manuscripts include the same two texts (the *Timaeus* lectures and a lecture on logic), which are in each case within a single quire copied by one hand. This suggests that one manuscript derives from the other, or, more likely, that they independently derive from the same source. At the end of the quire the Fermo manuscript contains a note by the scribe, whose name is Antonius, stating that he copied the text on 10 January 1554 (BCF, MS. 80 [4 CA 2/80], f. 105r: "Descripsi ego Antonius die 10 ianuarii 1554").

82 BUB, MS Aldrov. 56, vol. 2, f. 274 v.

which were addressed in Boccadiferro's commentary on Book I of Aristotle's *Meteorology*, with reference to the same passage from the *Timaeus*[83]. Three other aspects the *Timaeus* lectures shares with Boccadiferro's works are: the method of analyzing the texts in a critical way, an interest in the historical transmission of texts, and the inclusion of traditional *topoi* according to which Plato was *divinus*[84] and considered that philosophical knowledge makes us similar to God[85]. In addition, during his lifetime Boccadiferro was well known for his interest in Plato. He was a close friend of Achille Bocchi (1488-1562), a professor of humanities at the university and the founder of the Accademia Bocchiana, a school and literary academy sponsored by Cardinal Alessandro Farnese and active since 1526, with strong interests in the Platonic and Cabbalistic traditions[86]. In his funeral oration Giovanni Battista Camozzi, who was himself a disciple of Boccadiferro and the author of the *Alcibiades* commentary mentioned above, tells us that on his deathbed Boccadiferro spent around an hour praising Plato and wishing he had had the time "to write a treatise on Plato's *Laws*" (*epitomas librorum ipsius De legibus se collecturum*)[87]. A century later Cardinal Giacomo Filippo Tomasini wrote that Boccadiferro spent the last part of his life writing a commentary on Plato's *Laws*[88]. The presence of Plato is also noticeable in Boccadiferro's lectures on Aristotle. As Luca Bianchi has shown, Boccadiferro integrated in his teaching the new philosophical developments that took place in the fifteenth and sixteenth centuries. He consistently relied on medieval sources, but also showed a clear interest in the "new" commentators on Aristotle as well as in Galen, Plato and Ficino. His method was characterized by philological and historical criticism, which led him to criticize the interpretation of *auctoritates* (including Aristotle) if

---

[83] L. BOCCADIFERRO, *Lectiones super primum librum Meteorologicorum*, Venice, apud haeredem Hieronymi Scoti, 1590, pp. 161-162.

[84] L. BOCCADIFERRO, *Explanatio libri primi Physicorum Aristotelis*, Venice, apud Hieronymum Scotum, 1570, p. 3.

[85] *Ibid.*, p. 3. On this topos in Plato and its development in Aristotle's ethics, see D. SEDLEY, "The Ideal of Godlikeness", in G. FINE (ed.), *Plato 2: Ethics, Politics, Religion, and the Soul*, Oxford, Oxford University Press, 1999, pp. 309-328.

[86] At the university Bocchi taught Greek (*diebus festis*, 1508-12), rhetoric and poetry (1513-24 and 1527-39) and humanities (*diebus festis*, 1524-27 and 1539-62): see DALLARI, *I Rotuli dei lettori legisti e artisti dello Studio Bolognese*, I, pp. 202-212 (1508-1512) and II, pp. 9-156 (1513-62). On the Academy (earliest record in 1526, formal foundation around 1543), see WATSON, *Achille Bocchi and the Emblem Book as Symbolic Form*, pp. 26-63, with a list of visitors and members at pp. 153-154; ROLET, "L'Hermathena Bocchiana ou l'idée de la parfaite académie", pp. 295-323. On Achille Bocchi's interest in Cabbalah, see A. ANGELINI, *Simboli e questioni: l'eterodossia culturale di Achille Bocchi e dell'Hermathena*, Bologna, Pendragon, 2003, pp. 28-29.

[87] G. B. CAMOZZI, *Oratio in funere Ludouici Buccaferreae clarissimi philosophi Bononiensis*, Bologna, in officina Bartholomaei Bonardi et Marci Antonij Groscij, 1545, f. civ-ciir.

[88] TOMASINI, *Elogia virorum literis et sapientia illustrium ad vivum expressis imaginibus exornata*, p. 118.

it was not supported by the texts, and discuss in detail the opinions of authors that were not part of the traditional curriculum[89].

There is, however, an important aspect that makes the attribution to Boccadiferro difficult: in the final section of the third *Timaeus* lecture, the author mentions Lodovico Nogarola's *Timotheus sive de Nilo*, a dialogue on the periodic risings of the Nile, which was only published in 1552, that is, seven years after Boccadiferro's death. We find no references to Nogarola in Boccadiferro's published lectures, and we must discard the possibility that the *Timaeus* lecture was modified after Boccadiferro's death by one of his pupils, because the last sentence, which announces the topic of future lectures, indicates that the Nogarola section was part of the original text. It cannot be excluded that Boccadiferro knew Nogarola's work prior to its publication, since Boccadiferro and Nogarola studied at Bologna at the same time (around 1513-1515) and were both closely connected to the Gonzaga family[90]. It is more likely, however, that the author of the lectures was a pupil or a close associate of Boccadiferro and adopted a method of inquiry similar to the one we find in Boccadiferro's lectures[91].

The *Timaeus* lectures thus provide unmistakable evidence that a professor lectured on a Platonic dialogue in the context of a course on natural philosophy, and that he did so by engaging directly with the original text rather than relying

---

89 L. BIANCHI, "Fra Ermolao Barbaro e Ludovico Boccadiferro: qualche considerazione sulle trasformazioni della 'fisica medievale' nel Rinascimento italiano", in *Medioevo*, 29 (2004), pp. 341-378; Id., *Studi sull'Aristotelismo del Rinascimento*, Padua, Il Poligrafo, 2003, pp. 125-132. On Boccadiferro's interest in Plato, see also E. GARIN, "Note and notizie", in *Giornale critico della filosofia italiana*, 11, 3rd s. (1957), pp. 406-412: 407-408 and A. ROTONDÒ, "Per la storia dell'eresia a Bologna del secolo XVI", in *Rinascimento*, 2, 2nd s., (1962), pp. 107-154: 126-128 and 133-134.

90 Boccadiferro published under his hellenized name (Siderostomo) Guido Postumo Silvestri's *Elegiarum libri II* (1524) with a preface to Pietro Gonzaga; Nogarola's *Timotheus* was dedicated to Ercole Gonzaga. Boccadiferro was also in contact with Fracastoro, one of the protagonists in the *Timotheus*: in a letter to Ramusio dated 1541, Fracastoro writes that he hopes to publish in a reedition of his *Homocentrica* (which never appeared) an additional treatise in response to the objections made by Boccadiferro and Sabbatio: see D. ATAGANI, *Lettere di XIII huomini illustri*, Venice, per Francesco Lorenzini da Turino, 1560, p. 723: "Mi fu forza aggiunger'un trattatello a quei mei *Homocentrici* nel quale difendo molte obiettioni, che da diversi luoghi mi erano scritte, massime dal Boccadiferro et M. Basilio Sabbatio, et altre, che'l Reverando Cardinale Contareno già mi disse".

91 Although this anonymous professor was not necessarily teaching at the university of Bologna, we note that Boccadiferro's successors to the chair of philosophy in Bologna between 1552 and 1554 (i.e. between the date of publication of Nogarola's work and the date the Fermo text was copied) are Antonio Francesco Fava, Mainetto Mainetti, Piero Maria Baldi, Claudio Betti, Giovan Antonio Locatelli, Scipione Fava and Gabriele de Beatis. See DALLARI, *I Rotuli dei lettori legisti e artisti dello Studio Bolognese*, II, pp. 125-133 and more specifically on natural philosophy in Bologna, D. A. LINES, "Natural Philosophy in Renaissance Italy: The University of Bologna and the Beginnings of Specialization" in *Science and Universities of Early Modern Europe: Teaching, Specialization, Professionalization*, special issue of *Early Science and Medicine*, 6/4 (2001), pp. 267-323.

on Aristotle and the commentators. The aim of these lectures is to provide information about Plato and draw clear comparison between Plato and Aristotle, underlining their similarities and differences, evidently to teach Platonic doctrines to an audience that was more familiar with Aristotle. It also uses a typical scholastic method to interpret Plato, using syllogisms and logical deductions to discuss his arguments. The author's motivation seems, therefore, to inform students of the real differences between Plato and Aristotle without merely relying on the testimony of Aristotle and the Greek commentators. In several Aristotelian texts taught at university, students would encounter attacks against Plato. For instance, Book II of Aristotle's *Generation and Corruption*, contains strong criticism of Plato's *Timaeus*[92], and some themes mentioned in the *Timaeus* (the deluge, the rising of the Nile, and the creation of world) are central to Aristotle's *Meteorology*, another text that was part of the syllabus of natural philosophy (which however only makes one direct allusion to Plato, in Book II). One is tempted to speculate, therefore, that the anonymous professor, in the middle of his course on Aristotle, felt the need to pause and explain the *Timaeus* before analyzing Aristotle's criticisms, rather than simply relying on Aristotle's own reading of Plato's *Timaeus*.

The lectures also reflect an interest in textual and historical criticism. In the opening section the author considers the reasons why Plato did not enjoy the same popularity as Aristotle, an issue that, as we have seen, still baffles commentators to this day. "I do not know why no-one lectures on Plato's writings privately or publicly", he says, "for they do not lack philosophical insight, since the divine Plato excelled so much in every philosophical discipline that he was called the god of philosophers by Cicero, who also said that Aristotle was the one with the highest intelligence and talent, but after Plato". He further states that "in the investigation of natural things he was second to none; in fact, Proclus states that he was superior to Aristotle, because to the causes identified by Aristotle Plato added the exemplar and instrumental causes"[93]. Here the author not only invokes the idea, central in ancient Neoplatonic literature, that Aristotle adopted an incomplete set of Platonic causes (omitting the instrumental and paradigmatic causes)[94], he also underlines the fundamental difference between Plato and Aristotle regarding the study of meteorological phenomena, which is that Aristotle never discussed the existence of a final cause (namely, a purpose)

---

92 L. BOCCADIFERRO, *In duos libros Aristotelis de generatione et corruptione doctissima commentaria*, Venice, apud Franciscum de Franciscis Senensem, 1571, f. 148 r-v.
93 BUB, MS Aldrov. 56, f. 270r.
94 Later Neoplatonism posits six modes of causation: three true causes (*aitiai*), which are the efficient, final, and paradigmatic causes, and three auxiliary causes (*sunaitiai*), which are the formal, material and the instrumental, to be contrasted to Aristotle's four causes (material, efficient, formal and final, cf. *Physics* 2.3). Cf. SIMPLICIUS, *Commentary in Aristotle's Physics* 10.35-11.4 (Diels), where it is said that, according to Porphyry, Aristotle adopted an incomplete set of Platonic causes (the four Aristotelian causes) and omitted two further causes postulated by Plato: the paradigmatic and the instrumental causes.

for natural phenomena, whereas Plato did in the *Timaeus*. Aristotle's failure to identify final causes in the *Meteorology*, which threatened the Christian idea of the divine order of the universe, had been discussed in detail by Pomponazzi in his 1522 Bolognese lectures on Aristotle's *Meteorology* and later taken up, up to a certain point, by one of his students, Boccadiferro[95].

The author then reflects on the circumstances that led to the neglect of Platonic studies: according to him, this neglect is due to a lack of order and general confusion in Plato's writings, caused by Plato's habit to mix up matters related to natural philosophy with divine and mathematical doctrines, rather than treating them in separate treatises like Aristotle; the prevailing custom of reading Aristotle; and an ignorance of the Greek language. However, he argues, now that Greek literature has been revived, one can rely on a number of Platonic interpreters, among whom are Proclus, Porphyry, Calcidius, Iamblichus, Plotinus, and Marsilio Ficino[96].

The text consists of three different lectures, which are clearly distinct through closing statements marking the end of a lecture and announcing what will be taught at the next session[97]. The first one is an introductory lecture which typically explores the place of the *Timaeus* within the Platonic corpus, its subject, usefulness, structure and order; the second is an analysis of the opening section of the *Timaeus*, in which the author addresses the metaphysical significance of the dialogue's protagonists and the problem of the community of women and goods; the third one is on the myth of Atlantis in the *Timaeus* and its purpose for explaining physical phenomena, including the periodic flooding of the Nile. In terms of sources, the author mentions Aristotle, Cicero, Galen and the Neoplatonists, as well as Bessarion and Ficino. He also makes one allusion to "cabbalistic authors" whose tripartition of the world he compares with Plato's[98]. Finally, he mentions Girolamo Fracastoro and Lodovico Nogarola, the former as the protagonist of the latter's *De Nilo*.

The lectures adopt the traditional format of a classroom *expositio*, setting the work in its immediate context, clarifying the work's usefulness as well as the author's intention, and then providing a close reading of selected passages. The

---

95 On this important point, see C. MARTIN, *Renaissance Meteorology. Pomponazzi to Descartes*, Baltimore, The Johns Hopkins University Press, 2011, pp. 44-51: Pomponazzi explicitly contrasts Aristotle with Plato, whereas Boccadiferro notes the possibility for final causes to exist, even if the imperfect nature of meteorological phenomena makes it difficult to identify them.
96 *Ibid.*, f. 270r.
97 *Ibid.*, f. 270v and 272v.
98 *Ibid.*, f. 270v: "in naturalibus quoque posuit [sc. Plato] mathematica et divina, sicuti cabalistae qui tres mundos imaginantur, caelestem, supercaelestem et sublunarem, et unus in alio dicitur contineri". In addition to the Cabbalistic interests of the Accademia Bocchiana, it should be noted that the university of Bologna created in 1520 the first chair of "Hebrew and Chaldean letters", which was held by Giovanni Flaminio: DALLARI, *I Rotuli dei lettori legisti e artisti dello Studio bolognese dal 1384 al 1799*, II, p. 29 (the chair becomes vacant in 1526-27 and disappears from the rolls in 1532-33).

author's approach is mainly didactic and logical: he often recasts philosophical arguments in the form of syllogisms or *quaestiones*, presenting the *pro* or *contra* of each position. At times, he underlines the similarity between Aristotle and Plato[99]; at others, he rejects Aristotle's criticisms of Plato on the grounds that they are not logical[100].

The attempt to introduce Plato in courses of natural philosophy did not go unchallenged, as indicated by Federico Pendasio's lectures on the *Timaeus*. A close pupil of Boccadiferro who worked at the court of Ercole Gonzaga before holding a chair of natural philosophy at the universities of Pavia, Padua and Bologna, Federico Pendasio delivered several lectures on Plato, of which only one, entitled "On the differences between Plato and Aristotle", is preserved in the Ambrosiana library in Milan[101]. The lecture is not dated; it is part of a miscellaneous manuscript which includes various *reportationes* of Pendasio's lectures, each in a separate *quaderno* and copied by a different hand, collected by one of Pendasio's most faithful disciples, Gian Vincenzo Pinelli[102]. The lecture was probably delivered in the context of Pendasio's course of natural philosophy, since at the end of the lecture Pendasio explicitly refers to lectures on Aristotle's *Physics* he will give the same year[103]. This means that it was probably part of a set of introductory lectures on the differences between Plato and Aristotle he gave shortly before lecturing on the *Physics*, either in Padua (1565-1568) or Bologna (1573).

Pendasio's lecture emphasizes the differences between Plato and Aristotle and argues that Plato is not an appropriate author for students of philosophy. First, Pendasio provides a general paraphrase of Plato's *Timaeus*, followed by an analysis of his logical arguments. His aim is to show that, if one reduces Plato's theses to syllogisms, they are untenable and illogical. The tone is markedly different from the three anonymous *Timaeus* lectures analysed above: Platonic doctrines

---

99 *Ibid.*, f. 271v.
100 *Ibid.*, f. 273r.
101 BAM, S87 sup., f. 117r-122r: "Pendasius de differentia Platonis et Aristotelis lectio iiii". The complete text of the lecture is reproduced in E. DEL SOLDATO, *Early Modern Aristotle. On the Making and Unmaking of Authority*, Philadelphia, University of Pennsylvania Press, 2020, pp. 163-177, with analysis at pp. 66-67. On Pendasio's teaching in Pavia, see A. CORRADI, *Memorie e documenti per la storia dell'Università di Pavia. Vol. I*, Pavia, Bizzoni, 1878, p. 172; S. FAZZO, "Girolamo Cardano e lo Studio di Pavia", in M. BALDI and G. CANZIANI (eds), *Girolamo Cardano: le opere, le fonti, la vita*, Milan, Franco Angeli, 1999, pp. 521-574: 539-574. On his teaching in Padua, see A. RICCOBONO, *De gymnasio patavino*, Padua, Francesco Bolzeta, 1598, f. 22v and 73r. On his teaching in Bologna, see DALLARI, *I Rotuli dei lettori legisti e artisti dello Studio Bolognese*, II, pp. 182-282; FANTUZZI, *Notizie degli scrittori bolognesi*, VI, pp. 340-343.
102 The manuscript includes *Expositio digressionis Themistii De anima* (f. 47r-64v); *In digressionem de intellectu agente* (f. 66r-79v); *Lectiones libri tertii physicorum Aristotelis* (dated 1573, thus Bologna); *De differentia Platonis et Aristotelis lectio IV* (f. 117r-122r); *Summa libri Aristotelis de generatione et corruptione* (f. 123r-128v); *Ordo librorum Metaphysicorum Aristotelis* (f. 129r-130r); *Ex quaestione de toto et partibus* (f. 132r-134r).
103 BAM, S87 sup., f. 122r.

are not analysed for their content, but for their form, which is judged illogical, confusing and disorderly. In that context, Pendasio concludes that Aristotle's philosophy is more correct than Plato's and warns his pupils against the dangers of reading Plato[104]. Thus, after providing a summary of the central part of the *Timaeus* concerned with the creation of the Universe by the Demiurge, he notes the difference between Platonic and scholastic terminology, noting that Plato uses the word *corruptibilis* rather than *generabilis*[105]. Then he provides a judgement on Plato's method and approach, maintaining that Plato does not respect the principles of logic because he bases all his arguments on principles that have not been properly demonstrated[106]. Plato's method is of no help to those who wish to become philosophers, he concludes, whereas Aristotle's philosophy, which proceeds with order and method, allows us to gain a clear knowledge of the principles pertaining to natural philosophy[107].

In addition to philosophy, Plato was also introduced in courses on rhetoric. Between 1573 and 1575, the French humanist Marc Antoine Muret taught the first two books of Plato's *Republic* at the University of Rome. The two introductory lectures devoted to Plato's *Republic* that Muret delivered at the start of the academic years 1573-74 and 1574-75 are extant; they were printed posthumously in 1590 by Muret's former student Francesco Benci, with a dedication to Scipione Gonzaga[108]. Similarly, Muret's lecture notes on the first two books of the *Republic* have come down to us in an autograph manuscript, now in the Vatican Library[109]. They were also published in a separate edition by Adam Sartorius in 1602, together with other lecture notes on Aristotle and Xenophon[110].

---

104 *Ibid.*, f. 119v and 122r.
105 *Ibid.*, f. 117v.
106 *Ibid.*, f. 119v.
107 *Ibid.*, f. 121r and f. 122r.
108 M. A. Muret, *Orationum volumen secundum*, Verona, apud Hierony. Discipulum, 1590, pp. 1-11 ("Oratio prima, habita Romae pridie Non. Novemb. MDLXXIII") and pp. 12-25 ("Oratio secunda, habita Romae IV Kal. Martii MDLXXIV"). On this edition, see J.-E. Girot, *Marc Antoine Muret. Des Isles Fortunées au rivage romain*, Geneva, Droz, 2012, pp. 753-54.
109 BAV, Vat. lat. 11591, f. 207r-220r and 235r-280r; see J. Ruysschaert, *Codices Vaticani Latini 11414-11709*, Vatican City, Biblioteca Vaticana, 1959, pp. 362-366: 364-365 (§§ §18-21).
110 M. A. Muret, *Commentarii in Aristotelis X. Libros Ethicorum ad Nicomachum, [et] in Oeconomica. Aristotelis Topicorum Libri Septimi, et in eundem Alexandri Aphrodisiensis commentarii interpretatio. Commentarius In Lib. I. Et II. Platonis De Republica. Notae in Cyropaediam et Ἀνάβασις Xenophontis*, Ingolstadt, excudebat Adam Sartorius, 1602, pp. 615-740, reprinted in D. Ruhnken, *Mureti opera omnia, ex mss aucta et emendata cum brevi annotatione*, 4 vols, Leiden, apud Samuel et Johannes Luchtmans, 1789, III, pp. 517-586. In addition to the Platonic commentary, the 1602 edition includes Muret's commentary on Aristotle's *Ethics*; his annotations to the *Oeconomica* (together with his revised translation of the text by Jacques-Louis Strebée); his translation of Book VII of the *Topics* and of Alexander of Aphrodisias' commentary; his notes on Xenophon's *Cyropaedia* and *Anabasis* as well as notes on George Codinus' *De officiis* (an account of Byzantine ecclesiastical authorities *and* ceremonies). On this edition, see Girot, *Marc Antoine Muret*, p. 765.

Muret taught various disciplines (moral philosophy, literature, law, philosophy and rhetoric) at the Roman *studium* from 1563 until his death[111]. There he shared for several academic years the chair of rhetoric with Giovanni Battista Camozzi, the author of the *Alcibiades* commentary mentioned above[112]. An excellent Latinist and Hellenist, Muret produced numerous translations and commentaries stemming from his teaching, including on Aristotle's *Ethics*, Cicero, Seneca, Tacitus, Plato, Xenophon and Plutarch. Most of these have recently been studied in detail, with the exception of Muret's lectures on Plato[113].

Muret taught Plato's *Republic* for two years and decided to pair the reading of Plato with Cicero's most philosophical work, the *De finibus bonorum et malorum*. Muret himself justifies this unusual choice on the grounds that both works treat of the supreme Good: Plato's dialogue concerns the good of the city and Cicero's work deals with the good in individual citizens, which, Muret explains, are two identical forms of good, if one is to trust Plato and Aristotle[114]. This explains why he frequently establishes parallels between Plato and Cicero to elucidate grammatical, literary, as well as philosophical points. This mode of reading Plato through Cicero and other literary authors, motivated by the belief that rhetoric and philosophy are intrinsically linked, illustrates an important trend that we already encountered in Camozzi's commentary on the *First Alcibiades* and Valier's lectures.

The university rolls for the academic years 1573-74 are missing, but evidence indicates that the two texts were read in the context of a course on rhetoric: in the 1573 prolusion, Muret anticipates that many will take issue with the fact that a professor of rhetoric would take the liberty to lecture on philosophical texts rather than teaching one of Cicero's discourses or rhetorical treatises[115]. To this criticism he responds by stating that in Antiquity rhetoric and politics were intrinsically linked, and that most ancient authors considered that eloquence could not be acquired without in-depth knowledge of political and philosophical

---

111 On his teaching, see CONTE, *I maestri della Sapienza di Roma dal 1514 al 1787*, I, pp. 35, 41, 47, 54, 62, 68, 78, 92, 104-105, 111, 118, 123; LINES, *Aristotle's Ethics in the Italian Renaissance*, pp. 331-340; GIROT, *Marc Antoine Muret*, pp. 33-43; L. GUALDO ROSA, "L'insegnamento romano di Muret e il suo contributo di oratore e filologo alla controffensiva europea della Riforma cattolica", in L. BERNARD-PRADELLE, C. DE BUZON, J.-E. GIROT and R. MOUREN (eds), *Marc Antoine Muret, un humaniste français en Italie*, Geneva, Droz, 2020, pp. 281-294; I. PANTIN, "Le commentaire de Muret à l'*Éthique à Nicomaque*", in *Ibid.*, pp. 319-336.
112 CONTE, *I maestri della Sapienza di Roma dal 1514 al 1787*, I, pp. 89-92 [1574-75], 111 [1576], 116-18 [1579-80].
113 On Muret's interpretation of Plutarch, Sallust, Horace, and Latin poetry more generally, see, in addition to the sources cited at footnote 111, the various contributions in BERNARD-PRADELLE, DE BUZON, GIROT and MOUREN (eds), *Marc Antoine Muret, un humaniste français en Italie*.
114 MURET, *Oratio prima, habita Romae pridie Non. Novemb. MDLXXIII*, in *Orationum volumen secundum*, p. 1.
115 *Ibid.*, p. 2.

matters[116]. We also know that Muret lectured on Plato's *Republic* from the Greek text, as he did for Aristotle: in the same prolusion, Muret says that colleagues will probably take issue with his decision to teach Plato in the original[117], before launching into a passionate defence of Greek literature, which he deems to be the only one to have covered all knowledge necessary to civilisation; in addition, he argues, he will provide beginner students with additional guidance by referring to Ficino's Latin translation[118]. In fact, as we will see below, he expresses a very harsh judgement on Ficino's translation, and provide his own rendering of relevant passages in Plato.

Muret's decision to lecture on Plato's *Republic* is primarily motivated by his own pedagogical approach and his attempt to renew the conventional academic method of rhetorical teaching. Throughout his career Muret argued for the necessity to study *both* rhetoric and philosophy. Twenty years earlier, when he was teaching in Venice, he took the unusual step of lecturing on Cicero's rhetorical and philosophical works on alternate years, on the grounds that reading Cicero's rhetorical writings alone was not sufficient; Cicero himself, he argued, owed much of his eloquence from having studied Plato[119]. Muret makes a similar statement in the second Platonic prolusion, where he presents Plato's *Republic* as a powerful rhetorical defence of justice nourished by philosophical arguments that refute in detail the opinions of Socrates' opponents; in that respect, he says, Cicero's refutation of Carneades is indebted to Plato's *Republic* and *Gorgias*[120]. In fact, Muret made several attempts — often thwarted by the university authorities — to venture beyond the usual texts taught in university courses. For instance, university rolls indicate that, when teaching the *Pandects* as part of his law course, he requested (vainly) the permission to open up the curriculum to philosophical texts such as Aristotle's *Politics*[121]. Similarly, a few years after lecturing on Plato, he chose to teach Seneca and Tacitus, in a deliberate attempt to rehabilitate Silver Age prose authors; he later briefly taught Aristotle's *Politics*, before being requested by the authorities to stick to more conventional authors[122]. In this

---

116 *Ibid.*, pp. 4-5.
117 *Ibid.*, p. 2.
118 *Ibid.*, pp. 2-4. On Muret's defense of Greek, see GIROT, *Marc Antoine Muret*, pp. 128-132.
119 See MURET, *De philosophiae et eloquentiae coniunctione* (discourse held in Venice in October 1557), in RUHNKEN, *Mureti opera omnia*, I, pp. 32-44: 33 and 40.
120 MURET, *Oratio secunda*, in *Orationum volumen secundum*, p. 21.
121 CONTE, *I maestri della Sapienza di Roma dal 1514 al 1787*, I, p. 78. On Muret's lectures on *Politics*, see LINES, *Aristotle's Ethics in the Italian Renaissance*, p. 333, n. 49; on Muret's law teaching, GIROT, *Marc Antoine Muret*, pp. 109-119 and G. ROSSI, "Filologia e giurisprudenza nell'insegnamento romano di Marc Antoine Muret: alla ricercar di un nuovo metodo", in BERNARD-PRADELLE, DE BUZON, GIROT and MOUREN (eds), *Marc Antoine Muret, un humaniste français en Italie*, pp. 295-318.
122 See J. KRAYE, "Marc Antoine Muret as Editor of Seneca and Commentator on Aristotle", in J. KRAYE and R. SAARINEN (eds), *Moral Philosophy on the Threshold of Modernity*, Dordrecht, Kluwer, 2005, pp. 307-330: 313; GRENDLER, *The Universities of the Italian Renaissance*, p. 245.

context, he often argued for the necessity to teach political philosophy alongside rhetoric, in terms that strongly echo the alliance of eloquence and politics he promotes in the Platonic prolusion quoted above[123].

Muret's decision to lecture publicly on Plato's *Republic* did not go down well with the University authorities. In the prolusion delivered the following year, Muret explains that the University requested that he refrain from teaching Plato and concentrate exclusively on Cicero. He infers that the motivation behind the university's decision was that Plato was deemed too demanding an author for both teacher and students. This is surprising, perhaps, given that Muret had taught Aristotle's *Nicomachean Ethics* in the original and later obtained the permission to teach Aristotle's *Rhetoric* in Greek[124]. But this is not an isolated case: as we have seen, Muret's attempts to teach non-canonical authors were frequently frustrated by the university authorities, who admonished him on several occasions to stick to the standard curriculum[125]. As the prolusion makes clear, Muret complied with the university's request, but he also took the opportunity to reiterate his reasons for choosing to teach Plato: it is all the more necessary, he argues, to promote Greek studies that they have nearly disappeared from the curriculum; in addition, Plato, an author never taught before in Rome, is an excellent example of the union of eloquence and wisdom[126].

Muret's interpretation of the *Republic* is presented in the 1602 edition as a commentary, but it is actually a set of lecture notes that Muret primarily wrote for his teaching. In fact, the first section of the commentary is a direct continuation of the 1573 university prolusion. We know that this prolusion, as it appears in the 1590 edition, is incomplete, since the editor indicates at the end that a portion of the text is missing (*reliqua desiderantur*); however, the commentary, as it appears in the 1602 edition, elaborates on the discussion developed in the university prolusion regarding the *skopos* of the dialogue, thus suggesting that it is a continuation of the prolusion Muret delivered on Plato's *Republic*. In addition, the course outline described in the first prolusion corresponds closely to another

---

123 On Muret's alliance of rhetoric and political philosophy, see M. W. CROLL, "Muret and the History of 'Attic' Prose", in *Proceedings of the Modern Languages Association*, 39/2 (1924), pp. 254-309; F. LOVERCI, "Gli studi umanistici del Rinascimento alla Controriforma", in L. CAPO and M. R. DI SIMONE, *Storia della facoltà di lettere e filosofia de 'La Sapienza'*, Rome, Viella, 2000, pp. 199-243.
124 Muret taught *Nicomachean Ethics* in Greek, with the exception of Book V, which was deemed too difficult for students: LINES, *Aristotle's Ethics in the Italian Renaissance*, p. 333.
125 On the tensions between the university authorities and Muret, see CROLL, "Muret and the History of 'Attic' Prose', pp. 254-309; LOVERCI, "Gli studi umanistici del Rinascimento alla Controriforma", pp. 235-239; ROSA, "L'insegnamento romano di Muret", pp. 281-294.
126 MURET, *Oratio quinta habita Romae III Non. Novembris MDLXXIIII*, in *Orationum volumen secundum*, pp. 51-52.

section of the commentary, where Muret discusses in detail the dialogue's general features (purpose, character, and matter of the dialogue)[127].

The *Republic* lectures are to a great extent similar in format and approach to his commentary on Aristotle's *Nicomachean Ethics*, which also consisted of lecture notes[128]. It is divided into an introductory section, a summary of each book's arguments (*summa libri*), which are presented as a list of arguments for Book I and as a continuous summary for Book II, and a lemmatic commentary, which examines, phrase by phrase, the Greek text in detail. Muret's approach is highly didactic; it is designed to render Plato's text more accessible to students of various levels and linguistic proficiency: in most cases, he provides a Latin paraphrase of the Greek passage, peppered with key terms quoted in the original; he then explains in detail points related to Greek and Latin languages and cultures, and illustrates his explanations with parallel passages from ancient literary and historical sources. Muret's pedagogical concerns are also clear in sections where he clarifies Plato's arguments by recasting them in the form of formal syllogisms[129]. In fact, in the autograph manuscript, these formal syllogisms are supplemented by diagrams representing visually the logical structure of Plato's arguments.

At first sight, Muret appears to focus mostly on the literary interpretation of the text: he examines stylistic features of the text, solves grammatical points, discusses terminology and refers to historical examples, by drawing on a wide range of Greek and Latin sources. For instance, he discusses at length how Plato's εἰς Πειραῖα ("to the Peiraeus") should be translated into Latin (*in Piraeeum* or simply *Piraeea*), examining parallel passages in Cicero, Livy, and Servius Sulpicius[130]. Muret also focuses on philological aspects: he proposes his own emendations of the Greek text[131] and notes interesting variant readings[132]. On numerous occasions he criticizes Ficino on particular points of interpretation and translation, showing great philological acumen[133]. In fact, whenever he quotes a passage from Plato's *Republic* in Latin, he prefers to offer his own translation of the text rather than using Ficino's version[134].

But Muret is equally concerned with the philosophical content of Plato's *Republic*. In this context, Muret not only interprets the philosophical aspects of the text through the filter of philosophical sources (Plato, Aristotle and Proclus), but he also establishes frequent parallels with literary authors (Homer, Cicero,

---

127 MURET, *Oratio prima habita Romae pridie Non. Novemb. MDLXXIII*, in *Orationum volumen secundum*, p. 7. Cf. MURET, *Commentarius in libris I et II Platonis De republica*, ed. RUHNKEN, III, pp. 616-618.
128 On Muret's commentary on *Nicomachean Ethics*, see LINES, *Aristotle's Ethics in the Italian Renaissance*, pp. 331-340; PANTIN, "Le commentaire de Muret à l'*Éthique à Nicomaque*", pp. 319-336.
129 MURET, *Commentarius in libris I et II Platonis De republica*, ed. RUHNKEN, III, p. 586.
130 *Ibid.*, p. 521.
131 e.g. *Ibid.*, pp. 562 and 567.
132 e.g. *Ibid.*, p. 565.
133 e.g. *Ibid.*, p. 523; 527; 530-531; 533; 535; 536; 547.
134 e.g. *Ibid.*, p. 548.

Horace, Virgil) as well as biblical and patristic sources. This is not entirely surprising, given that professors of rhetoric usually drew moral precepts from a vast array of literary sources, but it is notable that Muret is here applying this humanistic method to discuss philosophical issues, juxtaposing sources as varied as Aristotle, Cicero, Proclus, Virgil and Augustine. Thus, he frequently draws moral precepts from Plato's doctrines and establishes parallels with other Platonic dialogues, Cicero and Aristotle: for instance, he provides a lengthy explanation of a passage where Socrates discusses with Cephalus the benefits of wealth (*Rep.* 330d) and the fear of the afterlife, drawing on several ancient sources (and in particular Cicero) to praise moderation and justice on earth[135]. Muret also offers longer explanations on specific themes, which appear to be digressions he made during his lectures on topics he deemed particularly relevant — even when they only occupied a marginal place in the original text. Some of these sections suggest that Muret was particularly interested in political philosophy, and more specifically in ethical or theological issues arising from the application of law. For instance, immediately following the lemmatic commentary on Book I (which breaks off abruptly at at *Rep.* 338c), a separate section is concerned with how laws can be intrinsically good, and at the same time punish, and thus do harm to, guilty parties[136]. Similarly, he compares in detail Socrates' definition of the good (*Rep.* 357b-358a) with Aristotle's: after examining closely the structure of the arguments developed by each interlocutor, he seeks to respond to the difficulties (*dissolutio quaestionis*) inherent to Socrates' position when it is compared with Aristotle's definition of happiness in *Nicomachean Ethics*: although Socrates' definition appears at first sight to be different from Aristotle's, this apparent discrepancy disappears when one considers that Plato's definition concerns all forms of good except happiness[137]. More generally, Muret frequently establishes parallels between Plato and Aristotle; in that context, he registers the points of agreement and disagreement between the two philosophers without endorsing one or the other[138].

Another important aspect of Muret's interpretation is its indebtedness to Proclus' *Republic* commentary, which he read extensively in Greek[139]. This is

---

135 *Ibid.*, pp. 537-540.
136 *Ibid.*, pp. 550-551.
137 *Ibid.*, pp. 553-556.
138 *Ibid.*, pp. 558 and 559. Muret presents his view of the differences between Plato and Aristotle in his *Ethics* commentary, criticising the commentators who wish to demonstrate the agreement between the two philosophers at all costs: see *Commentarius in Aristotelis Ethica*, ed. RUHNKEN, III, pp. 185-193.
139 See Muret's heavily annotated copy of the Basel edition of 1534 of Plato, now in Rome, which includes the first part of Proclus' *Republic* commentary: *Hapanta Platonos. Meth'hypomnematon Proklou eis ton Timaion, kai ta Politikà, thesaurou tēs palaias philosophias megistou. Platonis Omnia opera. Cum commentariis Procli in Timaeum & Politica, thesauro ueteris philosophiae maximo … Adiectus etiam est in Platonis omnia, sententiarum & uerborum memorabilium, index*, Basel, Johannes Walder, 1534 [Muret's copy is BNCR, 71. 2.F.5]. On Muret's annotations, see

particularly interesting, because, unlike his other surviving commentaries, Proclus' *In Republicam* is a collection of lecture notes used for the purpose of teaching rather than a fully developed commentary; it is composed of a mixture of introductory essays addressed to beginner students, and more advanced essays introducing steeper metaphysical speculations. In his own lectures, Muret paraphrases entire sections from Essays I and IV. He leaves aside the sections on the most complex Neoplatonic doctrines and concentrates instead on the didactic sections concerned with the setting and literary character of the *Republic*. We saw above that Camozzi's *Alcibiades* commentary appropriated a Late Antiquity pedagogic framework by adopting the format of the school lectures on the *Alcibiades* written by the ancient Neoplatonist Olympiodorus. But Muret's commentary is the first known example of the *translatio*, within actual university lectures and in relation to Plato, of the Neoplatonic teaching method and framework that was used in the Platonic schools of Late Antiquity, and which remained intriguingly absent from the medieval reception of Plato. This is not to say, however, that Muret adopts a mystical reading of the *Republic* comparable to that of Proclus: he mostly selects passages that concern the letter of Plato's text, and the parallels he establishes with Christianity do not go beyond the ones that can be found in patristic literature. Similarly, Muret is familiar with Ficino's *argumenta* to the *Republic*, but he never fully engages with his Neoplatonic reading of the dialogue, except in one passage where he rejects the allegorical interpretation of the protagonists' names[140].

Conclusion

These examples invite us to reassess the way in which some sixteenth-century interpreters envisaged Plato. Although Ficino remained the main vehicle for reading Plato well until the nineteenth century, several sixteenth-century commentators questioned his authority, both as a translator and an interpreter, and moved away from his theological interpretation to propose a more didactic version of Platonism, with strong emphasis on ethics, rhetoric and natural philosophy. In this context, the *Timaeus*, which was the only dialogue to be taught in the Middle Ages, remained central, whereas less "theological" dialogues, such as the *First Alcibiades*, the *Gorgias*, the *Apology* and the *Republic*, became particularly popular. In the cases presented here, the commentators have strong links with Aristotle and university teaching, and yet their attitude towards Plato cannot simply be reduced to a form of eclecticism. On the one hand, the religious crisis of the sixteenth century played an important role: with the realization that, to some extent, the

---

P. DE NOLHAC, "La bibliothèque d'un humaniste au XVIe siècle. Catalogue des livres annotés par Muret", in *Mélanges de l'école française de Rome*, 3 (1883), pp. 202-238: 217; P. RENZI, *I libri del mestiere: la Bibliotheca Mureti del Collegio romano*, Siena, Università degli studi di Siena, 1993, p. 149.
140 MURET, *Commentarius in libris I et II Platonis De republica*, ed. RUHNKEN, III, p. 518.

multiplication of Aristotelian commentaries and the new interpretative methods imported by humanism had failed to solve the tensions between philosophy and matters of faith, philosophers started to look at other schools — in particular Platonism — to find a philosophy that would better serve Christianity. On the other, the critical attitude towards ancient authorities, and the new method of interpreting an author through that author rather than through commentators, which were two of the most important advances of scholastic humanism, were themselves applied to Plato, leading to a transformation of Plato's dialogues into scholastic treatises that could be accessible to students of Aristotle. In this context, the oscillation between Aristotle and Plato suggests that Renaissance commentators were, in some cases at least, less concerned with defending one of the philosophers against the other, and more preoccupied with putting some order in the various philosophical traditions they had inherited.

In addition, contrary to what modern scholars have generally assumed, professors of Aristotelian natural and moral philosophy lectured on Plato's dialogues in university courses that were officially devoted to Aristotle's works. Despite the university statutes prescribing that the syllabus be based on Aristotelian texts, there was sufficient flexibility for professors to include lectures on non-Aristotelian authors. Some of these lectures might have been held privately, but we also have evidence that some of these lectures were delivered publicly. The anonymous lectures on the *Timaeus* and Pendasio's *comparatio* indicate that professors offered lectures on Plato in the context of a course on natural philosophy. Conversely, Muret's lectures (and to some extent Valier's) suggest that Plato's texts were not only taught in the field of philosophy, but also in the field of rhetoric. Somewhat paradoxically, perhaps, Aristotle is often the starting point of this increasing interest for Plato: several professors appear to have studied Plato in order to clarify some passages from Aristotle. In contrast, Muret taught Plato to promote Greek studies and the union of eloquence and wisdom; in that context, he established a close link between Plato and Cicero.

More generally, university professors were motivated by the wish to adopt a more "philological" attitude to the texts they were commenting upon, which led them to engage directly with Plato's dialogues rather than relying on Aristotle and the commentary tradition. In the case of the anonymous lectures on the *Timaeus*, the professor adopts the same teaching method used for Aristotle, through a word-by-word analysis and the use of syllogisms to clarify specific Platonic doctrines. Similarly, Pendasio's lecture on Plato's *Timaeus* uses syllogisms to demonstrate that Plato's arguments lack order and clarity and cannot be used to study philosophy. In contrast, Valier's lectures on Plato are motivated by a growing awareness that Aristotle, as Plato's pupil, was the heir of a long philosophical tradition, and that Plato's philosophy was important for ethics and eloquence, because it added a spiritual element absent from Aristotle's thought. Finally, Muret's reading of Plato is linked to the development of Greek philology, the progressive integration of new philosophical texts within the rhetoric curriculum, and the increased dissemination of ancient Neoplatonic commentaries on Plato.

As a result, Muret develops a novel approach to the Platonic tradition, which is characterized by a strong focus on Greek philology, a justifiably critical attitude towards Ficino's translation, a reading of Plato through literary sources (such as Cicero, Virgil and Homer) and, more importantly perhaps, the appropriation of some aspects of the pedagogic framework developed by the ancient Neoplatonic commentators. As Pendasio's lecture suggests, however, Plato's growing popularity within university halls did not go unchallenged: even as Pisa inaugurated the first official chair of Platonic philosophy, as the next chapter will now show, many dissenting voices challenged the very possibility of teaching Plato's dialogues on the grounds that they lacked method and order; others, as the fourth chapter explores in detail, chose instead to integrate Platonic material in their lectures or commentaries on Aristotle, in the context of a growing realization that Plato could no longer be ignored within academic circles.

SIMONE FELLINA

Teaching Plato in Sixteenth- and Seventeenth-Century Florence and Pisa[*]

From Francesco Cattani da Diacceto to Girolamo Bardi

No other place in the Renaissance is as intimately linked to Platonism as the city of Florence. It was here, in the second half of the fifteenth century, under Medici patronage, that Marsilio Ficino undertook a *restauratio platonica*. Ficino's translations and commentaries enabled Plato's return to the Latin world, along with his "predecessors", Zoroaster and Hermes Trismegistus, and his disciples and interpreters, Plotinus, Porphyry, Iamblichus, and Proclus. And it was also in Florence that Platonic thought officially made its way into university teaching, thanks to Ficino's student, Francesco Cattani da Diacceto (1466-1522). Cattani's university career began in 1502 when, after initially refusing an appointment with a stipend of 100 fiorini, he was awarded an ordinary lectureship with a salary of 200 fiorini. In this role, Cattani was to lecture in the morning (*de mane*) on "*De coelo et mundo* aut *Ethicam* vel aliam lecturam philosophiae moralis"[1]. He taught again from 1503 to 1504 when, according to previously unknown university records, he was brought "ad lecturam philosophiae moralis et Platonicae"[2]. Although this position required the teaching of Platonic (and moral) philosophy, it was not an official Platonic chair. But Cattani's situation was unique in that it constitutes one of the earliest instances, since the Middle Ages, in which a professor was permitted to

---

[*] This paper draws upon my recent monographs on Platonic teaching in Pisa (S. FELLINA, *Platone allo* Studium *Fiorentino-Pisano (1576-1635): l'insegnamento di Francesco de' Vieri, Jacopo Mazzoni, Carlo Tomasi, Cosimo Boscagli, Girolamo Bardi*, Mantua-Verona, Fondazione L. B. Alberti-Scripta Edizioni, 2019) and on Francesco Cattani da Diacceto (*Alla scuola di Marsilio Ficino: il pensiero filosofico di Francesco Cattani da Diacceto*, Pisa, Edizioni della Normale - Istituto Nazionale di Studi sul Rinascimento, 2017). I wish to thank Maude Vanhaelen and Eva Del Soldato for kindly revising the English text and providing suggestions to improve it.

[1] See A. F. VERDE, *Lo studio fiorentino (1473-1503). Ricerche e documenti. Vol.* II. *Docenti-dottorati*, Florence, Istituto Nazionale di Studi sul Rinascimento, 1973, p. 218.

[2] See the university records contained in the sixth book of "ufficiali dello Studio" in BMF, Bigazzi 109, f. 1r, and FELLINA, *Alla scuola di Marsilio Ficino*, pp. 21-22.

Simone Fellina • University of Parma

Teaching Plato in Italian Renaissance Universities, ed. by Eva Del Soldato and Maude Vanhaelen, Studia Artistarum, 51 (Turnhout: Brepols, 2024), pp. 59–90

teach Platonic texts in a university course on philosophy[3]. Records indicate that Cattani interrupted his teaching activities some time before Easter of 1504[4]. He then resumed teaching from 1516 to 1520, in the *Studium generale*, which by then had reopened in Pisa[5]. During this time, he was appointed ordinary lecturer. Though we lack sufficient evidence to determine the details of his lectureship, we can assume, on the basis of his extant work, that it focused on a reading of Aristotle filtered through the Platonic tradition[6].

Several years after Cattani da Diacceto's brief tenure, the teaching of Plato at the university was resumed by Francesco de'Vieri (1524-1591), known as il Verino secondo, who was granted a lectureship to teach Plato in Pisa, *in die festivo*, from 1576 to 1579. The teaching of Platonic philosophy was then interrupted for a period of ten years, after which time Baccio Valori, the influential senator and librarian of the Laurentian Library in Florence, revived the teaching of Plato, by creating a new Platonic chair. Though Verino lobbied hard for this appointment, his deteriorating health prevented him from teaching, and the position was given to Jacopo Mazzoni after Verino's death in 1591[7]. We know that Verino taught Plato's *Timaeus* and *Hipparchus* during the first, second, and third years of his

---

3 As mentioned in the Introduction and Chapter I of this volume (pp. 16 and 22), we know, from a letter Ludovico Ariosto sent to Aldo Manuzio, that Sebastiano Aquila taught Plato's *Timaeus* on holidays at the Ferrarese *Studium* in 1497: see P. O. KRISTELLER, *Supplementum Ficinianum Marsilii Ficini Florentini Philosophi platonici opuscula inedita et dispersa*, 2 vols, Florence, Olschki, 1937, II, p. 211 and *Id.*, "Marsilio Ficino e Venezia", in *Id.*, *Studies in Renaissance Thought and Letters IV*, Rome, Edizioni di Storia e Letteratura, 1996, pp. 245-263: 260-261. It is possible that Niccolò Leonico Tomeo taught Plato in Padua in the first years of the sixteenth century, see C. B. SCHMITT, "L'introduction de la philosophie platonicienne dans l'enseignement des universités à la Renaissance", in M. DE GANDILLAC and J.-C. MARGOLIN (eds), *Platon et Aristote à la Renaissance*. XVIe colloque international de Tours, Paris, Vrin, 1976, pp. 93-104: 99.
4 See VERDE, *Lo studio fiorentino. Vol. II*, p. 218. The sixth book of "ufficiali dello Studio" records Cattani's teaching stipend: see BMF, Bigazzi 109, f. 5r, 6v and 7r.
5 See P. O. KRISTELLER, "Francesco da Diacceto and Florentine Platonism in the Sixteenth Century", in *Id.*, *Studies in Renaissance Thought and Letters I*, Rome, Edizioni di Storia e Letteratura, 1956, pp. 298-299. From 1497 to 1506 the University of Pisa operated in Florence, see R. DEL GRATTA, "L'età della dominazione fiorentina (1406-1543)", in *Storia dell'Università di Pisa 1343-1737. I*, Pisa, Pacini Editore, 1993, p. 38. Though the *Studium generale* was established in Pisa in 1473, courses on Greek and Latin literature, poetry, and rhetoric — and in some cases philosophy — continued to be held at the *Studium florentinum*, see *Ibid.*, p. 38.
6 From what we know about his public and private teaching, Cattani most likely taught Aristotelian texts as prescribed by university statutes. A letter to Vincenzo Querini bears witness to Cattani's private teaching (published in F. CATTANI DA DIACCETO, *De pulchro libri III, accedunt opuscula inedita et dispersa necnon testimonia quaedam ad eumdem pertinentia*, ed. S. MATTON, Pisa, Scuola Normale Superiore, 1986, p. 320). On Cattani and his teaching see also D. A. LINES, *Aristotle's Ethics in the Italian Renaissance (c. 1300-1650): The Universities and the Problem of Moral Education*, Leiden, Brill, 2002, pp. 426, 498. See also the biography written by Eufrosino Lapini and included in F. CATTANI DA DIACCETO, *Opera omnia*, Basel, per Henrichum Petri et Petrum Pernam, 1563 (repr. Enghien-les-Bains, Éditions du Miraval, 2009).
7 See FELLINA, *Platone allo Studium Fiorentino-Pisano*, pp. 24-27.

appointment[8]. Verino's didactic project, outlined in his final work *Vere Conclusioni di Platone conformi alla Dottrina Christiana et a quella d'Aristotile* (1589) — with which he attempted to present himself to Baccio Valori as the best candidate for the renewed Platonic lectureship — provides insight into his decision to teach the *Timaeus*[9]. In Verino's view, the teaching of Plato should be conducted over a four-year period, during which Platonic doctrines are compared with Christian, Aristotelian, and Hippocratic tenets. The teaching of Platonic political and legal concepts should instead be reserved for the fourth year[10]. It is evident that Verino aimed to make Platonism compatible with university teaching and applicable to all areas of knowledge, including theology, natural philosophy, medicine, and law. Platonism could therefore take its place alongside Aristotelianism, and even be used to elucidate Aristotelian thought[11]. As an alternative, Verino suggested that the lecturer of Platonic philosophy could teach Alcinous' *Didaskalikos*, a comprehensive introductory manual (on logic, psychology, theology, politics, etc.) — strategic for emphasizing the agreement between Plato and Aristotle — or the *Timaeus*, the dialogue which, by virtue of its "systematic" nature, better allowed for the elaboration of themes pertaining to the fields of theology, natural philosophy, medicine, and politics[12].

---

8 Verino wrote to Baccio Valori: "Quanto alla lettura di Platone, io cominciai col favore di Dio, dipoi del Serenissimo Gran Duca Francesco e della serenissima reina Giovanna, sua consorte, nel 1576, et feci il principio nella scuola grande a XV di novembre et così seguitai tre anni ne' giorni festivi. Il primo io introdussi gli scolari con leggere quanto io potetti del *Timeo*; poi gl'altri duoi mi feci daccapo dall'*Iparco* esponendo solamente le conclusioni nelle quali si conformano esso Platone et Aristotele, le quali furono un numero grande". The letter is published in A. F. VERDE, "Il 'Parere' del 1587 di Francesco Verino sullo Studio pisano", in *Firenze e la Toscana dei Medici nell'Europa del '500*. Atti del colloquio internazionale di Firenze, 9-14 giugno 1980, 2 vols, Florence, Olschki, 1983, I, p. 92. Oddly, the university records indicate another Platonic lectureship granted to Verino for the years 1579-1580: see ASPi, Università 2, G 77, f. 192r (162r). This is interesting, considering that on several occasions Verino claimed to have taught Plato for only three years (see another letter to Valori published in VERDE, "Il 'Parere' del 1587 di Francesco Verino sullo Studio pisano", pp. 86-87, and F. DE' VIERI, *Vere conclusioni di Platone conformi alla dottrina Christiana et a quella di Aristotele*, Florence, appresso Georgio Marescotti 1589, pp. 4-5). Thus, we can presume that the lectures did not actually take place. For the years 1576-1579, see the university records in ASPi, Università 2, G 77, f. 185r (155r), 187r (157r), and 189v (159v). During those years Verino's salary was 350 fiorini.
9 On the revival of interest in the *Timaeus* during early Renaissance see J. HANKINS, "The Study of the *Timaeus* in the Early Renaissance", in N. G. SIRAISI AND A. GRAFTON (eds), *Natural Particulars: Nature and the Disciplines in Renaissance Europe*, Cambridge, MA, MIT University Press, 1999, pp. 77-119.
10 See DE' VIERI, *Vere conclusioni di Platone*, pp. 5-6.
11 See *Ibid.*, p. 21.
12 See *Ibid.*, pp. 89-90. Jacques Charpentier wrote a *concordia Platonis Aristotelisque* in the form of a commentary on Alcinous: see J. CHARPENTIER, *Platonis cum Aristotele in universa philosophia comparatio, quae hoc commentario in Alcinoi institutionem ad eiusdem Platonis doctrinam explicatur*, Paris, ex officina Iacobi du Puys, 1573. In a marginal annotation to his *Platonis opera*, specifically to the *Convivium* (p. 296), Verino quotes Charpentier, along with Plotinus, Alci-

Verino's selection of the *Hipparchus* for his lectures, an early dialogue on the love of gain, may at first seem surprising. But his reasoning becomes clear when we consider that Verino directly connects the *Hipparchus* with Aristotle's *Nicomachean Ethics*[13]. Thus, Verino not only considered the *Hipparchus* to be an important dialogue on moral philosophy, but also a text that could be used to compare Plato and Aristotle. The ethical implications of the "love of gain", explored in the dialogue, must have also attracted students interested in Aristotle's moral thought, considering the reevaluation of wealth in Italian culture in the works by Leonardo Bruni and Poggio Bracciolini[14]. Given the brevity of the dialogue, and scarcity of glosses in Verino's hand, it is unlikely that Verino devoted a full two years to teaching the *Hipparchus*. The dialogue was instead likely to be a point of departure that allowed him to deal more generally with the agreement between Plato and Aristotle. Verino in fact explored the matter in detail in another work, the *Compendio della dottrina di Platone in quello che ella è conforme con la Fede nostra*, published around the same time (1576). Several years later, in a letter to Baccio Valori, Verino implies that the *Hipparchus* allowed him to address a large number of *conclusiones* on the agreement between Plato and Aristotle: "[...] poi gl'altri duoi [years] mi feci daccapo dall'*Iparco* esponendo solamente le conclusioni nelle quali si conformano esso Platone et Aristotele, le quali furono un numero grande"[15]. This statement only makes sense if one considers that Verino's teaching of the *Hipparchus* included that of other dialogues or used the *Compendio* as a manual[16].

---

nous, and Syrianus: "De ideis ex platonicis: [...] Jacobus Carpentarius in *commentariis Alcinii*". On the *Platonis opera* owned by Verino see note 17.

13 In his proposal for the reform of the *Studium pisanum*, Verino remarks that the teaching of moral philosophy must include Plato's dialogues alongside the *Nicomachean Ethics*, see A. DEL FANTE, "Lo studio di Pisa in un manoscritto inedito di Francesco Verino secondo", in *Nuova Rivista Storica*, 64 (1980), p. 410. Maude Vanhaelen has pointed out to me that *Hipparchus* is the first dialogue in Ficino's *editio* of *Platonis opera* with the *Amatores* — and in his glosses Verino linked the two dialogues — and that a vernacular translation of these two dialogues, by Ottaviano Maggi, appeared in 1558. This suggests an interest in these texts, likely because they were considered easy entry-points into Plato's philosophy. On Verino Secondo and the joint attention to Aristotle and Plato in moral philosophy, see also LINES, *Aristotle's Ethics*, p. 237.

14 The glosses do not seem to support this assumption, see FELLINA, *Platone allo* Studium Fiorentino-Pisano, p. 69. On Poggio's revaluation of greed see E. GARIN, *L'umanesimo italiano. Filosofia e vita civile nel Rinascimento*, Roma-Bari, Laterza, 1994, pp. 54-56.

15 See the letter to Valori in VERDE, "Il 'Parere' del 1587 di Francesco Verino sullo Studio pisano", p. 92. The letter is undated, but was probably written at the beginning of 1590, when Verino was still teaching and before his health began to decline.

16 In the *Compendio*, in fact, where Verino addresses the agreement between Plato and Aristotle at length, the *Hipparchus* is only mentioned twice. See DE' VIERI, *Compendio della dottrina di Platone in quello che ella e conforme con la fede nostra*, Florence, appresso Giorgio Marescotti, 1576, respectively p. 48 and p. 131, "l'ultimo principio sia questo che il fine è quello che ogn'uno desidera et ciò nel primo dell'*Ethica* si mostra da Aristotile et nell'*Ipparco* da Platone [...]"; "[...] fà di mestiero ancora avvertire che l'amore retto è di due maniere, uno è desiderio de beni

Aside from his many writings, some of which only circulated in manuscript form, Verino's lecture notes on Plato are preserved in his own, heavily annotated copy of Plato's *Opera omnia*, now at the Laurentian Library in Florence[17]. We know that Verino gave importance to his notes on Plato. In his *Il Parere o vero Giudizio intorno alle cose del famoso et nobile Studio di Pisa* (1587) — a series of considerations on the reform of the *Studium pisanum*, addressed to Piero Usimbardi, first secretary of the Grand Duke Ferdinando I — and in a letter to Baccio Valori in February 1590, Verino requests that "his Plato" be preserved in the Ducal library; thus, he apparently considered it to be an important work in its own right[18]. In this copy of Plato's *Opera omnia* Verino made detailed notes in the margins of all of Plato's dialogues and Marsilio Ficino's commentaries. However, for the purpose of the present chapter, we will limit our investigation to those on the dialogues he taught, namely the *Timaeus* and the *Hipparchus*. A close examination of these *marginalia* indicates that they were lecture notes, which Verino used to both study and teach Plato's texts. A marginal note on the page preceding the beginning of the *Timaeus* in fact alludes explicitly to his Platonic teaching:

> Hac die XV mensis novembris aggressus publice in diebus extraordinariis doctrinam Platonis Ego Franciscus Verinus secundus, sic volentibus Serenissimo magno Aetruriae duce Francisco Mediceo et Serenissima eius uxore Joanna Austria. Utinam haec [*illegible*] ac profunda doctrina nunc exoriatur in mentibus eruditorum [*illegible*] modo olim exorta est <tem>pore Magni Cosmi patriae patris et Magnifici Laurentii De Medicibus[19].

---

creati per usargli honestamente, l'altro è l'amore di Dio per assomigliarsegli [...]; dell'amore delle cose create et prodotte da Dio et dalla natura et dall'arte inquanto si debbono usare parlò Platone nell'*Ipparco* quando ci mostrò, inducendo in ogni professione, che il bene è quello che si desidera da ogn'uno et Aristotile nel primo capitolo del primo dell'*Ethica*". The convergence between Plato and Aristotle is also recorded in the glosses, see note 52.

17 PLATO, *Omnia opera translatione Marsilii Ficini, emendatione et ad graecum codicem collatione Simonis Grynaei, summa diligentia repurgata*, Lyon, apud Antonium Vincentium, 1548 [henceforth PLATO, *Opera* 1548], first identified by R. PINTAUDI, "Il Platone di Francesco Verino secondo", in *Rinascimento*, 2nd s., 16 (1976), pp. 241-249. The shelfmark for the copy is BML, Acquisti e doni 706.

18 "Desidererei che almeno di detti scritti [of Verino the first] e del mio Platone se ne havesse cura et si mettessero nella libreria di Sua Altezza Serenissima et così il mio libro delle duomila distinzioni, acciocché tante et tante fatiche di esso mio Vecchio et mie non vadino male", quoted in DEL FANTE, "Lo studio di Pisa in un manoscritto inedito di Francesco Verino secondo", p. 411; and see another letter to Valori, "Se sua Signoria in questo et nelle figliuole mi aiuta, io le lascierò 8 o 10 libri miei tutti chiosati et riscontri con estrema diligenza et si potrebbero, dopo mia morte, mettere nella libreria; così altre mie fatiche non sono istampate et tra le altre, il Platone", published in VERDE, "Il 'Parere' del 1587 di Francesco Verino sullo Studio pisano", p. 85.

19 PLATO, *Opera*, 1548, p. 472.

As is expected, the marginal notes are primarily pedagogical in nature. They subdivide the dialogues into chapters, define key philosophical concepts, outline important themes, identify *suppositiones* and *rationes* — added in the margins and numbered throughout the text — and divide the dialogues into a series of *quaesita* or *quaestiones*, to help students better understand the text. Several annotations clarify passages that Verino has underlined in the text. These are mostly clarifications, or *nota bene*, and are generally preceded by the abbreviation *no* ("note"), which occasionally correspond to words within the text; several are asterisks that refer to relevant marginal glosses. On numerous occasions, Verino rearranges the arguments in the dialogue in the form of questions, introduced by *quare* or *nota quare*. He then writes the solution down, which is introduced by *respondit/responditur*, for the purpose of teaching. In most cases, Verino sketches, notes down, or summarizes the arguments. But he also sometimes refers to other Platonic dialogues. All of this suggests that Verino reformatted Plato's dialogues for a pedagogical purpose and adopted the approach traditionally used in university lectures on Aristotle, following a trend we already outlined in Chapter I of this volume.

In annotating the *Timaeus*, one of Verino's goals was to emphasize the agreement between Plato and Aristotle[20]. This he achieves by invoking Simplicius, Galen, and Themistius, whose commentaries include entire sections devoted to the comparison between Plato and Aristotle. Simplicius is, for instance, quoted as having affirmed that, according to Alexander of Aphrodisias, Plato and Aristotle used the word *caelum* as a synonym for *universum*[21], and that both philosophers believed that heaven exhibits "above" and "below"[22]. Galen, an author frequently used by Verino to interpret the medical doctrines in the *Timaeus*[23], is quoted to prove that Plato — like Aristotle — admitted the existence of a common material

---

20 With the exception of three cases in which Verino mentions Aristotle's disagreement with Plato (on the community of wives and children, divination, and respiration), he always underscores the agreement between the two philosophers regarding the unicity of the universe, the transformation of the elements, the determination of physical principles (matter, form and *compositum*), and the recognition of the shapeless and unknowable nature of matter, see FELLINA, *Platone allo* Studium *Fiorentino-Pisano*, pp. 61-63.
21 See PLATO, *Opera*, 1548, p. 476, PLATO, *Tim.* 28b2-4 and SIMPLICIUS, *In De Coelo* I, prooemium 2-8. Exceptionally Verino quotes *Tim.* 28b2-4 in Greek. The same lines appear at the beginning of Simplicius' *Commentary*.
22 See PLATO, *Opera*, 1548, p. 488 and PLATO, *Tim.* 62e ff. See SIMPLICIUS, *In Phys.* IV, 521.5 ff. e Id., *In De coelo* I, 63.25 ff.
23 Marsilio Ficino, Niccolò Leonico Tomeo, Sebastián Fox Morcillo, and Matthaeus Frigillanus also used Galen in commenting on the *Timaeus*. On Ficino's reading of Galen's *De placitis* see V. NUTTON, "De Placitis Hippocratis et Platonis in the Renaissance", in P. MANULI and M. VEGETTI (eds), *Le opere psicologiche di Galeno. Atti del terzo colloquio galenico internazionale di Pavia, 10-12 settembre 1986*, Naples, Bibliopolis, 1988, pp. 292-293. In his proposal for the third year of the course on Platonism, devoted to the comparison of Platonic and Hippocratic doctrines, Verino explicitly mentions Galen's *De placitis*: see DE' VIERI, *Vere conclusioni di Platone*, pp. 5-6.

substratum, having considered the reciprocal transformation of the elements[24]. Finally, Themistius' authority is invoked to explain why Plato situated the rational soul in the brain, and why Aristotle stated that the intellect comes from the outside[25].

More importantly, Verino frequently interprets Plato through John Philoponus and Thomas Aquinas. But Philoponus is also used to interpret Plato through Aristotle. For instance, in a passage in which Verino comments on the Demiurge's speech to the created Gods — at which point they are given the task of creating the three kinds of mortal beings (*Tim.* 41a7 ff.) — he refers to Philoponus' exegesis, which draws upon this passage to show that Plato, like Aristotle, believed that only the rational soul is separable and therefore immortal[26]. A second quotation is taken from Philoponus' *Commentary on Physics*, wherein he establishes the two ways (*per proportionem* and *per negationem*) in which knowledge of matter can be acquired[27]. The last reference is taken from Philoponus' *Commentary on Aristotle's De generatione animalium*. Herein, Verino stresses that the Platonic "pre-formation" theory mentioned by Philoponus — in contrast with Aristotle's theory *de semine et generatione animalium* — derives from *Tim.* 91a ff. The quotation of the passage containing the *opinio platonica* ends with the following remark: "Haec refert ipse Joannes Grammaticus in Commento suo super primo libro De generatione animalium super cap. 18ᵐ, in quo Aristoteles confutat illos qui putant semen exire ab omnibus partibus corporis"[28].

Verino similarly uses Thomas Aquinas to provide a Christian reading of the *Timaeus*. For instance, to explain *Tim.* 27c1 ff., Verino quotes a passage from the *Commentary on the Epistle to the Romans*, which addresses the impossibility of knowing the divine essence during earthly life even if, as Dionysius the Areopagite stated, man can know something of God *per causalitatem*, *per excellentiam*, and *per*

---

24 See PLATO, *Opera*, 1548, p. 483 and GALEN, *De elementis ex Hippocrate*, in *Operum Hippocratis Coi et Galeni Pergameni, medicorum omnium principum*. III, Paris, apud Petrum Aubouïn, 1638, p. 11.
25 See PLATO, *Opera*, 1548, p. 489, "Quare est quod Plato rationalem posuit in cerebro tanquam in suo habitaculo sitam, alias partes in aliis corporis partibus, et Aristoteles eam extrinsecus venire dixit 2° *De generatione animalium* cap. 3. Respondet Themistius in sua *Paraphrasi* in primo *De anima* capite penultimo quam utrique id consilii fuit ne quam offensionem turbam ne inmortalitas eius aut contagio mortalium partium aut vicinitate contraheret". See ARISTOTLE, *De gen. anim.* 736 b27-28 and 737 a7-10. Verino quotes from the translation by Ermolao Barbaro. See THEMISTIUS, *Paraphrasis*, Venice, apud Hieronymum Scotum, 1542, p. 246.
26 See PLATO, *Opera*, 1548, p. 480, "ex 24 et 25 [numbers refer to *quaesita* annotated by Verino on the edge of the page] particula eligit Joannes Grammaticus animam esse partim mortalem, scilicet plantalem et brutorum, partim inmortalem, scilicet innaturalem, in *prohemio* suo in primum *De anima*". See JOHN PHILOPONUS, *In De anim.* I, prooemium 11.29 ff.
27 See PLATO, *Opera*, 1548, p. 483, PLATO, *Tim.* 51a4 ff., JOHN PHILOPONUS, *In Phys.* I, 192,1 ff.
28 See PLATO, *Opera*, 1548, pp. 496-497 and JOHN PHILOPONUS, *In De gen. anim.* 25.20 ff.

negationem.[29] Another instance of appropriation occurs in the explanation of the *Timaeus* passage mentioned above, in which the Demiurge, addressing the created Gods, states that their nature is only indissoluble because of his will. Verino explains that one needs to read the passage through Thomas Aquinas, and he interprets the created Gods as a reference to heavenly bodies rather than separate substances — the angels — which are immortal. Verino then adds that even though two passages in the *Summa Theologiae* seem to advance a different position on this matter they actually reveal the meaning of Plato's words *Dii Deorum*. With the term "Dii" Plato in fact refers to heavenly bodies, while the term "Deorum" refers to separate substances[30].

When commenting on *Tim.* 66d ff., Verino mentions a passage from Ammonius' *Commentary on Aristotle's Categories* related to scents and the ways in which we perceive them[31]. Verino also quotes Michael of Ephesus' *scholia* on respiration when commenting on *Tim.* 79a ff[32]. And another interesting author Verino invokes in his *lectiones* is the Jewish philosopher Calo Calonymus. In particular, he refers to Calonymus' *Liber de mundi creatione* to provide three reasons why, according to the wise Jew Hasdai ibn Shaprut, Plato considered the generation of the world to be a *transitus* from disorder to order[33].

---

29 See PLATO, *Opera*, 1548, p. 476 and THOMAS AQUINAS, *In Epistolam S. Pauli super Romanos*, ch. 1 l. 6.

30 See PLATO, *Opera*, 1548, p. 480, "[*illegible*] Dii deorum sint sua natura corruptibiles [...] Respondit Divus Thomas quod hic Plato [*correxi* Aristoteles] per Deos intelligit corpora coelestia quae existimabat esse composita et ideo corruptibilia. Vide ipsum divum Thomam in prima parte *Summae* quaestione 50 de substantia angelorum absolute art. 5. At in prima parte *Summae* in quaestione 22 articulo 3° per deos intelligit substantias separatas. Sed non sibi contradicit, quia '*Dii*' sunt substantiarum separatarum corpora coelestia, '*Deorum*' substantiae separatae [*correxi* substantiarum separatarum]". See THOMAS AQUINAS, *Summa Theol.* I^a q. 50 a. 5 ad 2, "Ad secundum dicendum quod Plato per deos intelligit corpora caelestia, quae existimabat esse ex elementis composita, et ideo secundum suam naturam dissolubilia, sed voluntate divina semper conservantur in esse" and *Ibid.*, I^a q. 22 a. 3 co.: "Et secundum hoc excluditur opinio Platonis, quam narrat Gregorius Nyssenus, triplicem providentiam ponentis. Quarum prima est summi Dei, qui primo et principaliter providet rebus spiritualibus; et consequenter toti mundo, quantum ad genera, species et causas universales. Secunda vero providentia est, qua providetur singularibus generabilium et corruptibilium, et hanc attribuit diis qui circumeunt caelos, id est substantiis separatis, quae movent corpora caelestia circulariter". A third mention of Thomas Aquinas (*Summa Theol.* I^a q. 47 a. 3) is annotated at the edge of Chapter XVI of Ficino's *Commentary* titled *Cur mundus sit unus*, mentioned at note 34 below.

31 See *Ibid.*, p. 488 and AMMONIUS HERMIAE, *In Praedicamenta Aristotelis Commentarii*, Venice, apud Ioannem Gryphium, 1546, f. 9r-v.

32 See PLATO, *Opera*, 1548, p. 492 and MICHAEL EPHESIUS, *In Parv. Nat.* 120.18-121.18. Verino was reading the Latin translation of MICHAEL EPHESIUS, *Scholia in Aristotelem opuscula aliquot*, Venice, apud Hieronymum Scotum, 1552, ff. 35r-v.

33 See PLATO, *Opera*, 1548, p. 476 and CALO CALONYMOS, *Liber de mundi creatione physicis rationibus probata*, Venice, per Bernardinum de Vitalibus 1527, pp. 4-5 (mod. num.).

Two points are worth noting here. First, it is striking that the Neoplatonic tradition appears to be almost absent from Verino's glosses, and the same holds true for most of Verino's works. Marsilio Ficino, the only Florentine Platonist Verino mentions, is referred to only once, in a gloss that deals with the unicity of the world; but this gloss is mostly explicative and recapitulatory[34]. Proclus is only mentioned three times. On one occasion, Verino paraphrases a passage from John Philoponus' *De aeternitate mundi* wherein the Byzantine philosopher summarizes and refutes Proclus' second and third arguments in favor of the eternity of the world[35]. On two other occasions, Verino provides quotations from the *Commentary on the First Book of Euclid's Elements*, which address cosmological issues. The first is related to *Tim.* 34b3, where the Demiurge is said to place the World Soul at the center of the universe[36]. The second concerns *Tim.* 53b4 ff., and deals with the 'solid' nature of the elements, which Proclus considers to be the result of the emanation process[37]. Similarly, Plotinus is only mentioned

---

34 See PLATO, *Opera*, 1548, p. 460, "Ratio Marsilii Ficini hic sic potest formulari: si mundi plures, ergo Deus non dominaret toti materiae, aliqua vacua intercederent inter mundum et mundum, opera Dei dissipata existerent ordinis et unionis expertia, sed haec essent inconvenientia et contra Domini Dei potentiam, bonitatem et sapientiam, ergo antecedens omnino falsum et inconveniens. Ergo oppositum est verum, quod mundus est unus".

35 See *Ibid.*, p. 477, and JOHN PHILOPONUS, *De aet. mundi*, II-III, 24, 1-55, 23.

36 See PLATO, *Opera*, 1548, p. 478, "Anima, quoniam medium inter intelligibilia et sensibilia sortitur locum, idcirco quatenus intelligenti cohaeret naturae iuxta circulum agit, quatenus vero sensibilibus praeest iuxta rectum providet, ut dicit Proclus in suo secundo libro in definitione rectae lineae *In primum Elementorum Euclidis*, 62". Verino quotes from the translation of Francesco Barozzi: PROCLUS, *In primum Euclidis Elementorum librum commentariorum*, Padua, Gratiosus Perchacinus, 1560, p. 62. On Barozzi's translation see A. CARUGO, "L'insegnamento della matematica all'Università di Padova prima e dopo Galileo", in *Storia della cultura veneta. Dalla Controriforma alla fine della Repubblica IV.2*, Vicenza, Neri Pozza, 1984, pp. 155-157.

37 See PLATO, *Opera*, 1548, p. 484: "Termini et magnitudines secundum Platonem in mente impartibiliter habentur iuxta signi rationem. In anima iuxta lineae formam. In naturis iuxta superficiei rationem. Omnes demum in corporibus corporaliter. Unde ut notaret qualitates in animis esse iuxta lineae formam, ideo Timeus animam constituit ex lineis rectis et circularibus et Plato naturales rationes [continues on the lower edge of the page] corporum constituendorum vim habentes per plana manifestari iubebat. Totum hoc dicit Proclus *In primum Elementorum Euclidis* in secundo libro suorum commentariorum in expositione signi, id est puncti". See PROCLUS, *In primum Euclidis Elementorum librum commentariorum*, p. 53. Another passage of the *Commentary* Verino refers to quite often is *Ibid.*, p. 122, but his interpretation is almost original, see F. DE' VIERI, *Liber in quo a calumniis detractorum philosophia defenditur, & eius praestantia demonstratur*, Rome, apud Ioannem Angelum Ruffinellum, 1586, p. 40, "Geometriae similiter nonnullae utilitatis sunt, quarum una secundum Platonicos aliquos est illa, quae ex prima Euclidis in primo *Elementorum* demonstratione colligitur. Quemadmodum etenim super linea recta ope duorum circulorum se intersecantium triangulus aequilaterus constituitur, ita in corpore humano erectae staturae anima procreatur ope duorum circulorum, videlicet Dei, qui circulo assimilatur quoad intellectionem, et ope Caeli, quod circulare est". See also *Id., Delle stelle lezzioni due*, Padua, appresso il Bolzetta, n.d., p. 22 and *Id., Ragionamento intorno alle stelle recitato da esso nell'Accademia Fiorentina*, in BNCF, Panc. 126, f. 108r. A different reading occurs

once. Verino draws upon *Enn.* IV, 3, 23 to explain why Plato situated *mens* in the brain (*Tim.* 69c5 ff.) and shows that this opinion is consonant with Aristotle's[38]. Another commentator on the *Timaeus*, Calcidius, is mentioned by Verino twice: in a note on Ficino's *Commentary* regarding the *ordinatio* —the division of the dialogue in parts according to the topics covered[39] — and then as a quotation of a passage of Calcidius' *Commentary* on the Demiurge's creation of the human soul (*Tim.* 41d4 ff.)[40]. As will become clearer below, Verino's limited reliance on the Neoplatonic tradition revived by Ficino differs from the trend outlined in Chapter I of this volume, according to which interpreters seek to isolate Plato's "authentic thought" from that of his commentators.

Verino generally rejects doctrines deemed incompatible with Christianity, or interprets them allegorically. For instance, he allegorizes or refutes Plato's allusions to the preexistence and transmigration of the soul. Verino prefers to appeal to Avicenna's *De mahad* in order to interpret the preexistence and transmigration of the soul in an eschatological way, as relating to punishments and rewards in the afterlife[41]. Similarly, Verino refers to the Hermetic *Pimander*, to reject the doctrine of transmigration in animal forms[42]. In this respect, Verino echoes Ficino, who rejected the possibility that human souls transmigrate into

---

in *Id., Considerationes de anima,* in BNCF, Filze Rinuccini 18, f. 23v, "Ex Proclo *In primum Elementorum Euclidis* et partim ex Platone // Anima nostra est triangulus super linea recta constitutus ex duobus circulis se intersecantibus super lati linea ut semidiametro prodiens, ut eosdem cognoscens illos in operando imitetur et ita Deo assimiletur, quoad eius perfectionem et tranquillitatem, respectu vero aliorum quoad actus beneficentiae cum prudentia, justitia et sanctitate".

38 See PLATO, *Opera,* 1548, p. 489, "Ratio quare secundum Platonem mens fuit a Diis in capite collocata. Contra difficile est etiam fingere qua parte corporis intelligamus, ut inquit Aristoteles primo *De anima* non longe a fine. An est in capite quatenus utitur sensibus qui exercent suas operationes capite, ut dicit et Plotinus in 3° libro Quartae *Enneadis* capite 23°. Idem Aristoteles probat in libris *De partibus animalium*". See ARISTOTLE, *De an.* 411a 26 ff. and probably *Id., De part. anim.* 656a13-657a13.

39 See PLATO, *Opera,* 1548, p. 472, "Ordinatio libri et species ex Calcidio in interpretatione sua *In Timaeum* Platonis: vide ipsam a me appositam et scriptam in primis paginis albis huius operis". See CALCIDIUS, *In Tim.* VII.

40 See PLATO, *Opera,* 1548, p. 480, "'Haec fatus, in eodem rursus cratere'. Hic genituram humanarum prosequitur animarum ut natura eius liquido comprehendatur et perseverat in fabula quam interposuit, propterea ut quae dicuntur manifesta sint. Rursus enim cratera proponit et mixturam concretionemque earum potentiarum ex quibus mundi anima concreverat. Haec Chalcidius hoc in loco". See CALCIDIUS, *In Tim.* CXL.

41 See PLATO, *Opera,* 1548, p. 481: "Plato et Pythagoras intelligunt animam remanere cum habitibus bonis et malis ac si esset in corporibus foeminae, bestiae et cum eis puniri, ut exponit Avicenna in suo *Almahad,* idest in libro quem inscribit *de loco ad quem revertitur homo seu anima post mortem*". See AVICENNA, *De mahad, idest de dispositione, seu loco ad quem revertitur homo vel anima eius post mortem,* Venice, apud Iuntas, 1546, f. 60v-61r.

42 See PLATO, *Opera,* 1548, p. 481 "In *sermone* X° Mercurius 62 non concedere transmigrationem [...]". Verino quotes from the Parisian edition with Greek text HERMES TRISMEGISTUS, *Poemander,* Paris, apud Adrianum Turnebum, 1554.

animals, as shown in Chapter XLII of his *Timaeus' Commentary*, which contained one of the most articulated statements on the topic[43]. Marsilio Ficino returned to the passage on the creation and destiny of human souls (*Tim.* 41d4 ff.) years later, when he decided to further develop some of his commentaries, in light of a new expanded edition of Plato[44]. As such, Chapter XXV of the *Appendix* to the *Timaeus' Commentary* includes a conspicuous *resumé* that derives almost entirely from Proclus' *Commentary on the Timaeus* and addresses a wide range of topics: the doctrine of the three vehicles of the human soul[45] and the creation of the eternal one by God himself[46]; the need for the soul to descend into the *generatio* at least once in a cosmic cycle (*annus magnus*); the importance of the assignment to the stars and free choice as determining factors in other reincarnations[47]; and the return to one's own star and, potentially, from there to the intelligible[48].

Unlike Ficino, Verino does not seem to devote much attention to *Tim.* 41d4 ff., at least in the glosses. If we turn to his *Compendium*, written around the same time, we can instead see that Plato's words inspired Verino to discuss the topic of metempsychosis in animal forms; this is promptly rejected with arguments along the lines of Ficino's. More generally, he addresses the topic of the *vehiculum animae*, here presented in an eschatological context, aimed at clarifying how the souls of the dead — devoid of a body — can reach the place they deserve, and potentially experience ultramundane tortures. This opinion, advanced in the name of Platonists, leads Verino to assign three vehicles to the soul, in relation to its parts. The vegetative, the sensitive and the rational are assigned, respectively, to the earthly body, the aerial body, and the star to which the soul belongs. The aerial body allows souls to reach their respective destinations and experience the pain and affliction of the punishments. The star is instead the ultimate destination only of the rational part and, in this sense, its *proprio vehiculo*. The assignment to the stars, and descent through the spheres — with an eternal body of a celestial nature — imply the pre-existence of the soul. Conversely, according to faith the soul is created and infused by God within the earthly body, a position that Verino

---

43 See M. FICINO, *In Timaeum*, ch. XLII, in *Eiusd., Opera*, 2 vols, Basel, ex officina Henricpetrina, 1576, II, p. 1466. See also *Id., In Phaedonem epitome*, in *Opera*, II, p. 1392; *Id., In decimum dialogum de iusto epitome*, in *Opera*, II, p. 1438; *Id., Teologia Platonica*, ed. E. VITALE, Milan, Bompiani, 2011, XVII, 4, pp. 1741-1749. See also the letter sent to Giovanni Nesi on July 1, 1477, in *Epistolarum liber IIII*, in *Opera*, I, pp. 774-776.
44 Plato's new edition was never completed, whereas the *Commentaries on Parmenides, Sophist, Timaeus, Phaedrus* and *Philebus* were published in 1496, see KRISTELLER, *Supplementum Ficinianum*,I, pp. CXVII-CXIX. Specific additions on transmigration are found in FICINO, *In Timaeum*, Summa XXV, p. 1471 and Summa CIII, p. 1484; *Id., Commentaries on Plato, I. Phaedrus and Ion*, ed. and transl. by M. J. B. ALLEN, Cambridge, MA-London, Harvard University Press, 2008: *Phaedrus*, 3, ch. XXIV, p. 138 and ch. XXV, p. 146.
45 See FICINO, *In Timaeum*, summa XXV, p. 1470 and PROCLUS, *In Tim.*, III, 285.12-16.
46 See FICINO, *In Timaeum*, summa XXV, p. 1470 and PROCLUS, *In Tim.*, III, 267.19-28.
47 See FICINO, *In Timaeum*, summa XXV, p. 1470 and PROCLUS, *In Tim.*, III, 278.9-279.15.
48 See FICINO, *In Timaeum*, summa XXV, p. 1470 and PROCLUS, *In Tim.*, III, 291.17-292.9.

is at pains to reiterate in his writings, along with the belief that the soul does not have innate knowledge, as was also argued by Plato[49]. Deviating from the Ficinian reading, the assignment to the star (identified with the celestial vehicle) is thus traced back to a generic, Christianizing return to heaven by well-deserving souls[50].

If we closely examine Verino's notes on the *Hipparchus*, it becomes clear that his *modus operandi* is the same as the one used in his interpretation of the *Timaeus*. In this case, however, one of Verino's main goals is to consider the theme of the dialogue, namely greed, from an ethical point of view. In so doing, attention is paid to the logical aspects of the argument and its connection with other Platonic dialogues and Aristotelian works. In an explanation of Ficino's *argumentum* to the dialogue, Verino asserts that the *skopos* is to demonstrate that all men naturally pursue *bonum/lucrum*; however, if philosophy is to be considered as belonging to good things, that is a matter pertaining the following dialogue, the *Lovers*. For, he argues, according to Plato, and contrary to Aristotle, the knowledge of accidental qualities follows that of the essence, and the essence (*quid sit*) of philosophy is the goal of the *Lovers*[51]. There are two other references to Aristotle. In the first, Verino draws a parallel between the *incipit* of the *Nicomachean Ethics* and Plato's thesis that men's pursuit of the *lucrum* is *ipso facto* the pursuit of the good[52]. In the second, he emphasizes that the definition of food in *De anima* is similar to the one given by Plato[53].

Another important aspect of Verino's glosses on the *Hipparchus* is the explanation of the sayings of wise men (*dicta sapientium*), along with references to parallel passages or cues in other dialogues, evidently meant as an aid to elucidate key

---

49 See FELLINA, *Platone allo* Studium *Fiorentino-Pisano*, p. 51. In arguing *ad mentem Platonis* that the soul does not possess innate knowledge, Verino refers to *Phil.* 38e12-39a7, where, according to him, the soul is described as a tablet upon which nothing is originally written. See *Ibid.*, p. 48.
50 See DE' VIERI, *Compendio della dottrina di Platone*, pp. 168-172 and FELLINA, *Platone allo* Studium *Fiorentino-Pisano*, pp. 51-54.
51 See PLATO, *Opera*, 1548, f. 35v (mod. num. by Verino himself).
52 See *Ibid.*, p. 1, "Aristoteles primo *Ethicorum* capite primo probat quod omnes homines appetunt bonum [...]". See PLATO, *Hipparch.* 226e10-227d10 and ARISTOTLE, *Eth. Nic.* 1094a1 ff.
53 See PLATO, *Opera*, 1548, p. 2; PLATO, *Hipparch.* 230e3 and ARISTOTLE, *De an.* 414b6-14.

Platonic doctrines[54]. In the case of the saying *Ne amicum decipias* the discussion takes the form of a question, and addresses biblical *exempla*[55].

Another striking characteristic of Verino's glosses is the lack of comparison between Platonic teachings and Christianity. This is a significant contrast with the two major works directly related to Verino's Platonic *magisterium*, the *Compendio* and the *Vere conclusioni*[56]. In these works, Verino's position is unequivocal, and he relies mainly on Augustine's authority (*De civitate Dei* VIII, 1-12). He resolves that, among all doctrines, Platonism is the closest to Christianity by its very nature, rather than by virtue of interpretation, as in the case of Aristotelianism[57]. This is not to say that Verino considers Aristotelian philosophy to be intrinsically incompatible with Christianity. He simply believes that Aristotle focused more on natural things, which led him to lose sight of the divine truths elucidated by his master[58]. Verino also seems to rely on the Thomistic model, which he occasionally adapts to make room for Plato's teaching. Thus, he praises Thomas

---

54 See PLATO, *Opera*, 1548, p. 2 e *Id..*, *Hipparch.* 228e ff. In the upper margin Verino reports the *dicta* "Cognosce te ipsum, nihil nimis, perge quae iusta sunt curare, ne amicum decipias, non licet virum honestum ac bonum sapientum cuique inludere", precising on the margin: "Dicta sapientum Graeciae ut dicitur in *Protagora* 167". See PLATO, *Prot.* 343a ff. In the left margin, and in the lower one, Verino elaborates with references to other Platonic *dicta*: "Cognosce te ipsum, illud confert ad perfectionem intellectus // Nihil nimis ad perfectionem appetitus // [in correspondence to "Perge quae iusta sunt curare"] Istud est praeceptum de virtutibus ut hominem in se perficiunt. Quartum quod perficit hominem sic ad alium scilicet ad amicum // Se ipsum cognoscere est cognoscere animam suam, ex Platone in *Alcibiade primo de natura humana* 29 columna prima // Se ignorare contingit tripliciter. Esse tria bona: animae, corporis et externa. Vide in *Philebo de summo bono humano* 69". See PLATO, *Alc. I*, 132d sgg. and *Phil.* 48d8 ff.

55 See PLATO, *Opera*, 1548, pp. 2-3: "Utrum amici sint decipiendi, cum aliquando liceat uti deceptione, ut Joannes in vinculis cognoscebat Christum esse verum Messiam, quem alii<s> ostendet rato dicens 'Ecce agnus Dei, ecce qui tollit peccata mundi', sed vult hac sancta deceptione inducere discipulos suos ad Christum, ut visis miraculis illius fiant eius discipuli, cum ipse Joannes, ut lucerna adveniente lumine, deberet minui et (?) eos relinquere. Responditur quod deceptione mala qua quis intendat malum amico suo, hac non debet illum decipere, sed deceptione sancta, ut inducat illum ad bonum aliquod, licet eum decipere. Immo neque inimicus debet decipi, nisi gratia boni maioris, ut Judit decepit Olophernem a Deo inspirata et ut salvaret populum suum". The John the Baptist episode is described in *Matt.* 11: 2-6 and *Luk* 7: 18-23.

56 Moreover, according to Verino himself, the first year of the ideal Platonic course should be expressly dedicated to a comparison between Plato and Christianity, see *supra* p. 61.

57 See DE' VIERI, *Compendio della dottrina di Platone*, pp. 3, 5 (mod. num.), 35 (incorrectly numbered as 34); *Id.*, *Vere Conclusioni di Platone*, p. 95. For further references see FELLINA, *Platone allo Studium Fiorentino-Pisano*, pp. 29-30.

58 See DE' VIERI, *Compendio della dottrina di Platone*, pp. 20-21. The juxtaposition of Plato, the *theologus*, and Aristotle, the *physicus*, is a common exegetical key since Antiquity, either to reconcile their doctrines or stress their differences. In modern times, it was appropriated, among others, by Bessarion, Nicolaus Scutellius, Sebastián Fox-Morcillo, Jacques Charpentier, and Francesco Piccolomini, see E. DEL SOLDATO, *Early Modern Aristotle. On the Making and*

Aquinas, Bonaventura of Bagnoregio, Giles of Rome, and Cajetanus for showing that philosophy, as the handmaid and minister of Revelation, is fundamental in rejecting attacks on religion, by those who improperly and arrogantly employ reason. But he also remarks that only the Greek Church made use of Plato, whereas Scholasticism decidedly focused on Aristotle[59]. While it is true that this statement should be read within the context of a general defense and promotion of philosophical knowledge — whose usefulness for the cause of *religio* is reaffirmed — it nevertheless also carries with it a positive reconsideration of Platonism, even by virtue of its recognized "affinity" with Christianity.

The Ficinian conception of Platonism as a *pia philosophia* does not seem to have had a major impact on Verino's writings[60]. To be sure, we find echoes of Ficino's ideas in his works: the providential quality of Platonism is affirmed in the *Compendio*, and in a 1589 letter to Baccio Valori Verino quotes Ficino's introduction to the *Commentary on the Enneads*, specifically the famous passage on the *translatio* of the Academy in Florence. Nevertheless, these echoes seem mostly opportunistic and self-serving: Verino was interested in reviving the historical connection between the Medici and Platonism, in order to secure a teaching position. In 1576, at any rate, this strategy worked, thanks to the *Compendio*[61]. References to Zoroaster, considered to be the author of the *Chaldean Oracles*, and to Hermes Trismegistus prove that Verino embraced the genealogy of the Platonic doctrine established by Ficino. Yet this genealogy seems devoid of its original providential and exclusive character. Moreover, as we already noted in relation to Verino's *Timaeus* lectures, the privileged role Ficino ascribed to Plotinus and to the Neoplatonic tradition is also lacking. According to Ficino, the history of Platonism is divided into two periods: the pre-Christian period, which coincides

---

Unmaking of Authority, Philadelphia, University of Pennsylvania Press, 2020, pp. 26, 37, 44, 61, 63.

59 See DE' VIERI, *Compendio della dottrina di Platone*, pp. 4-5 and Id., *Vere conclusioni di Platone*, pp. 23-24.

60 See PLATO, *Opera. Accedit Theologia Platonica*, Venice, per Bernardinum de Choris de Cremona et Simonem de Luero impensis Andree Toresani de Asula, 1491, p. 2 (mod. num.); FICINO, *Teologia Platonica*, p. 4; Id. *Epistolarum Liber VIII*, in *Opera*, I, pp. 871-872; Id., *Commentaria in Plotinum*, in *Opera*, II, pp. 1537-1538. See also I. KLUTSTEIN, *Marsilio Ficino et la théologie ancienne*, Florence, Olschki, 1987; M. J. B. ALLEN, *Synoptic Art: Marsilio Ficino on the History of Platonic Interpretation*, Florence, Olschki, 1998; J. HANKINS, *Plato in the Italian Renaissance*, Leiden, 2 vols, Brill, 1990, I, pp. 282-287, and II, pp. 460-464; S. GENTILE, "Sulle prime traduzioni dal greco di Marsilio Ficino", in *Rinascimento*, 2nd s., 30 (1990), pp. 57-104; Id., "Considerazioni attorno al Ficino e alla *prisca theologia*", in S. CAROTI and V. PERRONE COMPAGNI (eds), *Nuovi maestri e antichi testi. Umanesimo e Rinascimento alle origini del pensiero moderno*. Atti del convegno internazionale di studi di Mantova, 1-3 dicembre 2010, in onore di Cesare Vasoli, Florence, Olschki, 2012, pp. 57-72; S. FELLINA, "Cristoforo Landino e le ragioni della poesia: il dissenso con Marsilio Ficino sull'origine della *pia philosophia*", in CAROTI and PERRONE COMPAGNI, *Nuovi maestri e antichi testi*, pp. 191-222.

61 See DE' VIERI, *Compendio della dottrina di Platone*, pp. 11-13; and the letter to Valori in VERDE, "Il 'Parere' del 1587 di Francesco Verino sullo Studio pisano", pp. 84-85.

with the wisdom of the *prisci theologi* and culminates in Plato's philosophy, and the period inaugurated by the advent of Christianity, of which Neoplatonists, despite being pagans, benefited. Though Plato had the historical merit of understanding, illustrating, and enhancing the theology of the ancients, he failed to clarify the divine mysteries. The *velamina* and the *figmenta* which, in the manner of the *prisci*, continue to envelop his teachings, are not only an expedient artfully used to conceal the divine truths from the uninitiated, but also the sign of a weakness yet to be fixed by the incarnation of the *Verbum* and yet to be illuminated by the light of Christian doctrines. According to Ficino, this is the reason for the superiority of Plotinus, who is celebrated as the first to have extracted Plato's theological teachings from the *velamina* with which they were originally covered. This was also thanks to the doctrines of Dionysius the Areopagite, which Ficino believes reached both Plotinus and Iamblichus, before temporarily disappearing as the result of some conjectural *calamitas Ecclesiae*[62]. Verino, for his part, establishes a clear break between the "obscure" theology of the *prisci*, and the "clear" theology of Plato:

> lasciate per lo più le favole e i numeri [Platone] parlò di Dio, de gli Angeli, dello stato, dell'anime nostre in questa et nell'altra vita molto chiaramente et dell'altre così fatte et importante verità, quelle per lo più cavando da' sopradetti Poeti e Theologi de Gentili et da Fisici, le quali erano conformi a quello che si dice creare della Divina Maestà, Bonta e Providenza [...][63].

Verino justifies the obscurity that characterizes Platonic teaching by the need to preserve the truth from popular consumption. This was a pious concern reserved for the divine doctrines of dialectics or metaphysics. But the same could not be said of practical philosophy (*attiva*), which is destined to be communicated to all as, he argues, a proper reading of the *Hipparchus* would suggest[64]. Verino, for the same purpose, quotes a passage from Justin Martyr's *Admonitorium gentium*, in the *Vere conclusioni*. The passage recounts that Plato, though he read the Old Testament, did not clearly express Catholic truths, for fear of breaking the laws of the Gentiles and sharing the fate of Socrates[65]. Nevertheless, it is not argued that Plato truly had a full knowledge of Christian truths. In the *Compendio* Verino maintains that Plato did indeed see the Old Testament but did not benefit from an explanation by God's chosen ones; this would account for the divergent view on Christian theology regarding the Trinity[66]. Furthermore, in the *Liber in quo a calumniis detractorum philosophia defenditur* (1586), dedicated to Pope

---

62 See ALLEN, *Synoptic Art*, pp. 51-92; HANKINS, *Plato in the Italian Renaissance*, I, p. 283; FELLINA, "Cristoforo Landino e le ragioni della poesia", pp. 220-221.
63 DE' VIERI, *Compendio della dottrina di Platone*, p. 20.
64 See Id., *Vere conclusioni di Platone*, pp. 57-58.
65 See Ibid., p. 103 and Id., *Compendio della dottrina di Platone*, p. 20; JUSTIN MARTYR, *Admonitorium gentium*, XX.
66 See DE' VIERI, *Compendio della dottrina di Platone*, p. 62 (incorrectly numbered as 46).

Sixtus V, Verino states that Plato and Aristotle, despite being princes among the philosophers — by virtue of providence — only arrived at a partial truth by means of natural illumination, since "gentiles extiterunt et doctrina divinitus revelata caruerunt"[67].

The second professor to hold the Platonic chair was Jacopo Mazzoni (1548-1598), an ordinary lecturer of Aristotelian philosophy at the *Studium* of Pisa from 1588 until his departure for Rome in 1597; as seen, from 1591 he was also appointed as a holiday lecturer on Plato[68]. Mazzoni's major work, the *In universam Platonis et Aristotelis philosophiam Praeludia, sive de Comparatione Platonis et Aristotelis*, was published in 1597, toward the end of his professorship in Pisa[69]. As the title suggests, Mazzoni's goal was to provide a systematic comparison of Plato and Aristotle. Herein, he abandons the youthful enthusiasm that had inspired his *De triplici hominum vita, activa nempe, contemplativa et religiosa methodi tres [...]* (1576), and particularly the belief in an intimate and universal accord between Plato and Aristotle. Without declaring allegiance to either of the two philosophers, he carefully weighs the reasoning of both, and chooses what is more consonant with the truth[70]. Mazzoni also undertook the task of demonstrating Plato's compatibility with the Christian faith in a way that strongly suggests that, by the end of sixteenth century, the teaching of Plato at universities still needed to be justified by arguing Plato's consonance with Christianity. This renewed apologetic effort indicates an enduring opposition toward Plato within academic circles; and Jacopo Mazzoni was certainly influenced by what was happening in Rome. As already mentioned in Chapter I of this volume, the conferral of the chair of Platonic philosophy to Francesco Patrizi elicited harsh reactions and resulted in the Inquisition's censorship of the *Nova de universis philosophia*. The 1594 publication in Rome of *De Platone caute legendo*, by Giovanni Battista Crispo from Gallipoli — the first *"quinario"* of a larger project, the *De Ethnicis caute legendis*, which was never completed — was the most successful attempt at upending the belief in the affinity between Platonism and Christianity[71].

---

67 See DE' VIERI, *Liber in quo a calumniis detractorum philosophia defenditur*, proemio, p. 2 (num. mod).
68 See D. BARSANTI, "I docenti e le cattedre dal 1543 al 1737", in *Storia dell'Università di Pisa 1343-1737.I*, p. 525. On Mazzoni's Platonic teaching, see ASPi, Università 2, G 77, fol. 218 (188). In the list of ordinary lecturers Mazzoni's name is accompanied by a note stating "Concedeseli Platone", f. 220 (190), f. 222 (192), f. 224 (194), f. 226 (196), f. 228 (198). Mazzoni's name appears again in the 1597 university record as an ordinary lecturer and teacher of Plato (on holidays). See, *Ibid.*, f. 230 (200), even though he had already left for Rome. From 1592 onwards Mazzoni received a stipend of 700 scudi.
69 J. MAZZONI, *In universam Platonis et Aristotelis philosophiam Praeludia, sive de Comparatione Platonis et Aristotelis*, ed. S. MATTEOLI, introduction by A. DE PACE, Naples, D'Auria, 2010 [henceforth MAZZONI, *De comparatione*].
70 *Ibid*, I, 1, pp. 10-12.
71 See A. ROTONDÒ, "Cultura umanistica e difficoltà di censori. Censura ecclesiastica e discussioni cinquecentesche sul platonismo", in *Le pouvoir et la plume: incitation, contrôle et répression dans*

Though Mazzoni condemns Plato's fallacy about the Trinitarian dogma[72], he nonetheless states that Plato was able to grasp many Christian truths with the sole *lumen naturale*. Consequently, his doctrines provided pagans the opportunity for a *praeparatio evangelica*, rather than being a heretical hindrance for Christians[73]. Mazzoni then stresses the usefulness of Platonism for Christian theology, and provides numerous examples taken from Marsilio Ficino, Eusebius of Caesarea, and Theodoretus of Cyrus[74]. Yet, Mazzoni's attitude toward Ficino's *pia philosophia* seems to echo that of Verino. There is, for instance, no mention of the providential and exclusive quality of Platonism as standard bearer of the

---

l'Italie du XVIᵉ siècle. Actes du Colloque international d'Aix-en-Provence-Marseille, 14-16 mai 1981, organisé par le Centre Interuniversitaire de Recherche sur la Renaissance italienne et l'Institut Culturel Italien de Marseille, Paris, Université de la Sorbonne Nouvelle, 1982, pp. 33-50; M. MUCCILLO, "Le *cautiones* antificiniane di Giovanni Battista Crispo", in S. GENTILE and S. TOUSSAINT (eds), *Marsilio Ficino: fonti, testi, fortuna*, Atti del convegno internazionale di Firenze, 1-3 ottobre 1999, Rome, Edizioni di storia e letteratura, 2006, pp. 339-380: 339-349; J. KRAYE, "Ficino in the Firing Line: A Renaissance Neoplatonist and His Critics", in M. J. B. ALLEN, V. REES, M. DAVIES (eds), *Marsilio Ficino, His Theology, His Philosophy, His Legacy*, Leiden, Brill, 2002, pp. 394-397; P. F. GRENDLER, *The Universities of the Italian Renaissance*, Baltimore, The Johns Hopkins University Press, 2002, pp. 304-306; J. HANKINS, "Plato's Psychogony in the Later Renaissance: Changing Attitudes to the Christianization of Pagan Philosophy", in T. LEINKAUF and C. STEEL (eds), *Plato's Timaeus and the Foundations of Cosmology in Late Antiquity, the Middle Ages & the Renaissance*, Leuven, Leuven University Press, 2005, pp. 387-406. While the chair of Platonic philosophy was vacant, Mazzoni took the initiative to send copies of the *De comparatione* to the Roman court, which garnered appreciation and led Clement VIII to make him chair: "Il Mazzoni ebbe l'avvertenza di mandar alcuni esemplari del suo libro in Roma, e particolarmente nella corte del Papa, sapendo che il Santo Padre era grande estimatore di Platone. L'opera piacque infinitamente, e i due Cardinali Nipoti, cioè Cinzio, detto il Cardinal S. Giorgio, e Pietro Aldobrandini, avendone fatta allo Zio una relazione molto favorevole, egli s'invogliò fortemente di riveder l'autore già da lui, come dicemmo, conosciuto in Macerata" (see P. SERASSI, *Vita di Jacopo Mazzoni patrizio cesenate*, Rome, nella stamperia Pagliarini, 1790, p. 106). After all, Mazzoni was indeed the best candidate, given his experience in Pisa and "moderate" profile, which was far from anti-Aristotelian. Mazzoni was soon destined for other, more urgent, assignments and, with his death in 1598, the teaching on Plato at the Roman *Studium* came to an end, see D. DALMAS, "Jacopo Mazzoni", in *Dizionario Biografico degli Italiani*, 72 (2008), permanent link at http://www.treccani.it/enciclopedia/jacopo-mazzoni_(Dizionario-Biografico)/ [last accessed December 13, 2021]. In fact, although initially inclined to maintain the Platonic chair, Clement VIII ultimately changed his mind upon the advice of Cardinal Roberto Bellarmino, according to whom Platonism was more misleading than other pagan philosophies, precisely because of its affinity to Christianity, see M. MUCCILLO, "Il platonismo all'Università di Roma: Francesco Patrizi", in P. CHERUBINI (ed.), *Roma e lo* Studium Urbis. *Spazio urbano e cultura dal Quattro al Seicento*. Atti del convegno di Roma, 7-10 giugno 1989, Rome, Ministero per i beni culturali e ambientali, 1992, pp. 235-236.

72 See MAZZONI, *De comparatione*, III, I, 2, p. 51 and particularly XXI, V, 3, p. 327.
73 See, *Ibid.*, XIX, V, 1, p. 309.
74 See *Ibid.*, XXI-XXII, V, 3-4, pp. 331-348 and FELLINA, *Platone allo* Studium *Fiorentino-Pisano*, pp. 101-107.

faith, even if Ficino's genealogy is once again invoked: Zoroaster, identified as the author of the *Oracula*, is used to confirm the Platonic positions, while Hermes Trismegistus is presented as the source from which Plato drew his teachings. The lack of quotations nonetheless suggests a disinterest in the *prisca theologia* and, consequently, in the founding moments of the Platonic doctrines. Alternatively, this absence can be read as a careful decision made by Mazzoni, in light of the controversies surrounding Patrizi in recent years[75]. Similarly, when compared to the Ficinian approach, the privileged role ascribed to Plotinus and the Neoplatonic tradition is again lacking[76]. Mazzoni does, however, show some interest in the works of Plotinus and Proclus, such as *De sacrificio et magia*, the *Commentary on the First Alcibiades* and *on the Republic*, all read in Ficino's translations. But his use of these sources is by no means linear. At times, he rejects their views[77] and, at others, he uses them to confirm his own philosophical interpretations. For example, he invokes these thinkers to demonstrate that there is no real distinction between essence and existence[78], and that human knowledge depends on divine *illustratio*[79]; but neither Plotinus nor Proclus constitute the main filter through which Plato's wisdom is interpreted.

Jacopo Mazzoni also relies on Renaissance authors, notably Marsilio Ficino[80] and Francesco Piccolomini, whose *Universa philosophia de moribus* contains important Platonic elements, as we have seen in Chapter I of this volume[81]. A prime example of Mazzoni's compilatory attitude is found in the discourse on the nature of the rational soul, developed by the Sixth Platonic Academy, or *Academia peregrina*, as a digression to the general question of Academic skepticism. Aside from the *Platonic Theology* of Marsilio Ficino, Mazzoni tacitly borrows arguments from Giovanni Pico's *Commento sopra una canzona de amore* and from two letters of Francesco Cattani da Diacceto to Cristoforo Marcello, which deal with the soul vehicle[82]. By contrast, Mazzoni has first-hand knowledge of Syrianus' *Commentary on Metaphysics*, which he uses strategically to highlight the

---

75 For the references to Hermes Trismegistus and Zoroaster, see MAZZONI, *De comparatione*, XX, V, 2, p. 313, p. 320 and VIII, III, 1, p. 160, p. 162 respectively.
76 See *Ibid.*, XIX, V, 1, p. 309, XX, V, 2, pp. 311-312, and FELLINA, *Platone allo* Studium *Fiorentino-Pisano*, pp. 78-81.
77 See MAZZONI, *De comparatione*, III, I, 2, p. 62, XVI, IV, 4, p. 265, XX, V, 2, pp. 314-315, XXI, V, 3, pp. 326-327.
78 See *Ibid.*, XI, III, 4, pp. 196-198, XX, V, 2, pp. 317-318 and FELLINA, *Platone allo* Studium *Fiorentino-Pisano*, pp. 88-89.
79 See MAZZONI, *De comparatione*, X, III, 3, pp. 181-190; IV, I, 3, p. 96, XXIIII, VI, 2, p. 374, and FELLINA, *Platone allo* Studium *Fiorentino-Pisano*, pp. 159-178.
80 See MAZZONI, *De comparatione*, V, I, 4, p. 105, III, I, 2, p. 60, XXI, V, 3, pp. 326-327, 329-330, and FELLINA, *Platone allo* Studium *Fiorentino-Pisano*, respectively pp. 139, 113, 120, 126-127.
81 See MAZZONI, *De comparatione* IV, I, 3, p. 87, XX, V, 2, p. 322, XVI, IV, 4, pp. 272-273, and FELLINA, *Platone allo* Studium *Fiorentino-Pisano*, respectively pp. 170, 93, 173-174.
82 See MAZZONI, *De comparatione*, VIII, III, 1, pp. 159-161, and FELLINA, *Platone allo* Studium *Fiorentino-Pisano*, pp. 150-159.

agreement between Plato and Aristotle and harmonize Platonic and theological-scholastic doctrines[83].

One of the distinctive characteristics of Mazzoni's Platonism is his use of scholastic philosophy to read and "correct" Plato. Yet, though Mazzoni echoes Thomas Aquinas and Thomas Cajetan with regard to metaphysics, he only does so to a certain extent. For Mazzoni there is no real distinction between existence and essence and for him matter *non signata* is not part of the essence of the composite substance.[84]. In terms of epistemology, Jacopo Mazzoni instead follows Henry of Ghent, though considering Thomas Aquinas to be a supporter of the *illustratio divina*[85]. In all these contexts, the Jesuit Benedict Pereira had a great influence on Mazzoni, especially with his *De communibus omnium rerum naturalium principijs et affectionibus*[86].

To fully understand Mazzoni's Platonism, it is necessary to highlight his divergence from Plato, on a number of metaphysical and anthropological matters. Mazzoni, for instance, demonstrates that the Platonic First Intellect, the second hypostasis outside the One, cannot exist[87]. He similarly rejects Plato's belief that the soul has an innate, eternal and heavenly vehicle, and that the soul has some innate knowledge. He rejects metempsychosis as well. More specifically, Mazzoni argues that Plato himself did not really believe in these doctrines. According to Mazzoni, metempsychosis, innate knowledge, and the soul vehicle are based on the assumption that the world is created *ab aeterno*[88]. Yet, in Mazzoni's view, Plato believed that the creation of the world in time or *ab aeterno* was a dialectical problem that cannot be solved by reason. Thus, in his dialogues he advances opposing doctrines. In other words, by maintaining that Plato argued *in utramque partem*, Mazzoni tried to save him from the accusation of adopting dangerous

---

83 See MAZZONI, *De comparatione* IV, I, 3, pp. 95-96, and FELLINA, *Platone allo* Studium *Fiorentino-Pisano*, pp. 135-136. In the attempt to shield Plato from the charge of being a Gnostic, Mazzoni follows Syrianus and argues that when Pythagoreans and Plato deal with the Dyad, they do not affirm the existence of a second principle. The Aristotelian question, whether principles are determined in number or species, does not apply to the first Principle, which is completely transcendent and pre-contains the cause of number and species. Following Thomas Aquinas, Mazzoni concludes that, among Pythagoreans and Plato, the Dyad means divine essence in relation to the things created, that is a kind of "multiplication" of God, which does not exist *per se* but only in relation to the creatures, see MAZZONI, *De comparatione*, III, I, 2, pp. 55-56, and FELLINA, *Platone allo* Studium *Fiorentino-Pisano*, pp. 112-114.
84 See MAZZONI, *De comparatione*, X, III, 3, pp. 179-180, and FELLINA, *Platone allo* Studium *Fiorentino-Pisano*, pp. 163-164
85 See MAZZONI, *De comparatione*, X, III, 3, p. 182, XXVIII, VII, 3, p. 419, and FELLINA, *Platone allo* Studium *Fiorentino-Pisano*, pp. 167, 175.
86 See FELLINA, *Platone allo* Studium *Fiorentino-Pisano*, pp. 91-93, 162-165.
87 See MAZZONI, *De comparatione*, XXI, V, 3, pp. 327-328, and FELLINA, *Platone allo* Studium *Fiorentino-Pisano*, pp. 120-123.
88 See *Ibid.*, pp. 93, 105-107, 154-155, 175-178.

doctrines, and present him as a supporter of more traditional philosophical and religious opinions.

Following Mazzoni's departure for Rome, Carlo Tomasi da Cortona (1558-1606) was appointed to teach Plato on holidays in Pisa. We know hardly anything about Tomasi, except that he was to teach medicine and philosophy — as indicated in university records — and give a course on Plato during the holidays from 1598-1599 to 1603-1604[89]. More information is instead available about Tomasi's successor, Cosimo Boscagli (1574-1621), who was a professor for two decades at the *Studium* in Pisa, and gave holiday lectures on Plato between 1609 and 1621[90]. Boscagli first lectured on the *Timaeus* from 1609 to 1610, then on the *Phaedo*, the *Statesman*, and the *Meno*[91]. He taught again the *Timaeus* from 1616 to 1617, the *Phaedo* from 1617 to 1618, and then lectured on the *Republic* from 1618 to 1619 and again from 1619 to 1620. The content of the lectures on the *Timaeus* (1616-1617), the *Phaedo* (1617) and the *Republic* (1619) are preserved in a Florentine manuscript in the form of a commentary[92]. University records confirm this chronology[93] and provide details regarding the final years

---

89 See BARSANTI, "I docenti e le cattedre dal 1543 al 1737", p. 536. University records for the years 1597-1598 indicate that Carlo Tomasi was appointed to teach "medicina teorica ordinaria", with a salary of 130 fiorini, and lecture on Galen's *Ars medica*, see ASPi, Università 2, G 77, f. 229v (199v). During the years 1598-1606 he was an ordinary lecturer in philosophy and taught *On the Heavens, On the Soul, On the Heavens, On the Sould, Physics*, then again *On the Heavens, On the Soul, Physics*, and finally *De caelo*, and probably *De anima*, but there is no indication of the latter lectureship. From 1601 on, Tomasi's salary was 160 fiorini. See *Ibid.*, f. 232r (201r), f. 233v (203v), f. 235v (205v), f. 237r (207r), f. 239r (209r), f. 241r (211r), f. 243r (213r), f. 244v (214v).

90 See BARSANTI, "I docenti e le cattedre dal 1543 al 1737", p. 510. In 1609 Boscagli obtained an extraordinary lectureship with a salary of 145 fiorini and an additional 25 fiorini for his lessons on Plato, given on holidays and on Thursdays ("Lecturam Platonis // D. Cosmus Boscaglius Florentinus bis in hebdomada"), see ASPi, Università 2, G 77, f. 252v (222v) and f. 253r (223r). In 1610 Boscagli obtained an ordinary lectureship with a salary of 200 fiorini, but "obbligato anco all'estraordinario di Platone", see *Ibid.*, f. 255v (224v). In 1614 Boscagli received a salary increase of 100 fiorini, see *Ibid.*, f. 264v (234v) and ASPi, Università 1, 18, f. 489. He was given another raise of 100 fiorini in 1618, making his final, and highest, salary 400 fiorini, see ASPi, Università 2, G 77, f. 278v (248v), and ASPi, Università 1, 19, f. 641, Università 1, 20, f. 201r and f. 380v.

91 See BNCF, Pal. 1025 vol. II, f. 8r. See the note below for the manuscript.

92 See BNCF, Pal. 1025 vol. II, ff. 3r-40r, 41r-86r, 88r-97v respectively. See also P. L. RAMBALDI and A. SAITTA REVIGNAS (eds), *I manoscritti palatini*, Rome, La libreria dello Stato, 1950, pp. 26-27, and P. O. KRISTELLER, *Iter Italicum: A Finding List of Uncatalogued or Incompletely Catalogued Humanistic Manuscripts of the Renaissance in Italian and Other Libraries*. Vol. V, London, The Warburg Institute, 1990, p. 584a-b. The commentaries on the *Phaedo* and on the *Republic* are dated 1617 and 1619 respectively, see BNCF, Pal. 1025 vol. II, f. 41r, 88r. I have edited the text of the three commentaries with introductions and notes in my *Platone allo Studium Fiorentino-Pisano*, pp. 199-324.

93 See ASPi, Università 2, G 77, fol. 271v (241v; year 1616): "Platonis Timeum // D. Cosmus Boscaglius Florentinus" and ASPi 1, 1, f. 121v: "Extraordinarie diebus Iovis et Festivis //

of Cosimo Boscagli's tenure: they show that he lectured on the *Charmides* and the *Laches* between 1620 and 1621[94]. This chronology is further confirmed by Girolamo da Sommaia, *provveditore* or governor of the *Studium* (1614-1636), in his diary entitled *Dello studio overo università*[95].

In his *Commentary* on the *Timaeus*, Boscagli explains that he decided to teach this dialogue again to follow the curricular program of a "vir clarissimus huius platonicae scolae, in hac universitate auctor"[96], who maintained that the *Timaeus* be taught for four years. Though Boscagli does not explicitly mention his name, he is clearly referring to Francesco de' Vieri[97].

Of the extant commentaries, only the one on the *Phaedo* is complete. Those on the *Timaeus* and the *Phaedo* provide a detailed explanation of Plato's text, in Marsilio Ficino's translation, which is arranged into *lemmata*, in the format of scholastic commentaries on Aristotle. Conversely, the *Moralia Platonis in libris De republica* deliberately adopts the format of a continuous commentary, as Boscagli explains at the beginning of the work. In all three, we find the same pedagogical apparatus: in the left margin, Boscagli provides titles and numbers that correspond to arguments or subdivisions within the commentary; in the right margin, he provides additional notes. The commentaries on the *Timaeus* and *Phaedo* are divided into several *lectiones*, while the *Commentary* on the *Republic* is divided into thematic chapters.

For the most part, Boscagli's lectures appear to tacitly borrow from a number of sources. He inserts references to classical authors such as Cicero, Horace, Tacitus, and Aulus Gellius. He also frequently references Aristotle, either to emphasize his different points of view or, more often, to confirm Plato's doctrine.

Thus, in his commentary on the *Timaeus*, in an attempt to defend the dogmatic (not aporetic!) nature of Plato's doctrines, and reconcile Plato with Aristotle, Boscagli silently draws upon Mazzoni's *De comparatione* to outline the historical evolution of the Academy. He also tacitly borrows from Mazzoni to explain why Plato failed to complete the discussion planned on the fifth day of the

---

[...] Excellentissimus D. Cosmus Boscaglius Florentinus" and beside "tres priores dialogos De republica Platonis hora prima pomeridiana", and f. 130r: "Extraordinarie diebus Iovis et Festivis // [...] Excellentissimus D. Cosmus Boscaglius Florentinus Moralia Platonis in libris De republica hora prima [i] [*sic*] pomeridiana". University records are dated "in stile pisano" 1619-1620 and 1620-1621, which corresponds to the years mentioned above. The university record for the year 1618-1619 specifies that Boscagli's teaching covered the first three books of the *Republic*.

94 See *Ibid.*, f. 137v : "Extraordinarie diebus Iovis et Festivis // Excellentissimus D. Cosmus Boscaglius Florentinus" and beside "Platonis Charmiden seu de temperantia // Lacheten seu de fortitudine hora prima pomeridiana".

95 See BUP, MS 384, f. 38v: "1619 // Leget moralia Platonis in libris de Republica" and below "1620 // Boscaglia? [*sic*] Platone // Charmidem seu de temperantia // Lachetem seu de fortitudine".

96 See BNCF, Pal. 1025 vol. II, f. 8r.

97 See *supra* p. 61.

Panathenaic Games. Lastly, Boscagli follows Mazzoni, but without mentioning him, when he addresses the allegorical and mystical interpretation of the dialogue characters[98].

Cosimo Boscagli also draws heavily upon Ficino's *Commentary on Timaeus*, again without acknowledgment, particularly when dealing with the main theme, or *skopos*, of the *Timaeus*[99]. However, his main source is undoubtedly Paolo Beni's *Commentary on Timaeus*, an important work partially published in 1594, which is explored in more detail in Chapter III of this volume. Nearly half of Boscagli's *Commentary* is a *verbatim* reproduction of Beni's published commentary, even if Beni is mentioned only twice. Nevertheless, Boscagli shows a great deal of independence and originality. For instance, most of Beni's attacks on Ficino are usually refuted or toned down[100]. Boscagli's view of the *Timaeus* markedly differs from Beni's commentary, even when Boscagli appropriates discussions, digressions, and quotations from it. Boscagli, for example, observes that the *Timaeus* is not only a dialogue about natural philosophy, but also about theology, while Beni considers the *Timaeus* to be a work concerned with the *universa rerum series*, or Aristotle's natural philosophy[101]. Moreover, Boscagli follows Ficino's Latin translation of the *Timaeus*, rather than Beni's version.

Other sources used by Boscagli, without attribution, include Justus Lipsius' *Politicorum sive civilis doctrinae libri sex*, the source for a digression on the nature of wisdom (*prudentia*) and the importance of history[102]; Francesco Vimercato's *Commentary on Meteorology* and Benedict Pereira's *Commentaries on Genesis*. From these commentaries Boscagli lifts entire exegetical and doxographical sections to prove that celestial motions can only cause local deluges (such as the Deucalion deluge alluded to in the *Timaeus*) rather than universal ones, as testified by Plato, Aristotle, and the Scriptures[103].

Boscagli's approach in the commentary on the *Phaedo* is threefold. He identifies logical and demonstrative methods used by Plato; he harmonises Plato and Aristotle; and he underscores Plato and Aristotle's compatibility with Christianity. A striking feature of Boscagli's commentary is the effort he makes to express — in a logical-syllogistic way — the complex order of the arguments, replies, and counterreplies, made by Socrates and his interlocutors. This approach to philosophical texts was well-established in academic contexts in Late Antiquity and the Renaissance, as we have seen in Chapter I of this volume, and Boscagli here applies it to Plato's dialogues. One of the main purposes of Boscagli's commentary is to teach students the skills Plato uses to develop a truly demonstrative science, and the order of his arguments. In other words, Boscagli implicitly refutes two

---

98 See BNCF, Pal. 1025 vol. II, respectively f. 4v-5r, 12v-14r, 18v-19v.
99 See *Ibid.*, f. 8r-v.
100 See for example *Ibid.*, f. 31r.
101 See *Ibid.*, f. 16v-18r.
102 See *Ibid.*, f. 33v.
103 See *Ibid.*, f. 35r-35v and 36v-37v.

charges that were often formulated against Plato since the Middle Ages: that Plato lacks *rationes* and *ordo* and is therefore not fit to be taught in the university. By focusing on the order and method of Plato's philosophy, Boscagli emphasizes its didactic value. For instance, he states that at the beginning of the *Phaedo* Plato changes the *ordo compositivo* in favor of the easier *ordo resolutivo*[104].

As already mentioned, the *concordia* between Plato and Aristotle is among the main goals of Boscagli's *Commentary*. Consequently, Aristotelian quotations often follow the doctrines of Plato to confirm them. Boscagli, for example, presents the Aristotelian proofs in *De anima* against the soul as harmony, or the importance of music in education, to confirm the *Phaedo*'s doctrines[105]. Aristotelian quotations are also used to enrich the textual exegesis or strengthen Boscagli's interpretation of Plato, like when he argues that the *Phaedo* is a metaphysical dialogue[106]. Generally speaking, Boscagli adopts a very traditional image of Plato and Aristotle, according to which the former is fully oriented toward the Divine, while the latter is a true master *in naturalibus*[107].

This does not mean, however, that Boscagli always distorts their thoughts to emphasize their agreement. Indeed, he openly admits that Plato's anthropology and epistemology are irreconcilable with those of Aristotle. The same is true for their relationship with Christianity, and Boscagli stresses the differences between the two Greek philosophers and the Christian faith. In the case of Plato, Boscagli admits that the recollection argument that proves the immortality of the soul is not valid, because the soul cannot have innate knowledge. To confirm his view Boscagli quotes Thomas Aquinas and tacitly includes a passage from Francesco Piccolomini's *Universa philosophia de moribus*, which, as we have seen in Chapter I, attempted to provide a more balanced account of the *comparatio* between Plato and Aristotle[108]. However, Boscagli stresses Plato's affinity with Christianity concerning three important themes: God can be known only in the afterlife, Grace is a necessary requirement to gain the eternal life, and suicide is unlawful[109]. Boscagli's theological positions are always confirmed by references to Thomas Aquinas' *Summa Theologica*, Augustine's *De genesi ad litteram*, or *De civitate Dei* with Juan Luis Vives' commentary. The similarity between Platonism and Christian faith is supported by references to numerous *auctoritates* which are lifted, without attribution, from Jacques Charpentier's *Platonis cum Aristotele in universa philosophia comparatio* and Jacopo Mazzoni's *De comparatione*[110].

As in the *Commentary on Timaeus*, Boscagli borrows heavily (and tacitly) from several recent works: Francesco Piccolomini's *Universa philosophia de moribus*;

---

104 See *Ibid.*, f. 42r-v.
105 See *Ibid.*, respectively f. 80v-81r and f. 52v.
106 See *Ibid.*, f. 42v.
107 See *Ibid.*, f. 43r. See supra note 58.
108 See *Ibid.*, f. 77r.
109 See *Ibid.*, respectively f. 67r, 46v ff., 59v.
110 See *Ibid.*, f. 43r-v.

Sebastián Fox Morcillo's *In Platonis dialogum qui Phaedo seu de animorum immortalitate*; Jacopo Mazzoni's *De comparatione*; Stefano Tiepolo's *Academicarum contemplationum libri X*; Marsilio Ficino's *argumentum on the Phaedo*; and Jacques Charpentier's *Platonis cum Aristotele in universa philosophia comparatio*. To these, he occasionally adds quotations from Horace, Diogenes Laertius, Cicero, Aulus Gellius, and Tacitus.

Though he appropriates heavily from these works, Boscagli also shows a great deal of independence from his sources. On many occasions, he even expresses his own point of view. For example, he criticises Augustine and Lactantius' interpretation of the Socratic daemon, whom he considers to be angelic rather than evil in nature[111]. Finally, like some of his predecessors Boscagli is not interested in developing a genuine Neoplatonic exegesis; indeed, he very rarely refers to Plotinus, Porphyry, Iamblichus, or Proclus.

In the opening section of the final commentary, the *Moralia Platonis in libris De republica*, Boscagli offers insight into his *modus operandi*. Instead of providing a lemmatic commentary on the dialogue, he selects relevant moral *excerpta* or *morales sententiae*, and excludes doctrines related to politics, natural philosophy, and theology. Additionally, Boscagli states the two goals that inform his explanation: the *concordia* between Plato and Aristotle, and the exposition of *theologica veritas*[112]. The commentary is brief and certainly does not cover all the lectures of the course; it abruptly ends with two *sententiae* which are left uncommented upon, probably the last ones dedicated to book I (*Rep.* 350d ff. and 352d ff.)[113]. As a result, it only covers part of Book I of the *Republic*, beginning with the words of Thrasymachus (*Rep.* 336b ff.). Thrasymachus' attacks on Socrates and his persistent and ironical questioning are examined carefully, along with Socrates' profession of ignorance. Here Boscagli plagiarises Ficino's *argumenta* on the *Protagoras* and the *Republic*, and Piccolomini's *Universa philosophia de moribus*. In addition, as in the case of the *Phaedo*, Boscagli consistently focuses on the logical-syllogistic aspects of Socrates' reasoning, and often underscores Plato's agreement with Aristotle. For example, he argues that both philosophers believe that errors due to ignorance are unintentional[114].

More than ten years after Boscagli's death, the holiday teaching of Plato resumed in Pisa, thanks to Giuliano de' Medici, archbishop of Pisa, and Ascanio Piccolomini, archbishop of Siena, who hired Girolamo Bardi (1603-1675?). Bardi was awarded an extraordinary lectureship on philosophy and a holiday lectureship on Plato for the period of 1633-1635[115]. Personal circumstances, however, quickly

---

111 See *Ibid.*, f. 52r-v.
112 See *Ibid.*, f. 88r and 89r.
113 See *Ibid.*, f. 96v and 97v.
114 See *Ibid.*, f. 91v.
115 See M. GIUSTINIANI, *Gli scrittori liguri*, Rome, appresso di Nicol'Angelo Tinassi 1667, p. 417; F. CAGNETTI, "Girolamo Bardi", in *Dizionario Biografico degli Italiani*, 6 (1964), http://www.treccani.it/enciclopedia/girolamo-bardi_(Dizionario-Biografico)/[last accessed, Decem-

prevented him from teaching and he was eventually forced to leave Pisa. Despite his brief career, Bardi is an interesting figure who provides insight into the evolution of Platonic teaching during the seventeenth century. Bardi was in contact with prominent intellectuals of the time, including Galileo Galilei, with whom he exchanged letters. In one of them, Bardi provides details about his teaching of Plato and the works he wrote:

> Stamparò quanto prima il mio primo Ingresso, e ne farò parte a V. S., come è mio debito; e sarei di pensiero di stampare anco la prima lettione di Platone, che è in forma di apologia contro Aristotile, e mi son valso di molte sue galanterie; ma temo li denti de' cani rabbiosi, essendo noi troppo pochi, e chi vuole farli partire con ragioni dal testo, è un volere stuccicare le vespe che dormono e trattare dell'impossibile[116].

As the letter suggests, Bardi intended to publish his *Prolusio philosophica*[117], the academic prolusion publicly delivered at the beginning of his Platonic course, as well as the *Anteloquium platono-apologeticum*, his first lecture of Plato, which he describes as an apology in defence of Plato and against Aristotle[118]. We know that he also wrote two commentaries on the *Timaeus* (*In Platonis Timaeum propedeumata et dilucidationes*, the *Vestigium libertatis philosophicae in Platonis Timaeum*)[119], and translated Plato's dialogues[120]; unfortunately, none of these works survives. Their titles, however, suggest that Bardi wished to develop a strong anti-Aristotelian interpretation of Plato, which was a far cry from the harmonising approach of his predecessors.

Bardi's most important work, the *Medicus politico-catholicus*[121], printed in 1643 in Genoa, provides additional clues about his teaching. Like his predecessors, Bardi explores the affinity of Plato with Christian faith. Thus, he repeats the

---

ber 3, 2023]; G. L. BRUZZONE, *Girolamo Bardi (1603-1675) tra filosofia e medicina*, Genoa, Accademia Ligure di Scienze e Lettere, 2004, pp. 8-9, and BARSANTI, "I docenti e le cattedre dal 1543 al 1737", pp. 508 and 562.

116 Letter from G. Bardi to G. Galilei, October 26, 1635, in *Le opere di Galileo Galilei, Edizione Nazionale*, ed. A. FAVARO, 20 vols, Florence, Barbera, 1905, XVI, p. 328. See BRUZZONE, *Girolamo Bardi (1603-1675)*, p. 11.

117 *Prolusio philosophica habita in Pisarum celeberrimo Athaneo XI mensis novembris 1633, antequam Platonem et Aristotelem explicandos accederet*, Pisis, in aedibus Francisci Tanagli, 1634.

118 See GIUSTINIANI, *Gli scrittori liguri*, pp. 420-422 and BRUZZONE, *Girolamo Bardi (1603-1675)*, pp. 23-25. We know that Galilei appreciated the prolusion and owned a copy: see the letter from G. Bardi to G. Galilei, April 12, 1634, in *Le opere di Galileo Galilei*, XVI, pp. 82-83.

119 However, in the list of Giustiniani, the *Vestigium libertatis philosophicae in Platonis Timaeum* and the *Anteloquium platono-apologeticum* seem to be a unique work, see GIUSTINIANI, *Gli scrittori liguri*, p. 421.

120 The translation of Plato's dialogues is mentioned in a letter addressed to Gabriel Naudé, now at the Morgan Library, PML, MS 2841, f. 1 (mod. num.).

121 G. BARDI, *Medicus politico-catholicus, seu Medicinae sacrae tum cognoscendae, tum faciendae idea* [...], Genoa, typis Ioannis Mariae Farroni, 1643.

traditional apologetic *topos* according to which Plato, despite having made a great number of mistakes, derived his doctrines from Moses and the Holy Scriptures[122]. However, as is evident in the letter to Galileo Galilei, Bardi fiercely attacks Aristotle, and claims that in his *Anteloquium platono-apologeticum*, and his *In Platonis Timaeum propedeumata et dilucidationes*, he proved in detail that Aristotle was a cuttlefish[123]. In the same treatise, he quotes Jacques Gaffarel's *Catena cabalistica*, according to which a Spanish rabbi, Iactilia Ben Ioseph, stated that Aristotle delivered a palinode at the end of his life, and conceded that "verissima omnino esse ea omnia et a philosophis amplectenda quae scripta sunt in libro legis Mosys"[124]. Bardi also states that he does not understand the reason for Aristotle's philosophical success[125]. By contrast, Plato is always mentioned in a positive light in the *Medicus politico-catholicus*, and is often used as an *auctoritas* to confirm Bardi's point of view. For instance, Bardi quotes Isaiah, 3,7 ("And the other answers: 'Who, I? Nay, I have no doctor's skill. As for my house, there is neither bread nor coat in it; ruler thou shalt never make of me'"), to say that the verse contains the same teaching found in Plato's *Republic* and *Statesman*[126], namely that kings should devote themselves to philosophy, an argument Bardi claims to broadly address in the *Prolusio philosophica*. Bardi is nevertheless convinced that this *axioma* pertains more to physicians "qui animam et corpus curare debent, in quorum iusta symmetria, quae non nisi a medico potest haberi, totius reipublicae et dominii microcosmi oeconomia rectaque administratio consistit". Bardi again refers to Plato's statements on the utility and necessity of medicine[127], and on the role of the physician, who must care for both soul and body[128]. Ficino is also mentioned in a positive way, when Bardi wants to emphasize the connection between medicine, theology, and moral philosophy[129], or stress that physicians

---

122 See *Ibid.*, p. 7.
123 See *Ibid.*, pp. 7-8. On the cuttlefish epithet attributed to Aristotle, see C. B. SCHMITT, "Aristotle as a Cuttlefish: The Origin and Development of a Renaissance Image", in *Studies in the Renaissance*, 12 (1965), pp. 60-72.
124 See BARDI, *Medicus politico-catholicus, prolusio*, p. 8. Bardi quotes explicitly from F. LICETI, *De Quaesitis per epistolas a claris viris responsa*, Bologna, typis Nicolai Tebaldini 1640, ep. 15, p. 88. See E. DEL SOLDATO, "Saving the Philosopher's Soul: The *De pietate Aristotelis* by Fortunio Liceti", in *Journal of the History of the Ideas*, 78 (2017), pp. 531-547.
125 See BARDI, *Medicus politico-catholicus, prolusio*, p. 9.
126 See *Ibid.*, pp. 18-19. Bardi refers to *Rep.* 473d-e and to the Ficinian argument on the *Politicus* (p. 138), a precise reference that suggests he used PLATO, *Opera omnia Marsilio Ficino interprete*, Lyon, apud Antonium Vincentium, 1557.
127 See BARDI, *Medicus politico-catholicus*, pp. 248-249. References are to *Charm.* 171a8-9, *Alc. II* 138d-139a, *Men.* 72d8-e8, *Gorg.* 451d9 ff., *Clit.* 408e2 ff., *Gorg.* 500e3-501a3, *Euthyd.* 291e4-6, *Pol.* 293a9-c1, *Symp.* 186c5-9, *Leg.* IV 720a6 ff.
128 See BARDI, *Medicus politico-catholicus*, pp. 301-303 and *Rep.* 405e-d, *Phaedr.* 270c1-5.
129 See BARDI, *Medicus politico-catholicus*, pp. 334, 336 (on the link between medicine and moral philosophy Bardi refers to the Ficinian *argumentum* on *Protagoras*).

must have a holistic knowledge of man, to care for the soul and body[130]. The quotations from Plato, Ficino, and the Platonic tradition all regard medicine, alchemy, and astrology — Bardi's main interests at the time — as is proven by what should have been his *opus maius*, the *Iatrochimia*, in five volumes[131].

This concludes our investigation of the development of Platonic teaching at the University of Florence-Pisa. University records do not mention any other Platonic appointments after 1635. The approach to Platonic teaching presents notable continuities and discontinuities from Cattani to Verino and the other professors of Platonism. Francesco Cattani conceived the teaching of Plato in the form of a *concordia* with Aristotle in a way that echoes, to some extent, what Verino, Mazzoni and Boscagli did. Yet Cattani did not display any apologetic effort to underline the agreement between Platonism and Christian faith, an attitude consistent with his lack of engagement with the Ficinian *pia philosophia*. Neither was he interested in the question of *methodus* and *ordo*, two themes that became particularly central in philosophical discussions from the middle of the sixteenth century onwards, and eventually represented a new chapter in the *concordia* between Plato and Aristotle and a key to ensuring Plato's entry into academic *curricula*. As a consequence of these discontinuities only the general trends in the history of Florentine Platonism between the second half of the sixteenth century and the first three decades of the seventeenth century will be considered.

The first major trend is the constant effort to reaffirm the compatibility between the truths of Christianity and Platonic philosophy which, in the eyes of Verino, Mazzoni, Boscagli, and Bardi, justifies the inclusion of Platonism in the academic *curriculum*. This approach does not aim, therefore, at a compilation of a Platonic doctrinal *corpus*, but is instead apologetic. Indeed, many Platonic doctrines on metaphysics and anthropology are manipulated or even rejected in favour of Christianity. This is the case of metempsychosis, the *vehiculum animae*, the innate knowledge and the existence of a *Prima Mens*. Ficino had not intended his *restauratio platonica* to be simply a scholarly enterprise, but rather an authentic reform of Christian dogmas. In contrast, the Platonism of Verino, Jacopo Mazzoni, and other Platonic professors, is linked to more established orthodox positions. After all, the philosophical *Weltanschauung* of their time was not represented by Platonism, but by the tradition of the *scholae*, mainly Thomas

---

130 See *Ibid.*, p. 300. Bardi quotes Ficino's interpretation of the *Charmides* passage dealing with Zalmoxis' medicine (156d-157b). Even though Bardi refers to the *argumentum* on *Charmides*, he nonetheless follows Ficino's *Platonic Theology*, see FICINO, *Teologia Platonica*, XIII, 1, p. 1170. For a full list of the *loci* on Plato and Ficino see FELLINA, *Platone allo Studium Fiorentino-Pisano*, pp. 335-336.
131 The *Iatrochimia* partially survives in BNCR, S. Pantaleo 37-38. See also FELLINA, *Platone allo Studium Fiorentino-Pisano*, pp. 336-339 for a complete list of Bardi's Platonic quotations. Bardi only published the framework of *Iatrochimia*, see G. BARDI, *Theatrum naturae iatrochymicae rationalis. Opus dogmaticum theorico-practicum, quo quidquid in universo naturae ambitu medicarum continetur facultatum, ob oculos curiosi, et novitatum amatoris, et melioris medicina studiosi exponitur*, Rome, typis Angeli Bernabò, 1653.

Aquinas. In addition, even when these authors mention Ficino's *prisca theologia*, the providential qualities conferred by Ficino upon the *pia philosophia*, and which constituted the core of his proposal for reform, are entirely lost. In other words, their Platonism is now connected to a more general ancillary conception of philosophy.

Another notable feature we have encountered among all these professors of Platonism, with the partial exception of Verino and Mazzoni, is the fact that the Neoplatonic tradition is scarcely present. It should be noted, however, that this trend differs markedly from the various attempts made in the second half of the sixteenth century to separate and contrast Plato's "authentic" thought from that of his Neoplatonic followers, as was done by Chrysostomus Javelli, Jean de Serres, and Paolo Beni (as discussed in Chapters I and III of this volume)[132]. In other words, despite rejecting some significant aspects of Ficino's *pia philosophia*, the Florentine Platonism of the sixteenth and seventeenth centuries continued to embrace its tenets. From the very beginning, these authors considered Platonism as a continuous tradition, and a homogeneous corpus of doctrines, which included those of the *prisci theologi* and of the Neoplatonic successors of Plato, who were more or less faithful interpreters of Platonic teachings[133], rather than an autonomous philosophy that had to be apprehended without recourse to the commentary tradition.

The third important aspect lies in the emphasis on Plato's scientific and didactic merits, evidently intended to justify his introduction into university *curricula*. From the second half of the sixteenth century, the issue of the agreement between Plato and Aristotle was no longer limited to an examination and conciliation of their respective doctrines for philosophical or theological reasons. It was also addressed in discussions of *methodus* and *ordo*. Verino, Mazzoni, and Boscagli echo ideas previously formulated by Sebastiano Erizzo, Theodor Zwinger, Gabriele Buratelli, Jean de Serres, and many others, who compared the method and order of each philosopher, sometimes in favour of Plato[134]. Verino deals with the question of method in some of his writings[135]. The more articulated discussion — which certainly reflects his hope of being hired to teach the new Platonic course — is contained in his final work, the *Vere conclusioni*. Aside from acknowledging Aristotle's demonstrative and didactic superiority — which is why the *magister* of Platonic philosophy must also be an Aristotelian[136] — Verino maintains that Plato

---

132 See E. N. TIGERSTEDT, *The Decline and Fall of the Neoplatonic Interpretation of Plato: An Outline and Some Observations*, Helsinki, Societas Scientariarum Fennica, 1974, pp. 38-43; B. BARTOCCI, "Il Platonismo di Paolo Beni da Gubbio e la critica della tradizione Neoplatonica", in *Accademia* 12 (2010), pp. 75-108.
133 See FELLINA, *Platone allo Studium Fiorentino-Pisano*, pp. 29-33, 80-81, 188.
134 See *Ibid.*, pp. 9-16.
135 See *Ibid.*, pp. 18-19.
136 See DE' VIERI, *Vere conclusioni di Platone*, p. 7. Aristotle's demonstrative and didactic superiority is a firm point for Verino, and it is also confirmed by his considerations on the reformation of

shared Aristotle's concern for the four "ufizii intorno al vero", namely, definition, demonstration, distinction, and order[137]. Furthermore, Plato and Aristotle both employ natural order with respect to knowledge – from the universal to the particular — and human knowledge — from the particular to the universal, or from things that are simple to things that are more complex[138]. Thus, Verino does not hesitate to respond to the traditional accusation against the inclusion of Plato in university education on the grounds that he lacks order:

> Altri dicono che Platone non merita di essere publicamente esposto per gli Studii si perché e' non procede con methodo o vero ordine, che conferisce alla memoria, si ancora perché le sue ragioni son topiche et probabili et non come quelle di Aristotile demostrative e producitrici negli animi nostri di scienza[139].

Two of Verino's replies are worth noting. Plato is said to be "per lo più ordinato", as in the *Philebus*, the *Parmenides*, the *Symposium*, the *Timaeus*, and the *Hipparchus*, according to a gloss in his copy of the *Platonis Opera*[140]. Verino also recognizes the utility of Plato's use of probable reasons, being convinced that the truth can be legitimately exposed in at least six different ways. In his opinion this is true of the Platonic tradition, which includes the "Aristotelian way", characterized by a refutation of false opinions and demonstration of truth. Verino concludes:

> [...] è manifesto che a gran torto ell è stata et è ancora ripresa o lasciata in tutto o quasi in tutto da professori dell'humana sapienza. Et in contrario di qui è chiaro che da ogni banda è giusto et honesto che se ne faccia et publicamente et privatamente dagli scienziati grandissimo conto [...][141].

In *De comparatione* Jacopo Mazzoni instead begins with the distinction between *methodus per se* and *methodus per accidens*, tacitly borrowing from Theodor Zwinger[142]. In considering the *methodus per se*, Mazzoni distinguishes two meanings by referring to Averroes. Method in the broad sense includes both the *demonstratio* and the *ordo*, while according to the specific meaning it only coincides with the *via doctrinae*, since the order exclusively concerns the arrangement of

---

the *Studium* pisanum, see DEL FANTE, "Lo studio di Pisa in un manoscritto inedito di Francesco Verino secondo", p. 407.
137 See DE' VIERI, *Vere conclusioni di Platone*, pp. 27-28.
138 See *Ibid.*, pp. 32-33.
139 *Ibid.*, p. 97.
140 This gloss is not on the dialogue but on the *Vita Platonis*. Verino maintains that, in *Hipparchus*, Plato applies the *ordo studi*. See PLATO, *Opera*, 1548, f. 19r (mod. num.): "In Hipparco de lucri cupiditate studi ordo a Platone servari videtur. Primo volens demonstrare bonum ab omnibus hominibus appeti et acquisitum lucrum existimari a definitione luchri exorditur, quod definitio principium. demonstrationis est. Secundo perpendit plures luchri definitiones et corrigit, ostendens non qualecumque et a quolibet expetibile esse verum luchrum, sed cum sapientia et bonitate exemplo Hipparci [...]".
141 DE' VIERI, *Vere conclusioni*, p. 102.
142 See FELLINA, *Platone allo* Studium *Fiorentino-Pisano*, pp. 10-12.

the *scibilia*. On the topic of order, Mazzoni maintains the full convergence of Plato and Aristotle, since both, in fact, order knowledge starting from what is best known (*notiora*)[143]. The same is true for the method, assumed in its specific meaning: according to both Plato and Aristotle, the method of division is not a demonstrative one in itself, but only useful for scientific reasoning[144]; again, their differing opinions on the resolutive method (*demonstratio quia*), and their different use thereof, is due to their peculiar approach to understanding the passage from sensibles to intelligibles. For Plato, this is a form of purification, whereas for Aristotle it represents the very form of scientific knowledge[145]. In terms of the *methodus per accidens*, relative to the stylistic and rhetorical characteristics of discourse[146], the comparison between Plato and Aristotle seems to suggest that, even if the latter put aside the esoteric *modus philosophandi* of Plato and Pythagoras, comprised of *fabulae*, mathematical symbols, and other *involucra*, the characteristic conciseness of the Stagirite's *oratio* was nonetheless artfully employed for the same purpose, namely to shield the truth from the uninitiated[147]. Plato had to resort not only to the strength of arguments, but also to the attraction of rhetoric to address the threat posed by sophistry; once the latter was defeated, Aristotle no longer required stylistic trimmings, nor did he need to devote himself to refutation and could entirely dedicate himself to the teaching the truth[148].

These discussions show an important concern for the logical-demonstrative aspects of Platonic dialogues, especially in the texts prepared for teaching, as in the cases of Verino and Boscagli. The common methods consolidated in the university teaching of the Aristotelian texts are thus transposed onto Platonic dialogues, in accordance with normal practice. This enables to highlight the scientific merits of Plato *in vivo*, and ultimately proves the suitability of Platonism for the academic *curricula*. The effort to bridge the gap between Plato and Aristotle (whose superiority *in docendo* was historically recognized) can already be seen in Verino's decision to consolidate the Platonic doctrines in a compendium, and in conclusions and propositions — containing *auctoritates* and arguments —, that is in formats adapted to a university audience[149].

---

143 With a clarification: "Aristoteles semper a notioribus quo ad sensum et rationem auspicatur, Plato vero idem in paedia quidem facit, sed si sibi constare debet, in scientia ab iisquae sola ratione notiora sunt exordiri debet [...]". See MAZZONI, *De comparatione*, XVI, IV, 4, p. 267.
144 See *Ibid.*, pp. 267-268.
145 See *Ibid.*, pp. 268-269. Mazzoni says he prefers Aristotle's position: the *demonstratio quia* pertains in its own to science.
146 *Ibid.*, p. 269: "Nunc transeamus ad methodum accidentalem, quae considerari solet in quodam orationis modo".
147 See *Ibid.*, pp. 269-270.
148 See *Ibid.*, p. 271. The explanation is once again tacitly borrowed from Zwinger, see FELLINA, *Platone allo* Studium *Fiorentino-Pisano*, pp. 10-12, 17.
149 The same concern is widely shared by all those who promoted the teaching of Plato's at universities. It is in this context that we must consider Zwinger's intention to reduce Platonic dialogues to analytical tables, or embrace some of the editorial peculiarities of the *Platonis opera* edited by

Another common feature is that the academic teaching of Plato at the *Studium* is influenced by the philosophical *genre* of the *comparatio*[150]. With the notable exception of Girolamo Bardi, the teaching of Plato is generally approached as a *concordia* with Aristotle.

A final feature that we find in the authors envisaged in this chapter, and particularly in Verino, is their common humanistic formation, which is evident in the style of their works. This attitude was certainly influenced by the Tuscan cultural *milieu*, characterized by mutual exchanges between the *Studium* and institutions like the Accademia Fiorentina[151].

Thus, the introduction of Platonism into university teaching, and the creation of a course on Plato's dialogues, remained a complicated matter, even in Ficino's Tuscany. This is all the more striking since in the Tuscan context these Platonic courses were intimately linked to Ficino's heritage of the *translatio Academiae* and tied to the tradition of the Medicean patronage . Yet, even if the teaching of Plato remained restricted to an intermittent and poorly paid holiday lectureship, it developed a number of complex and varied strategies and proposed new, sometimes original interpretations of Plato, in silent dialogue with contemporary Aristotelian authors like Francesco Piccolomini or in a perspective that was strikingly similar to that of the proponents of "scholastic humanism".

Estienne and de Serres. See C. GILLY, *Theodor Zwinger e la crisi culturale della seconda metà del Cinquecento*, 2012, p. 111, http://www.saavedrafajardo.org/Archivos/LIBROS/Libro0844.pdf [last accessed, December 13, 2021], and FELLINA, *Platone allo* Studium *Fiorentino-Pisano*, pp. 21-22. On Boscagli see *supra* p. 78-82.

150 On the genre of *comparatio* see DEL SOLDATO, *Early Modern Aristotle*.
151 Verino "il primo" (grandfather of Verino "il secondo") delivered the inaugural lesson at the Accademia Fiorentina on February 17, 1541. See M. PLAISANCE, *L'Accademia e il suo principe. Cultura e politica a Firenze al tempo di Cosimo I e di Francesco de' Medici*, Rome, Vecchiarelli Editore, 2004, pp. 13-14 and 96. Verino, Mazzoni and Boscagli had several academic affiliations and gave lessons at academies, see FELLINA, *Platone allo* Studium *Fiorentino-Pisano*, pp. 18, 40 ff., 75, 183-184.

BARBARA BARTOCCI

Shifting Away from Aristotelianism towards Platonism[*]

Paolo Beni's Project

Introduction

In the second quarter of the sixteenth century, many voices were raised against scholastic Aristotelianism, which at the time constituted the basis of curricula for lay and religious higher education, and many attempts were made to introduce Platonic philosophy in the universities, especially in Italy. This chapter focuses on the project of the Platonist philosopher and theologian Paolo Beni da Gubbio (1552–c. 1625), who shifted away from Aristotelian philosophy and established a new Christian philosophy based on Platonism. I argue that for Beni Platonism was the pillar on which rested his new philosophy, religion and politics.

First as a student and then as novice and lecturer at various Italian Jesuit colleges, Paolo Beni gained a deep knowledge of scholastic Aristotelian philosophy. But already in its youthhood he was more sympathetic towards Platonic philosophy, perhaps as a result of the intellectual influence of the Paduan and Roman learned circles he belonged to. In the first section I reconstruct Beni's intellectual biography with special attention to his writings and teaching activity. In the second section I outline Beni's twofold strategy for making Plato's thought systematic and teachable. The first step was to present Plato's *corpus* as a doctrinally systematic and coherent whole. The second step was to clarify, by means of a running commentary, the obscurities of Platonic dialogues and to show the consistency of the Platonic system. Beni's project itself includes critical and constructive elements. In the third section I present the *pars destruens*, that is the charges he levels against Aristotle and the arguments he develops to show that

---

[*] I thank Maude Vanhaelen and Eva Del Soldato for inviting me to contribute to this volume and I am deeply grateful for their very insightful comments. I am also thankful to the anonymous reviewers whose suggestions improved the text in many ways. Obviously, any mistakes are all mine. All transcriptions from Beni's unedited works are my own, unless otherwise specified; I have standardized spellings and I have followed modern punctuation.

Barbara Bartocci • University of Edinburgh

Aristotelianism is irreconcilable with the main teachings of Christianity. In the fourth and last section, I delineate his positive program of proving the perfect compatibility between Platonic philosophy and Christian doctrine.

Teaching Plato via Aristotle across Italy

The philosopher and theologian Paolo Beni was born in Gubbio in 1553 into a noble family[1]. At the age of five he was sent to the Jesuit Collegio Germanico in Rome, where he received a humanistic education centred on grammar and rhetoric. In 1566, his father sent him to Perugia to study civil law; he only remained there for a few months, since the same year he decided to enrol at the University of Bologna to study philosophy and theology. Then, in 1573-1576, he continued his theological studies at the University of Padua, where he earned his doctorate in theology in 1576. During his Paduan years, Beni became a member of the Accademia degli Animosi, where he got acquainted with many leading intellectuals of the time, such as Torquato Tasso, Bernardino Tomitano, Antonio Querenghi, Giovanni Vincenzo Pinelli and Cinzio Aldobrandini[2]. It is probably in this Platonically oriented intellectual environment that Beni planned to translate and comment on all the dialogues of Plato, a project of which, however, he only completed a small part. In the following years, Beni worked in Rome as a secretary, first for Cardinal Cristoforo Madruzzo, then for the Duke of Urbino Francesco Maria II della Rovere, before entering the Jesuit novitiate in 1581. In the years 1584-1586 he was lecturer (*tutor*) in *Umanità* at the Roman Seminary and was subsequently (1586-1590) sent to various Northern cities, including Venice and Padua, where he taught moral theology (or cases of conscience) and philosophy. From May 1590 Beni was in Milan and lectured at one of the Jesuit schools in Milan, perhaps at S. Mary of Brera, which had a university status and was one of the most important Italian Jesuit colleges[3]. We do not have any information concerning Beni's teaching activity in 1590-1591, but we know that in the spring term of 1592 he taught moral philosophy based on Aristotle's *Nicomachean*

---

1 P. B. DIFFLEY, *Paolo Beni. A Biographical and Critical Study*, Oxford, Clarendon Press, 1988, pp. 9-18.
2 P. BENI, *Il Cavalcanti overo La difesa dell' Anticrusca di Michelangelo Fonte*, ed. G. DELL'AQUILA, Bari, Cacucci, 2000, p. 50. On the Accademia degli Animosi, established in 1573 by Ascanio Martinengo de' Cesareschi da Brescia, and aiming at building a new science inspired by the Hermetic and Platonic traditions, see S. O. SECCHI, "Laici ed ecclesiastici fra sogno e ragione in un'accademia padovana del '500: gli Animosi", in *Archivio Veneto*, 130 (1988), pp. 5-30; U. MOTTA, *Antonio Quarenghi (1546-1633): un letterato padovano nella Roma del tardo Rinascimento*, Milan, Vita e Pensiero, 1997, pp. 13-33.
3 On Jesuit teaching activity in Milan in the second half of the sixteenth century, see F. RURALE, *I Gesuiti a Milano. Religione e politica nel secondo Cinquecento*, Rome, Bulzoni, 1992, ch. 5.

Ethics[4]. It is widely acknowledged by scholars that, since its foundation, the Jesuit order saw Aristotelian philosophy, or rather "Christian Aristotelianism", as a means to support and "confirm theological truths"[5] in opposition to the secular Aristotelianism taught in Italian universities, which relied on newly discovered (or re-translated) ancient Greek and Arabic sources. Jesuits discouraged their teachers from addressing in lectures controversial topics and authors, such as Alexander of Aphrodisias and Averroes. This meant that Aristotle had to be taught following the (by then old-fashioned) medieval tradition and medieval commentators, mainly Thomas Aquinas[6]. However, Beni did not work within the guidelines and often introduced challenging subject matters into the classroom, as can be seen from parts of the unedited *Commentationes ac notae in eam Aristotelicae philosophiae partem, quae ad vitam pertinet ac mores* which relates to his teaching of Aristotle's ethics in Milan[7]. Here, rather than relying on the medieval commentary tradition, Beni engages with the secular philosophers of his time, like Jacopo Zabarella and Marcantonio Zimara, who were criticized by his Jesuit fellows. And he did not limit himself to comment upon Aristotle's words and on philosophical issues related to them, but he often added long digressions where he compared the views of Aristotle and Plato on various topics in ethics, such as the theory of happiness of the two ancient philosophers[8]. Clearly, Beni had some reasons for introducing these parallels. One was to show that Aristotelian philosophy is deeply rooted in, and draws heavily on, Plato's works, following a trend that we also encountered in the other chapters of this volume[9]. In the inaugural

---

4 The inaugural lecture of his course on moral philosophy entitled *De moralis philosophiae praestantia et utilitate. Habuit hanc Mediolani kalendiis Martii MDXCII cum Aristotelis libros de moribus explicandos aggrederetur*, is preserved in P. BENI, *Orationes quinquaginta*, Padua, per Franciscum Bolzettam, 1613, Oratio VI, pp. 48-59; see D. A. LINES, *Aristotle's Ethics in the Italian Renaissance (c. 1300-1650)*, Leiden, Brill, 2002, p. 519. On the teaching of Aristotle's *Ethics* at the Jesuit Collegio Romano see *ibid.*, ch. 9.2, pp. 348-376.
5 P. F. GRENDLER, *The Jesuits and Italian Universities*, Washington, D.C., Catholic University of America Press, 2017, 402-403.
6 *Ibid.*, ch. 14; RURALE, *I Gesuiti*, ch. 5.
7 The *Commentationes ac notae in eam Aristotelicae Philosophiae partem, quae ad vitam pertinet ac mores* are now preserved in the collection Beni II in the Vatican Archives in Rome (hereafter abbreviated as ASV, ABII), MS 89. On the relation of this work to Beni's teaching in Milan see DIFFLEY, *Paolo Beni*, p. 35; the *Notae* seems to have been reworked for Beni's teaching on the *Nicomachean Ethics* in Padua (*ante* 1610).
8 Unsurprisingly, in his commentary on Aristotle's *Nicomachean Ethics* Beni often approaches the theme of happiness, especially at the beginning of the second volume of the commentary, where he devotes many chapters to the "disputatio de foelicitate ex Platonis Aristotelisque sententia".
9 P. BENI, *Commentationes ac notae in eam Aristotelicae philosophiae partem, quae ad vitam pertinet ac mores*, f. 32v-33r: "Aristoteles in moralis philosophiae ordine ac methodo Platonis methodum atque ordinem secutus est [...]. Aristoteles in naturali philosophia sic Platonis vestigia secutus est ut *Timaeus* Platonis seu liber de universitate aut de natura totius Aristotelicae physiologiae fuerit seminarium; ita quae in suis libris de *Republica* et de *Legibus* scripsit Plato, activae Aristotelis philosophiae suppeditarunt argumentum. Quo circa quemadmodum ea, quae Plato

lecture of his course on Aristotle's ethics, Beni openly claimed that in ethics as well as in poetry Aristotle either took his ideas from Plato or developed them in opposition to the Platonic view: "Princeps ingenii ac doctrinae Plato cum alibi sepe, tum in *Phaedro* et in libris de *Republica* de poesi nobis praecepit, quae cum exinde Aristoteles partim usurpaverit ac pro suis usus sit, partim etiam de more oppugnarit ac repudiaret"[10]. But if one considers the *Notae* in their entirety, there emerges another major reason for Beni's comparison between the two ancient authors: to suggest the superiority of Platonic philosophy over Aristotelianism by exposing the flaws of the latter. This idea is sometimes explicit, as at the beginning of the *Notae* where Beni, referring to Patrizi, raises doubts about the Aristotelian authorship of the *Nicomachean Ethics* for stylistic reasons[11]. This attitude is most surprising, because a Jesuit like him was supposed to avoid teaching topics that could show Aristotle in a negative light, lead to difficult discussions and upset the status quo.

In November 1592 Beni started teaching two classes per day, Greek language on Plato's dialogues in the morning, and Aristotle's *Rhetoric* in the afternoon. In the inaugural lecture to his Greek course, Beni echoed the arguments used by Agostino Valier and Marc-Antoine Muret (see Chapter I of this volume) by introducing Plato to his students as the chief exponent of Greek rhetoric, a fact, he said, acknowledged even by his zealous imitator Aristotle. Beni then continued his praise by claiming that Plato was more than a mere model of Greek eloquence: he was the greatest philosopher of ancient and modern times, the "philosophorum deus"[12]. Beni's extensive tribute to Plato should not be interpreted as a mere teaching strategy to increase student engagement with the course subject matter, but rather as part of Beni's project to present his "Christian Platonism" to students, and to familiarize them with the idea that Plato's thought could well be an alternative to "Christian Aristotelianism". For, Beni argued, already the Fathers of the Church, *in primis* Augustine, had emphasized the natural affinity between Platonic philosophy and Christian doctrine, which made Platonism more suitable to serve theology than Aristotelian philosophy: "Etiam Augustinus, vir acumine

---

breviter ac tanquam compendio disputaverat de universitate incipiens a principiis, theorematis, affectionibusque communissimis, et ad individuos usque partes progrediens, id Aristoteles copiosissime (pro suo nimirum admirabili ingenio) prosecutus est longa librorum serie. Sic sane in morali atque adeo activa philosophia universa Platonis decreta, eaque physicis ampliora Aristotelicis longe ac late aperuerunt campum".

10 BENI, *Orationes quinquaginta*, Oratio VI, p. 67.
11 BENI, *Commentationes ac notae*, f. 6v: "Videtur libros hos Aristotelis non esse quia ordo ac methodus longe videtur abhorrere ab Aristotelis consuetudine et stylo, id quod fuse probat (si tamen probat) Franciscus Patritius, libro nono suarum *Discussionum* prope finem". The reference is to F. PATRIZI, *Discussiones peripateticae*, Basel, ad Perneam Lecythum, 1581, Book 9, p. 126.
12 BENI, *Orationes quinquaginta*, Oratio III: "De Graecae linguae dignitate atque in primis de Platonicae orationis praestantia, habita Mediolani noniis Novembris anno MDXCII cum Plato Graece esset explicandus", p. 32.

ingenii morumque sanctitate clarissimus, Platonis libros ad sacrarum rerum scientiam moresque conformandos testatur esse perutiles, neque ullum esse ex veteribus qui ad Christianam pietatem ac veritatem proprius accesserit"[13]. Despite being a topos, these words would have sounded strangely out of place in many classrooms of sixteenth-century secular universities and surely in a Jesuit school, where students had to assimilate the principles of "Christian Aristotelianism" and learn how to put them in good use in their life. And Beni's numerous claims about the superiority of Platonic over Aristotelian philosophy might have acted as a trigger for the students of his afternoon course on Aristotle's *Rhetoric*[14]. Evidently, Beni was navigating a tricky territory. His barely hidden preference for Plato and his ambitious project to shift from the institutionalized Aristotelianism to a form of "Christian Platonism" must have disturbed many of his Jesuit fellows. And it might have been a crucial factor that led the General of the Society of Jesus, Claudio Acquaviva, to recall Beni to Rome in the spring of 1593 — precisely at the time when his fellow Jesuit Benedetto Giustiniani was examining Patrizi's *Nova Philosophia*, a manifesto for Neoplatonic philosophy — and, subsequently, to dismiss Beni from the Jesuit Order for unspecified "legitimate reasons" (*iustas ob causas*) in September 1593, before he could take his vows[15].

In the years following his dismissal from the Jesuit order, Beni was comfortably established in the Roman academic and intellectual environment. In 1594, he was involved in the activities of the literary and political Academy organized by Cardinal Cinzio Passeri Aldobrandini, the nephew of Pope Clement VIII[16]. Its members were all leading intellectuals — including Beni's Paduan acquaintances Querenghi, Tasso, Pinelli and Lelio Pellegrini[17]— who shared a common interest in Platonic philosophy as a source of political renovation[18]. The same year, Beni printed the first part of his most important philosophical work, the *In Platonis Timaeum*, which is probably the most extensive commentary on Plato's *Timaeus* ever written. It comprises 30 books, running to more than 3000 pages, arranged in three major units of ten books each (entitled *decades*), which Beni started

---

13 *Ibid.*, p. 34.
14 *Ibid.*, Oratio IIII: "in qua brevissime Aristotelis Aristoteleaeque *Rhetoricae* laus attingitur, habita Mediolani noniis Novembris anno MDXCII pomeridiano tempore, cum matutino alteram de Graecae linguae praestantia deque Platonis eloquentia laudationem habuisset", and p. 35: "Aristoteles qui quemadmodum in philosophiae studio caeteros facile omnes, uno fortasse Platone excepto, superaverat".
15 See DIFFLEY, *Paolo Beni*, p. 28.
16 On the Academy, see A. E. BALDINI, "Botero e la Francia", in *Id.* (ed.), *Botero e la "ragion di stato"*. Atti del convegno in memoria di Luigi Firpo (Torino 8-10 marzo 1990), Florence, Olschki, 1992, pp. 335-359.
17 Lelio Pellegrini was professor at the University of Rome and granted the permission to publish the first decade of Beni's *In Platonis Timaeum* in 1594.
18 See A. E. BALDINI, "Aristotelismo e platonismo nelle dispute romane sulla ragion di stato di fine Cinquecento", in *Id.* (ed.), *Aristotelismo politico e ragion di stato*. Atti del convegno internazionale di Torino (11-13 febbraio 1993), Florence, Olschki, 1995, pp. 201-226.

writing in Padua in 1576 and reworked throughout his entire life[19]. In 1595 Beni became professor of natural philosophy at the University of Rome, partly thanks to the support of Francesco Patrizi, who had been appointed Professor of Platonic philosophy at the Roman Studium in 1592 by the then newly elected Pope Clement VIII[20]. Patrizi and Beni shared an anti-Aristotelian attitude, even though Beni's criticisms were less virulent than Patrizi's; moreover, both men devoted all their efforts to promote the dissemination of Platonic philosophy, which for Patrizi included also Middle and Neoplatonism, and to favour the replacement of Aristotelianism with Platonism. As far as we know from some student notes (*reportationes*) preserved in the Vatican Archives, Beni taught a course on Aristotle's *On the Heavens* in 1595[21], *Generation and Corruption* in 1596[22], *On the Soul* the following year[23], *Meteorology* in 1598[24], and finally *Physics* in 1599[25]. In this new secular environment Beni continued to use the same teaching methodology and hermeneutic approach to Aristotle's text that he had adopted when teaching in the Jesuits' schools. In his explanation of the Aristotelian text, Beni introduced long comparisons between Plato and Aristotle on the subject matter at hand and,

---

19 The first decade was printed in Rome in 1594 and 1605; the two books of the second decade were printed as *Platonis et Aristotelis Theologia* in Padua in 1624. The rest of the work (18 books) remains in a manuscript now in the ASV, ABII, along with the majority of Beni's numerous unpublished works. A detailed description of Beni's works preserved in the ASV is in P. P. PIERGENTILI, *L'Archivio dei conti Beni di Gubbio. Note storiche e inventario*, Vatican City, Archivio Segreto Vaticano, 2003, and B. BARTOCCI, "*L'In Platonis Timaeum* e le altre opere inedite di Paolo Beni da Gubbio", in *Recherches de Théologie et Philosophie médiévales*, 80 (2013), pp. 165-219.
20 On the relationship between Beni and Patrizi see B. BARTOCCI, "Paolo Beni and His Friendly Criticism of Patrizi", in T. NEJESCHLEBA–P. R. BLUM (eds), *Francesco Patrizi Philosopher of the Renaissance*, 2014, Olomouc, Univerzita Palackeho, pp. 261-295. On Patrizi's teaching in Rome, see M. MUCCILLO, *Il Platonismo all'Università di Roma: Francesco Patrizi*, in P. CHERUBINI (ed.), *Roma e lo Studium Urbis. Spazio urbano e cultura dal Quattrocento al Seicento*. Atti del convegno, (Roma, 7-10 giugno 1989), Rome, Ministero per i beni culturali e ambientali, 1992, pp. 200-247.
21 ASV, ABII, MS 70, f. 1r: "Pergratum mihi quidem fuerit in primum Aristotelis motorem, hoc est in eum qui hanc rerum universitatem temperat ac moderatur, mentem cogitationemque defigere quod anno primo Aristotele duce prestitemus [...] quod insequenti anno Aristotele item duce perfecimus"; the lecture notes of this course are preserved in ASV, MS 112, f. 1-93 and, partially, in MS 69, f. 1r-38r.
22 ASV, ABII, MS 113, f. 1r: "Lectio introductoria in Aristotelis libros qui *De ortu et interitu* inscribuntur, Romae habita MDXLVI"; the *reportationes* are in *Ibid.*, f. 1r-10v and MS 69, f. 63r-73v.
23 *Ibid.*, f. 11r-22v, f. 11r "In Aristotelis libros *De Anima* praefatio habita in almo Urbis Gymnasio noniis Novembris MDLXXXXCVII"; cf. ASV, ABII, MS 70.
24 ASV, ABII, MS 113., f. 23r "In Aristotelis libros *Meteororum* praefatio habita in Romae in publico Sapientiae Gymnasio anno MDLXXXXIX [*pro* MDLXXXXVIII] pridie noniis Novembris"; more material from this course is found in ASV, ABII, MS 131, f. 76r-150v.
25 ASV, ABII, MS 70, f. 1r "Physicae Disputationes habitae in Almo Urbis Gymnasio MDLXXXVIII [...] fieret explicandos Aristoteles libros *De Naturali Auditiones* postremus".

under the guise of establishing the harmony between the two ancient philosophers, Beni emphasized his preference for Platonism by stressing that several principles and ideas of Aristotelianism were unsuited to, if not incompatible with, Christian doctrines. I will only give one example of this method, which Beni used when teaching Aristotle and when writing on Plato. In *In Platonis Timaeum*, Beni devotes an entire book to Plato and Aristotle's views on ten doubtful issues in physics, the second of which is whether there is only one world, a plurality or an infinite number of worlds, which was a hotly debated question at that time. Both Plato and Aristotle thought that there is just one world ("pari consensione respondent unicum omnino esse et singularem"); however, Plato's treatment of the issue at *Tim*. 30-31 might lead someone to infer the existence of many worlds, despite Plato's subsequent claims about the unicity of the world (*Tim*. 31a3ff and 92c4-9). Beni promptly dispelled this possibility and went on to discuss the points of contact and the differences between the two philosophers and between each of them and Christian doctrine. Eventually, he set the question about which of the two philosophers offers a better interpretation: undoubtedly, it was Plato. For, Beni states, Plato adopted what we would call today a rationalist stance: to gain knowledge, he proceeded by postulation and by deduction from principles (e.g., necessary true propositions), and not by sense-data:

> Quisnam rectius in hoc theoremate [*scil.* Utrum mundus sit unus vel plures aut etiam innumeri] philosophatus sit. Quamobrem re tota diligenter inspecta, minime dubitarim in hoc theoremate rectius philosophatum esse Platonem; cum praesertim Aristoteles in suis hisce ratiocinationbus disputet subtiliter quidem et ingeniose, sed tamen interim totus in motu, sensu, naturaque ipsa infixus sit. Quod philosophandi genus, ut infirmi sunt hominis sensus, non sine Christiani theologi iudicio ac censura adhibendum est in veritatis conquisitione. Plato contra ex Dei sapientia, virtute, probitate, caeterisque huiusmodi initiis, passim ducit suas argumentationes. Quae philosophandi ratio mirifice excitat attolitque animum ad Deum. Ut propterea Platonica ratio divina quodammodo, Aristotelica humana potius censenda sit[26].

The incompatibility between Aristotelianism and Christian teachings seems to have been a crucial issue for Beni, who systematized his numerous critiques of Aristotle — which are scattered throughout the *reportationes* of his courses on Aristotle — in his *In Platonis Timaeum*, and more specifically in Books I-III of the first Decade, and Books I, II and VII of the second Decade. Beni presented a set of critiques against Aristotelian metaphysics, and particularly Aristotle's conception that God is on the same ontological level as the celestial intelligences, and that

---

26 P. BENI, *In Platonis Timaeum, decadis secundae liber septimum*, ASV, ABII, MS 99, f. 20v; the second question covers f. 16v-21v: "Utrum mundus sit unus vel plures aut etiam innumeri. Pari consensione respondent unicum omnino esse et singularem [...] Declaratur quibusnam inter se conveniant Plato et Aristoteles in hoc theoremate, quibus dissentiant [...] Ostenditur quo consentiant cum Christiana religione, quod aberrent ab ea".

both obey the laws of celestial physics. It is easy to see that these alleged views of Aristotle lead to impious consequences — on the basis of such doctrine, one would infer that God and celestial intelligences are deprived of freedom, and that God does not have any efficient potency and does not intervene in human affairs[27]. Another set of severe criticisms concerns Aristotle's physics and psychology and specifically his position on the world's eternity and the mortality of the soul, two questions central among ancient and scholastic commentators[28]. Actually, many passages of the Aristotelian *corpus* contained strong arguments which gave solid foundations for the heterodox views that the world is eternal and the soul mortal, which both had highly problematic religious, moral and political consequences. Indeed, they undermined the foundations of Christian piety and human society and promoted instead Aristotle's naturalistic ethics, which not only allowed, but also justified misconduct such as divorce, eugenics, birth control, slavery and tyranny[29]. Thus, Aristotelian philosophy contained numerous potential risks Platonism was devoid of, provided it was correctly understood, especially Plato's *Republic* — a fact which Beni greatly emphasized in order to refute well-established criticisms against Plato (see *infra* §3.1).

At the turn of the century, Beni left Rome and went to Padua, where he taught rhetoric, poetics, history, politics, and moral philosophy at the university until the end of his life, in 1625. Things started well. Shortly after his arrival, Beni became part of the intellectual elite of Padua, attending the meetings organized by Gian Vincenzo Pinelli and Antonio Querenghi in their homes. For a brief period, he was member of the Accademia dei Ricovrati, along with his colleague Galileo Galilei. But then, stormy years followed. His theological treatise on predestination, *De efficaci Dei auxilio*[30], was condemned in 1604 by the Inquisition; in addition, he was often involved in literary polemics. Despite all these troubles, the Paduan interlude was his most prolific period: during that time, he wrote and published most of his works, principally his commentaries on Aristotle's writings. His commentaries on Aristotle's *Nicomachean Ethics, Politics, Poetics, Rhetoric* and on Cicero's *Orations, Tusculan Disputations, Dream of Scipio*, as well as the monograph *De historia*, share the same characteristics of Beni's earlier works: disguised or overt criticisms of Aristotle and a clear preference for Platonic philosophy, which justify the introduction of numerous digressions promoting the superiority of Plato.

---

27 P. BENI, *In Platonis Timaeum sive in naturalem omnem atque divinam Platonis et Aristotelis philosophiam decades tres*, Rome, ex typographia Gabiana, 1594, p. 91.
28 BENI, *In Platonis Timaeum*, p. 13.
29 *Ibid.*, pp. 92-100.
30 P. BENI, *Qua tandem ratione dirimi possit controversia quae in praesens de efficaci Dei auxilio et libero arbitrio inter nonnullos Catholicos agitatur*, Padua, In officina Laurentii Pasquati, 1603.

Shifting paradigms[31] in philosophy: from Aristotelianism to Platonism

In those years, Beni was not the only one to reject Aristotle. In addition to the well-known crisis resulting from the Patrizi affair and the question of the immortality of the soul, Aristotelian philosophy was experiencing a crisis caused by its failure to accommodate some astronomic phenomena and by its lack of scientific methodology. Signs of this crisis can be seen in the various attempts to shift away from the Aristotelianism paradigm, by philosophers like Patrizi, Bernardino Telesio, Giordano Bruno and Tommaso Campanella. More specifically, Beni was convinced of the need for a paradigm shift from Aristotelianism toward Platonism to ground a new Christian philosophy. This became a lifelong project that he tried to realize through his teaching and editorial activities, which are the two sides of the same coin, since most of Beni's edited and unedited writings (commentaries, notes and inaugural speeches) resulted from his school and university lectures. However, his call to replace Aristotle with Plato never succeeded because, despite the crisis it underwent, Aristotelianism remained the prevalent philosophy in and outside academia throughout Europe; as the Introduction to this volume shows, Plato was only officially introduced in a few universities, even though he was constantly discussed in lectures which were part of the traditional "Aristotelian" curriculum, and enjoyed a wide circulation outside academia[32].

As we have seen in Chapter I, since the Middle Ages, one of the major impediments to the spread of Platonism across university classrooms was the perceived lack of systematicity in Plato's thought, which was even more evident when compared with Aristotle's[33]. This asystematicity was due, at least in part, to the dialogical form of Plato's philosophical works, which made them pleasant to read but unsuited for teaching purposes, at least according to Plato's critics. In addition, Plato never devoted a dialogue to the treatment of a single discipline but scattered in different dialogues ideas pertaining to a wide range of disciplines. As a result, it was felt impossible to map the subject matter of a course to a specific dialogue. Finally, the various doctrines were neither spelled out nor presented in

---

31 I understand the notion of "paradigm shift" in the Kuhnian sense, namely as the replacement of a dominant theory at a given time by a new theory that fits the observations and evidence available which the old theory was not able to accommodate.
32 BENI, *In Platonis Timaeum*, pp. 35-36: "Aristoteles non modo privatim [...] evolvitur [...] verum etiam in publicis Academiis legitur passim, idque diligenti commentatione adhibita et studio. [...] Id ipsum fere de Platone affirmari potest; etsi enim hoc tempore in pubblicis Gymnasiis non usque adeo frequens est eius usus atque tractatio, privatim tamen nusquam non volutatur. [...] Quin apud Gallos, Germanos, Transalpinosque pene omnes nostris quoque temporibus serio ac diligenter evolvitur".
33 See L. BIANCHI, "L'acculturazione filosofica dell'Occidente", in *Id.* (ed.), *La filosofia delle università. Secoli XIII-XIV*, Florence, La nuova Italia, 1997, pp. 17-21. On the shift from Plato to Aristotle in the Middle Ages, see J. HANKINS, "Antiplatonism in the Renaissance and the Middle Ages", in *Classica et mediaevalia*, 47 (1996), pp. 359-376.

a philosophical way, namely using unambiguous words, clear concepts and sound arguments, making Platonic texts difficult to teach students without preparation. Therefore, a prerequisite for the successful realization of Beni's project was, like for many sixteenth-century Platonists, to render Plato's thought teachable. Beni admitted that Platonic dialogues were not written according to a clear and straightforward methodological stance but remarked — rightly — that this was also true of the Aristotelian *corpus*, especially the parts concerning metaphysics[34]. However, he maintained that Plato's writings covered the major areas of philosophy. Natural philosophy was dealt with in the *Timaeus*, ethics mainly in the *Republic* and the *Laws*, partly in the *Charmides*, *Laches*, *Lysis*, *Crito*, *Meno*, and metaphysics was the subject matter of the *Parmenides*. Moreover, Plato also touched upon dialectic in the *Phaedrus* and *Gorgias*, grammar in the *Cratylus*, and poetics and history sparsely in the other dialogues:

> Certe Timaeus et mundo et universitate, seu de natura, verba facit ita ut physiologiam breviter complectatur omnem. Libri *de Republica* et *de Legibus* moralem partem si non explent omnem, magna tamen ex parte illam prosequuntur, praesertim si dialogi quidam qui de virtutibus et moribus docent cum illis coniungantur, cuiusmodi est *Charmides*, *Laches*, *Lysis*, *Crito*, *Menon*, et alii huiusmodi. Quod si non ea negligas quae de ideis et rerum omnium principio obscure satis effert in *Parmenide*, habeas praecipuam hinc philosophiae partem, quam divinam appelles. Ita sane tripartitam philosophiae varietatem si non omnibus numeris ac coloribus expressit et absolvit, at certe adumbravit expressitque magna ex parte […] Ita sane hac partitione atque hoc ordine Platonis libros distribuere ac lectitare possis non inutiliter quantumvis philosophica methodo conscripti non essent, vel philosophico inter se ordine iuncti et copulati[35].

Beni took two major steps to accomplish his goal of making the Platonic corpus a doctrinally systematic and coherent whole, apt to be introduced in the university curricula. In this respect his attitude is strikingly similar to what Javelli attempted to do in the first half of the sixteenth century, as we have seen in Chapter I. The first step was to throw down the gauntlet on the asystematicity accusation, by showing the systematic character of Platonic philosophy. This could be easily done with physics, since it was the only part of philosophy that Plato presented in one single book, the *Timaeus*, and treated in a more or less systematic way, namely by starting from general principles from which he deduced conclusions

---

34 BENI, *In Platonis Euthyphronem*, ASV, ABII, MS 116, f. 5v: "Crediderim quidem Aristotelis methodum forsitan ex Platonis doctrina fluxisse […] Neque vero id dixerim quod Aristoteles, etsi methodi studiosissimus videri possit, non interdum ipse etiam ab ea declinasse censeatur, ita ut interdum magnopere sit requirenda, ut in Divina Philosophia contingit in primis, quemadmodum perspicuitas in eo requiritur passim, ita ut multa in eius schola versentur in controversia inter quae est sententia de immortalite animi".

35 *Ibid.*, f. 5r-v.

about particulars and individuals. In his commentary on that dialogue, Beni tried to define the basic tenets of Platonic natural philosophy and to show how they were tightly interrelated into a coherent and systematic whole. For all the other areas of philosophy, first it was necessary to identify where exactly, in the Platonic corpus a treatment of the different branches of philosophy was to be found; then one had to extrapolate Plato's position on their various topics from these passages. This is what Beni tried to do by extracting the fundamental building blocks of Plato's thought on metaphysics, ethics, rhetoric, poetics and history and putting them together[36]. Since Antiquity it was acknowledged, though not unanimously, that Plato had considered metaphysical themes, such as the notion of Good and the doctrine of Ideas, in his *Parmenides* and, to a lesser extent, in his *Timaeus*. Starting from these two textual sources and adopting the same approach he had used when dealing with Plato's physics, Beni collected the fundamental principles underpinning Platonic metaphysics and arranged them in an axiomatic system in his *Platonis et Aristotelis Theologia*. But he had to adopt an approach other than the axiomatic one when it came to reconstructing Plato's view on practical philosophy and sub-disciplines like rhetoric, poetics or history. Indeed, Plato's thought on each of these subjects had been articulated in many dialogues. Consequently, a full understanding of each subject required that all the relevant passages concerning it be seen in relation to each other, which is precisely what Beni set out to do. For each discipline, he collected a set of relevant quotations from Platonic dialogues and provided a systematic reconstruction of Plato's thought (or rather what Beni believed Plato's view on that subject was), which he added to his commentaries on Aristotle. Thus, in the *De historia libri quatuor* (Venice, 1622) he discussed a digression on what "de historia senserit Plato"; in his *In Aristotelis Ethicam, Politicam, Oeconomicam commentaria et notationes* (Venice, 1623) he devoted a section on the ethical thought of Plato and Platonic philosophers[37]; similarly,

---

36 BENI, *Curriculum Platonicum*, f. 134r: "Multa ex facultatibus singulis cursim saltem in Platone collegi, quae varias philosophiae partes aut disciplinarum illustrant. Itaque invenias in primo lucubrationum nostrarum volumine multa de historia ex Platone [ed. 1622]; in Aristotelicae vero *Poeticae* commentariis [ed. 1624] ad extremum Platonis poeticam. Eiusdem rhetoricam denique in morali et naturali philosophia illius decreta varia [ed. 1623] et in opusculis seu miscellaneis conferri multa quae Platoni illustrando plurimum valent".

37 As far as we know from the *Beniana Bibliotheca*, which is a reasoned catalogue where Beni comments on all the books he wrote and owned, Beni refers to his discussion of Plato and Aristotle's theories of governance in his (now lost) *Discorsi Politici*: see BENI, *Beniana Bibliotheca*, in BMV, MS lat. IX.52 (= 3167), f. 58r: "Ego vero dum Platonicum quoddam Aristotelicumque opus de vita ac moribus urgeo, alicubi etiam morales Platonis libros in aciem educo, civile hasce vigilias italice saltem conscriptas propono atque offero: *Discorsi politici accommodati allo stato e governo degli Ottimati*. Harum vero disputationum ex italica oeconomia percipies quae est eiusmodi: Sommario et ordine de Discorsi Politici. [...] Nel quarto si conferma la fermezza e perfettion [...] e si risponde agli Argomenti recati all'incontro per la della Politia e Democratia. Con che si dà largo conto dell'opinione dei più lodati Maestri di Repubblica intorno al perfetto Civil governo; e particolarmente di Platone et Aristotele; dichiarando con diligenza i lor detti

he added some "decreta ex Platone de rhetorica" to his *In Aristotelis Rhetoricen commentarii* (Venice, 1624) and integrated remarks on Plato's poetics in his *In Aristotelis Poeticam commentarii* (Venice 1624):

> De poetica vel rhetorica. Aristoteles enim haec certis quaeque voluminibus est persecutus, Plato non ita quod si tamen quaedam sparsim de tota poesis et eloquentiae ratione observavit Plato, haec tum perpauca sunt, praesertim si cum Aristotelicis conferantur, tum obiter fere ac per transennam in dialogis illis disseminantur. Nos tamen Platonis poeticam ex dispersis illius praeceptionibus collegimus, et commentariis, quos in Aristotelis *Poeticam* mandavimus typis, subiecimus, ut ea quisque perlegere possit et ad suam utilitatem convertere, praesertim quia in multis aliter sentit, quam deinde praeceperit Aristoteles. [...] Nos eodem exemplo Platonis *Rhetoricam* conscripsi[mus], et iis commentariis adiunxi[mus], quos in Aristoteleam *Rhetoricen* edidimus. Atque haec etiam rhetorica Platonis decreta non paucis dissident ab Aristotelicis ita ut Aristoteles data opera videri possit, tum in his, tum in poeticis a praeceptore discedere. Atque haec sunt quae non ita attinguntur a Platone, ut perfecte quis in iis instrui possit, quemadmodum ab Aristotele. [...] Quod pertinet ad historiam, historiaeque praecepta atque decreta, ieiunus est uterque, vix enim perpauca, atque has aliud plane agentes, attingunt isti de historia et rerum antiquitate. Nos haec collegimus in iis monumentis, quae de historia conscripsimus[38].

The second step Beni undertook to realize his project was to interpret the dialogues in order to show the consistency of the Platonic system. The Platonic Greek text was sometimes obscure because of Plato's use of poetic license and metaphorical language. Beni tried to address the issue through a long running commentary, using the typical scholastic format of the *quaestio*, where words and sentences were disambiguated, and complicated passages disentangled. The commentaries were supposed to accompany the Greek Platonic texts, together with Beni's new Latin translation, with which Beni wished to replace that of Marsilio Ficino. As we have already seen in Chapter I of this volume, Ficino's translations were the object of frequent criticisms in sixteenth-century philosophical circles, although they remained the reference version all across Europe well into the nineteenth century. For Beni, Ficino's translations were influenced by his adherence to Middle- and Neoplatonism and, accordingly, did not present Plato's genuine thought, but rather Ficino's preconceived views about Platonic philosophy. Thus, in his original project, which as we have seen should date to his years in Padua as a student, Beni planned to translate, and comment on, all the *Corpus Platonicum*. However, other commitments prevented him from completing this project: he only produced a commented translation for the *Euthyphro*, the *Axiochus* — which,

---

e sentenze e concludendo per lor giuditio ancora che fra i Governi Civili l'Aristocratia sia il più commodo e più perfetto".
38 *Ibid.*, f. 114r.

until now, has not been identified — and of the *Timaeus*. He also compiled a short introduction to Platonic philosophy, the *curriculum Platonicum*. This unedited booklet, which is bound to the manuscript containing his *Euthyphro* translation[39], is an annotated bibliography aiming at teaching people interested in Platonism how to navigate the Platonic dialogues and the large body of ancient and modern works devoted to interpreting Plato's thought[40].

What is wrong with Aristotelianism and what is not wrong with Platonism

Beni's principal aim was to shift away from Aristotelianism toward Platonism in order to build a new Christian philosophy based on Platonic principles that, to his mind, were more consistent with Christian doctrine. Consequently, his project rested on two pillars: to show that the main tenets of Aristotelian philosophy were incompatible with Christian religion and had potentially ill-fated political effects, and to prove that Platonism fitted better with Christian doctrine than Aristotelianism. But Beni went far beyond the trend that had been initiated more than a century earlier by Bessarion: there were clear political undertones in his project, which echo the more general trend, already outlined in Chapter I, of using Plato to serve the new Christian ideals of the Catholic Reformation. In other words, Beni's aim was perhaps to (re)establish the unity of Christianity and a new social and political order. This project was not entirely original. According to Baldini, Patrizi too thought that Platonism was a body of common knowledge on which there could be universal consensus, offering therefore the perfect ground for rebuilding Christian unity[41]. This explains why Beni's attacks against Aristotle had a more theological and political than philosophical significance: they targeted what Beni believed to be Aristotle's major mistakes with respect to Christian doctrine and politics, namely, to have rejected the creation *ex nihilo* and to have elaborated a detailed theory of tyranny. From a philosophical viewpoint, these two doctrines did not create any problem within the Aristotelian system, in the

---

39 ASV, ABII, MS 116, f. 136r-147v. Between the *Euthyphro* and the *Curriculum Platonicum*, MS 116 contains another longer introduction to Platonic philosophy.
40 BENI, *Miscellanea sive opuscula varia*, ASV, ABII, MS 132, f. 9r-14v, written in 1624, f. 11r-v: "Ego ea cogitatione primum hunc Platonis dialogum [*scil. Euthyphronem*] de Graecis converti adolescens et commentariis illustravi, quod Platonis dialogos convertere et explanare statuissem. Sed sententiam mutavi et opere gravissimo supersedi, quod animadverterem tempus utilius impendi posse iis quibus a me deinde transmissa sunt. His tamen commentariis, quos extrema aetate absolvi, lucubrationes quasdam subieci in quibus ad Platonicos dialogos reliquos introducitur et instruitur lector, et ita instruitur, ut percommode illos peragrare possit universos".
41 On Patrizi's use of Platonism for political purposes see A. E. BALDINI, "Ragion di stato e platonismo nel dibattito politico italiano di fine Cinquecento", in F. B. NALIS (ed.), *Studi in memoria di Enzo Sciacca*, 2 vols, Milan, A. Giuffrè Editore, 2008, I, pp. 57-70: 60.

sense that they did not produce any inconsistency within it. From a theological and political standpoint, however, they raised serious concerns. In fact, since the recovery of Aristotle's writings in the twelfth and thirteenth centuries, scholastic philosophers and theologians acknowledged that Aristotle's claims about the eternity of the world were in contradiction with biblical creationism. Although they noted the problem, and authorities banned perilous interpretations of Aristotle's texts, Aristotelianism continued to be the privileged theoretical framework for philosophical and theological discussions. And scholastic commentators attempted to find plausible justifications for Aristotle's claims, or to elaborate interpretations of Aristotle's texts that supported the creationist hypothesis. None of these attempts convinced Beni, who decided to go in another direction. He argued that the Christian creation out of nothing was fundamentally incompatible with Aristotelian philosophy, as Christian authors said from Augustine onwards, and that, accordingly, for Aristotle the world could not but be eternal.

We could flesh out Beni's argument for supporting his claims as follows. Aristotle did not admit a creation out of nothing and conceived the world as constituted only by sensible substances (i.e., physical objects) and as resting upon physical change ("sensibus ac mutationibus physicis nitebatur totus; creationem non agnovit"). Physical objects are material — if they were not constituted of matter, we could not perceive them; all material objects are subject to physical changes and particularly to the kind of change called generation and corruption. Physical change is defined by Aristotle as the passage from potentiality to actuality, thus a necessary condition for change to happen is the existence of a potential 'substance', namely matter, which is eternal since change is eternal. That change is eternal is proved by a *reductio*. Let us assume that change c_1 is not eternal, then either c_1 has been produced by a prior change (c_2) or by something unchanged. But there are no unchanged (physical) objects, since all physical objects are subject to change, so c_1 has to be produced by c_2; c_2 is produced by a prior change, c_3, which in turn has been produced by a prior change and so on in an infinite regress; therefore, change is eternal. Insofar as time follows change, time is eternal as well. Since matter (*corpus mobile*) too is eternal, all material beings, from the simplest (i.e., the four elements), to the most complex compound being, the world, are eternal[42]. For Beni, all the exegetical efforts made by Aquinas and other medieval thinkers to read traces of the creationist view in Aristotle were not only wrong but, what was worse, they introduced a series of unsolvable problems and inconsistencies in his system[43]. From Beni's theological perspective, the absence of creation in Aristotle's physics, and the correlated eternity of change and matter, caused a cascade of errors in Aristotle's physics and in all the other areas of Aristotelian philosophy. In physics, Beni argues, Aristotle had to account for the

---

42 BENI, *In Platonis Timaeum*, pp. 147-148.
43 *Ibid.*, p. 150: "Mundi aeternitas, divina efficientia, animi immortalitas, praesertim pro hominum numero multiplicati, materiae subiectae necessitas in effectione rerum, cohaerere non possunt ac conciliari".

incorruptibility of the celestial realm while maintaining its changeability, and precisely its local change, so he had to postulate different elemental compositions and, accordingly, different physical laws for the lunar and sublunar worlds. The lunar sphere was made of aether, which moved by circular motion only, and was subject to local change alone; the sublunar sphere was made of the four elements (heart, fire, water, air), which undergo three different types of change, including coming to being and passing away. This state of permanent change in the sublunar sphere had also heavy repercussions on Aristotelian epistemology, which was totally sense-based. In addition to assuming the senses (which from Beni's Platonic perspective were unreliable and uncertain) as the sole source for human knowledge the only epistemic objects admitted by Aristotelian epistemology were physical objects, which are ontologically unstable and contingent and thus cannot be the object of proper knowledge[44]. In metaphysics, the eternity of change and matter diminished God's power by depriving it of its causal activity. Indeed, given that there is no production out of nothing but only change in pre-existing, eternal matter, the action of every efficient cause is dependent on change and cannot be free nor infinite nor undetermined. Similarly, in psychology, the eternity of change and of matter implied the mortality of the human soul; since human souls belong to the sublunary worlds, just as the bodies they ensoul, they are subject to generation and corruption like all sublunary beings:

> Et quoniam visus est hic Author [*scil.* Aristoteles] Deum coelo movendo abstringere nec coelo impellendo tantum obstringere, sed certis finibus illius vim ac facultatem circumscribere quin naturae quoque necessitate illum implicare, quasi necessario moveat non libere, immo vero, quod multo deterius est, rerum inferiorum curam illi adimit aliquando, nec toti mundo facit praesentissimum, sed veluti in puncto primi orbis, ubi scilicet incitatissimum sit motus, eum collocat; quia inquam haec etsi quid huiusmodi visus est de Deo disseminare coelestium quoque mentium numerum, munera, vim, naturam, praepostere definire ac declarare ambigue insuper atque adeo callide ac vafre de daemonibus deque humano animo suam sententiam promulgare de sentiendi et intelligendi initio et facultate pugnantia scribere, discas qua iis occurras via, ut scilicet vel eum ab huiusmodi calumniis purges, si forte id tulerit ratio, et dilucides, aut contra ei resistas strenue, illius rationes ac paralogismos diluens[45].

But, as noticed previously (§1.2), the thesis of the eternity of the world and the following denial of the immortality of human souls had also strong implications for morality and politics. In the Aristotelian eudaemonist virtue ethics, the life's end for an individual agent is happiness; since the human soul is mortal, men's true happiness can only be achieved in this life and does not consist of afterlife

---

44 *Ibid.*, p. 618.
45 BENI, *Beniana Bibliotheca*, f. 84r-v.

rewards and punishments. Echoing the same argument Javelli had made in the first half of the 16th century, Beni underlines that Aristotle's secular notion of happiness was completely incompatible with Christian ethics, which was based on worshippers' beliefs in punishments and rewards in the afterlife. And for Beni, these same beliefs were at the foundation of, and guaranteed, social stability[46].

Here Beni's other chief charges against Aristotle enter into the picture: Aristotle's appeal to emotion in rhetoric and his treatment of tyranny in politics. Aristotelian popular rhetoric aimed at producing irrational persuasion in the audience; to achieve this it used arguments meant to trigger emotional responses that interfere with rational decision-making. In other words, Beni argues, by separating rhetoric from justice, virtue, and law, Aristotle denied rhetoric its role as a means for preserving justice and the virtuous political order and made it a powerful tool for subverting political and civil organization, if used by ill-intentioned orators and politicians like aspiring tyrants[47]. Tyranny was the other black sheep in Aristotelianism. Minimizing the fact that Aristotle despised tyranny as one of the degenerate forms of government, Beni harshly attacked Aristotle, perhaps targeting through him Machiavelli, whom he considered to be a follower of Aristotle, and the late sixteenth-century supporters of Machiavelli's political doctrine[48]. The main charge against Aristotle was that his theorization of the extreme and mild forms of tyranny in *Politics* had provided generations of rulers, including the politicians of his time, with a guide for establishing and preserving despotic governments that generated violent political environments, which were contrary to Christianity and prevented men from becoming virtuous[49]. As a consequence of these central errors, Aristotle's philosophy contained many doctrines that were either incompatible or hardly harmonizable with Christianity and made it ill-suited to being the philosophical framework within which theological theorising had to take place and, perhaps, new and more stable political orders had to be established.

In his commentary on Plato's *Timaeus*, where the pros and cons of Aristotelianism and Platonism are analysed, Beni tried to keep the discussion balanced, at least formally, by pointing out the Platonic doctrines which seemed to clash with Christian teachings. Yet, a mere glance at the number of pages

---

46 Beni's attacks against Aristotle on these topics are present, in more or less detailed manner, in the unpublished *reportationes* of his lectures for the years 1592, 1595-1599, in the unpublished *In Politicos Aristotelis libros*, ASV, ABII, MS 91. Since in all these works Beni refers the reader to his commentary on Plato's *Timaeus*, particularly to Book III of Decade I, where the critiques against Aristotle are expressed systematically, we rely on BENI, *In Platonis Timaeum*, pp. 119-136 and 154-173.
47 BENI, *In Platonis Timaeum*, pp. 141-145.
48 On the spread of Machiavelli's views among late sixteenth-century Aristotelians and Platonists see BALDINI, "Ragion di stato e platonismo nel dibattito politico italiano di fine Cinquecento", and Id., "Aristotelismo e platonismo nelle dispute romane sulla ragion di stato di fine Cinquecento".
49 BENI, *In Platonis Timaeum*, pp. 145-147.

containing arguments *contra* Aristotle and *contra* Plato makes clear which philosopher Beni favoured: the pages presenting anti-Aristotelian arguments are ten times more numerous than those providing arguments against Plato (36 against 3 and a half). Among the opinions of Plato that appeared incompatible with Christian religion, two emerged as possibly extremely harmful, which critics of Plato had considered as potential sources of heresy. Firstly, Plato's writings seemed to foreshadow the Christian Trinity; in the Middle Ages and the Renaissance, commentators of Plato's *Timaeus* elaborated exegesis of the dialogue which matched the *Timaeus* triad of God, Intellect and World Soul with the Christian Trinity. However, this alignment raised problems since, while the persons of the Trinity were on the same level, the *Timaeus* triad saw a pattern of subordination within the Trinity. This was evidently unacceptable for Christians, since it paved the way to heresies, such as Arianism. Secondly, the Platonic account of the production of the world, according to which God, *summus opifex*, seemed to have created only the essential parts of the world, leaving the production and ordering of the unessential parts to secondary divinities, could be perceived as a form of Manicheism, as if God created what is good and demons what is bad. In the *Timaeus*, indeed, Plato had attributed a soul to the world and to the celestial bodies, making both animated and divine beings. Moreover, in his account of the origin of the world it was unclear whether Plato thought it was created *ex nihilo* or from a pre-existing matter and, in that case, if such pre-existing matter was created or eternal. Although Plato had undoubtedly advanced the thesis of the immortality of the soul, his psychology contained erroneous views, like metempsychosis or the transmigration of the souls from a body to another and seemed to attribute to men three numerically distinct souls, each of which was dislocated in a specific part of the human body. And the body, according to the *Timaeus*, had not been produced by God directly, like the human soul, but by intermediate, minor divinities; accordingly, the body was axiologically inferior to the soul, a conclusion that was unacceptable for Christians, for whom body and soul occupy the same axiological plane[50].

Although Beni tried to present himself as an objective arbiter, he did not play this role particularly convincingly. In the replies to the arguments against Aristotelianism and Platonism, Beni concluded that it was impossible to refute some anti-Aristotelian arguments, particularly the ones related to the eternity of change, matter and the world. In contrast, in the hundreds of pages he devoted to refuting the charges against Plato, he was able to offer satisfactory answers, providing philological elucidations and textual supports to show that the accusations arose from Plato's metaphorical language and, broadly speaking, from linguistic misunderstandings: "Tolle igitur nomen, ac nullus superest offensionis locus [...] Solo nomine dissidemus" (*In Platonis Timaeum*, pp. 103 and 105). Since Beni replied to each charge in a very detailed manner, we need to cut a long story

---

50 BENI, *In Platonis Timaeum*, pp. 100-103.

short. In reply to the criticism against Plato's possible heterodoxy, Beni rejected all the interpretations of Plato's theology that presented it as a prefiguration of the Christian Trinity, on the grounds that they were philologically and exegetically baseless[51]. Accordingly, he also refuted the well-established doctrine of *prisca theologia*, on the grounds that it was not acceptable to merge theology with philosophy, divinely inspired wisdom with human wisdom. Instead, he elaborated his own genealogy of the *prisca sapientia*, in which none of the revealed doctrines was identified with any pagan author and declared as illegitimate any use of Plato in theology. In that respect, Beni's Platonism was markedly different from the theologized Platonism developed by the ancient Neoplatonists and by Ficino and closer perhaps to Javelli's attitude[52]. As to the philosophical and theological critiques, Beni argued that Plato had clearly acknowledged the existence of only one God, or first cause, endowed with efficient causal power, who had created the whole world out of nothing, including the human body and the alleged minor divinities. These divinities had to be understood as being second causes cooperating with God, identical with the celestial bodies and moved by motive forces that Plato called 'moving Minds' and the angels of the Bible. Broadly speaking, Beni claimed that the difficulties pointed out by Plato's critics did not pose serious doctrinal issues since they concerned a superficial, linguistic level. For example, Plato made an improper use of the name 'divinity' for denoting celestial physical objects, but if one did not qualify them as divine, then the creative power of God was unaffected, the distance between Plato's thought and the Christian doctrine was bridged and the risk of Manicheism vanished: "sat nobis esse debet Platonem, si non falsitatis, impietatis certe culpa vacare" (*In Platonis Timaeum*, p. 107). By rejecting all the accusations against Platonism, Beni was also trying to legitimize the study of Plato in the university. Not only he adopted a format used in the university in commenting Plato's dialogues, especially the *Timaeus*, that is, he split the text in numerous short sections each of which was accompanied by paraphrases, lexical and doctrinal explanations. But he also offered a clear elucidation of Plato's thought in order to clarify obscure philosophical points, show its systematicity and refute the charges against it.

---

51 BENI, *Curriculum Platonicum*, ASV, ABII, MS 116, f. 140r: "Quod si de dogmatibus quaeris, haec vero in Platone illustriora sunt, etsi sparsim adhuc occurrant, nec argumentis satis probata et confirmata videri possint. De qua tamen re universa nos in secunda *Timaei* decade distincte et copiose, ubi tamen sic Platonem suspicimus ut, pace aliquorum, veram triadis cognitionem, eam Christianae fidei ac doctrinae reservantes, denegemus".

52 BENI, *In Platonis Timaeum*, p. 697: "[Philo] Moysis *Genesim* in Platonis *Timaeum* convertisset. Quod philosophandi genus eo magis nobis est detestandum, quod ex liberiore hac atque coacta dogmatum coniunctione, Christianorum deinde culpa multae inter fideles irrepserint opiniones, quae ecclesiam non mediocriter labefactarunt". On Beni's strategy for reconstructing Plato's genuine thought and for separating philosophy, mainly Platonism, from theology see BARTOCCI, "Paolo Beni and his friendly criticism of Patrizi"; *Ead.*, "Il Platonismo di Paolo Beni da Gubbio e la critica della tradizione neoplatonica", in *Accademia*, 13 (2011), pp. 75-108.

Why study Plato?

Beni's project to shift paradigm in philosophy was obviously costly, for it implied leaving aside the conceptual tools and philosophical framework that for centuries had provided the foundation for dealing with philosophical and theological issues. Thus, the replacement of the current dominant Aristotelianism with Platonism had to be justified by sufficiently strong reasons and by improvements, such as a more elegant and parsimonious theory of the universe capable to accommodate celestial phenomena that did not fit the Aristotelian cosmology. Showing that Platonism fitted better with Christian doctrine than Aristotelianism and, consequently, provided more adequate philosophical grounds for building a renewed Christian religion, was a crucial step towards realizing that project. And this is what Beni tried to demonstrate in all his writings. There, he constantly highlighted the principles of Aristotelianism that were incompatible with Christian beliefs and dogmas and, in doing so, he achieved a twofold result: to weaken Aristotle's philosophy and, at the same time, to set fundamental groundworks for the second pillar of his project. Every critique of Aristotle was preceded or followed by textual and philological arguments showing that Plato adopted a better view on the question at hand. As we have seen, Beni argued that a central error of Aristotle was the doctrine of the eternity of change and matter and, accordingly, of the eternity of the world. Following Hermes Trismegistus, Beni argued, Plato had endorsed ontological dualism[53] and this prevented Plato from making the same mistake as Aristotle. In Platonic ontology, as Beni presents it, there are two separated spheres of beings, the one comprising all beings existing prior to the world's creation, and the other including all created corporeal beings. The sphere of incorporeal beings is inhabited by the God of the *Timaeus*[54], the Ideas contained in His mind, and the souls of the world and of human beings, all of which enjoy the highest mode of existence: they are stable, self-sufficient, self-identical over time and eternal. Conversely the world of objects perceived by the senses enjoys an inferior type of existence with respect to incorporeal beings, for it is populated by unstable beings which are not identical over time, and it is created by God through the exemplars (i.e., the Ideas) contained in his mind[55]. This ontological dualism provided ground for Plato's creationism, since the existence of the phenomenal, generated world necessarily implied the existence of at least a first efficient cause that created it, as Beni proved through the following *a priori* argument. Whatever is generated, is brought about and so is an effect; since the notions of effect and cause are relative to each other and imply each other, when the one is posited, the other is posited altogether, therefore necessarily the phenomenal world, which is an effect, has at

---

53 When talking about ontological dualism, Beni refers to *Tim.* 27d6-28b3 and to the *Parmenides*. For the Hermetic origin of Platonic dualism see BENI, *In Platonis Timaeum*, p. 589.
54 Beni proposes an *a posteriori* argument that proves the existence of an immaterial and eternal being, although in a *plausible* and not certain way ("ratio probabilis"), *Ibid.*, p. 604.
55 *Ibid.*, pp. 587-605.

least one efficient cause. This efficient cause is the God which Plato introduced at the beginning of his *Timaeus*, where he provided a description of the production of the world that fully agrees with biblical creationism:

> Neque vero minor ei debetur laus dum de mundo philosophatur; sive enim huius decreta cum caeterorum philosophorum monumentis sive cum divinis literis conferas, invenies profecto ex ethnicis ad Christianam fidem ac veritatem propius accessisse neminem, ac vel ob id unum Attici Mosis nomen (si tamen dignare ethnicum fas est) iustissime meruisse. Quamobrem apud eum statim mundum et a Deo, et in tempore, et boni causa, et libere, et perfectum audies conditum, atque in eodem tandem hominem dominum collocatum, quae sunt Mosis dogmata germanissima[56].

As the absence of a creationist model was the source of flaws and weaknesses in Aristotle's philosophy, so Plato's adoption of creationism accounted for the superiority of his philosophical system. In metaphysics, unlike Aristotle, Plato acknowledged that God is the only essentially omnipotent being, namely that God actually has all power a being can possibly have by virtue of His very essence. God exercises His omnipotence freely. Moreover, Plato's God is omniscient and, accordingly, has foreknowledge of everything that happens in the world, including human free actions. About this issue, Beni concludes, "egregie philosophatus est Plato"[57].

In physics, Plato's recognition of the corruptibility of the world not only agreed with the Holy Scriptures, but also made it possible to adopt a more economical cosmological model than Aristotle's. For once the perishability of the world, and *a fortiori* of the lunar region, is accepted, it becomes unnecessary and superfluous to posit — as Aristotle had done — the existence of a fifth unperceivable element, the aether, whose only role in Aristotelian physics was to account for celestial incorruptibility and the world's eternity. Moreover, when one rejects the ethereal composition from the lunar region, the Aristotelian bipartition of the world into two heterogeneous regions, each governed by its own physical laws, is eliminated altogether. The Platonic cosmos was a homogeneous whole filled with the four elements, air, fire, earth and water. Consequently, the perceived differences between the terrestrial and lunar regions did not originate from an essential diversity, but from a different concentration of the four elements: heavens, planets and stars contained a much higher percentage of fire and a much lower percentage of the other three elements than items in the "sublunar" region. Beni was not the first to attack the Aristotelian doctrine of the ethereal composition of the heavens, nor was he alone in preferring Plato's cosmological framework which, for various reasons, gained increasing favour among sixteenth-century natural

---

56 *Ibid.*, p. 101.
57 *Ibid.*, p. 107; for Beni's comparative analysis of Aristotelian and Platonic metaphysics see BENI, *In Platonis Timaeum*, Decade 2, Books 1-2 and the *reportationes* preserved in ASV, ABII, MS 69, f. 1r-38r, MS 70, MS 112, f. 1-93.

philosophers and astronomers[58]. This suggests, as already mentioned in Chapter I, that eclectic Aristotelianism was not the only way of handling the crisis resulting from new celestial discoveries, as claimed by Schmitt. One reason was parsimony or simplicity: in Plato's homogenous cosmos, there was no need to postulate epicycles and additional orbs, like the crystalline, in order to explain the visible movements of stars and planets. A further reason was that Aristotle's cosmological physics, which did not admit any change in the lunar region but only local motion, could not accommodate some celestial phenomena that testified to changes in the heavens. During Beni's life, a decisive challenge to Aristotle's doctrine of the incorruptibility of heavens came from the appearance and disappearance of the 1572 and 1604 supernovas (i.e. explosions of stars). Tycho Brahe situated the 1572 supernova (named after him today) in the most external celestial sphere, namely that of the fixed stars. Johannes Kepler and Galileo Galilei — who at that time was Beni's colleague at Padua — situated the 1604 supernova in Sagittarius. Beni sided with the astrologers, who stated that these new stars proved that the heavenly region is necessarily subjected to corruption ("caelum non posse non esse alterationi et varietati substantiali subiectum"[59]). In his unpublished commentary on Cicero's *Dream of Scipio*[60], Beni brought as further evidence against the Aristotelian cosmological model the latest astronomical discoveries which his colleague Galileo had made in 1609-1610 and described in the *Sidereus Nuncius*. Thus, when discussing a passage of the Ciceronian dialogue set in the Milky Way, Beni stated that the Galaxy is in the heaven and not in the sphere of air, as Aristotle said, and claimed that it contains a total number of stars greater than the number of stars visible to the naked eye, as had been only recently

---

58 See for example W. H. DONAHUE, *The Dissolution of the Celestial Spheres 1595-1650*, New York, Arno, 1981; M. A. GRANADA, *Sfere solide e cielo fluido: Momenti del dibattito cosmologico nella seconda metà del Cinquecento*, Milan, Guerini, 2002.
59 *In Platonis Timaeum*, ASV, ABII, MS 100, Decade 2, Book. 9, f. 421v-422r: "Quod vero nulla adhuc transmutatio facta sit in caelo, non temere videtur asserendum. [...] Superiore quoque saeculo, anno scilicet MDLXXII in Cassiopea per biennium nova stella conspecta est tantae magnitudinis ac splendoris, ut Venerem superaret: tametsi tantam splendoris ac magnitudinis vim praetulit primis mensibus solum; paulo vero post decrescere visa est, tum denique evanescere. Quo factum est, ut astrologi plerique iique clarissimi eo confugerint, ut voluerint caelum revera non posse non esse alterationi et varietati substantiali subiectum. Id quod nunc demum hoc anno MDCIV in nova quadam stella Marti et colore et magnitudine primum non dissimili eademque interdiu scintillante, sic renovatum est, ut peritissimi quique Astrologi eam et novam et in octavo orbe non longe a Sagittario sitam, pari consensione affirmaverint: cum tamen post aliquot menses sese ab hominum conspectu subtraxerit et evanuerit". It is extremely likely that Galileo was among the "peritissimi Astrologi" mentioned in this passage, for in the public lectures delivered at the University of Padua in December 1604 he situated the supernova in 18° Sagittarius.
60 Beni's *In Somnium Scipionis commentarii* is preserved in two manuscripts in ASV, ABII: 1) MS 115, f. 1-31 and f. 43-48, which does not include Cicero's *Dream of Scipio* VI, 17-29; 2) MS 131, f. 151-168, covering Cicero's *Dream of Scipio* VI, 21/22-26. Both manuscripts lack the part of the commentary concerning the planetary arrangement, namely VI, 17-20.

detected by means of the telescope ("Nam conspicilio nuper invento frequentissimae illae quidem sed utcunque inter se distinctae cernuntur"[61]). Despite his open-mindedness towards astronomical and technological novelties, which he used to dismantle Aristotelian cosmology, nowhere in his work does Beni adopt Copernicus' heliocentric system, perhaps because it could not be harmonized with Platonic physics[62].

Turning now to epistemology, following the earlier (Aristotelian-based) tradition, Beni assumed that knowledge in its proper sense does not concern individuals but only universals that, from a Platonic perspective, are the Ideas belonging to the incorporeal realm. These assumptions led him to claim that, within the Aristotelian ontological framework, human beings could not achieve knowledge at all since their only epistemic objects where physical items, namely ontologically unstable individual beings. A less hopeless scenario, in which men could aspire to attain true knowledge, although not in their embodied state, was provided by Plato's ontological dualism, which lays at the root of Plato's epistemological dualism ("abstruso quodam modo duo <Plato> efficit humanae cognitionis genera et formas"). According to Beni's reconstruction of Platonic epistemology, there are two kinds of epistemic objects: objects perceived by the senses, which are unable to enjoy cognitive success since men can only have opinions about them, and eternal objects, like the Ideas, which are suited to enjoy full cognitive success, or knowledge[63]:

> Plato suas ideas statuit esse seiunctas ab iis quorum sunt ideam, ac re ipsa per se existere, ita ut Τὸ ὅσιον, verbi gratia, sit quid abstractum ac separatum ab iis omnibus quae dicuntur sancta, ac re ipsa per se existat. Addit idearum notitiam non esse huius vitae, sed animi ab huius corporis contagione separati ac propterea si quis forte eam assequatur in hac vita, summo quodam Dei beneficio contingere: rerum naturas quas cernimus ac

---

61 BENI, *In Somnium Scipionis commentarii*, ASV, ABII, MS 115, f. 19r: "Satis constat Ciceronem eos sequi omnino qui galaxiam in caelo collocarent. Ac profecto videtur non in aere (Aristotelis pace) sed in caelo collocanda [*scil.* Galaxia], cum ex dissitis regionibus ac plagis cernatur [...]. Fateamur igitur cum Ptolomaeo galaxiam seu circulum lacteum esse in caelo, sive esse partem aliquam Firmamenti: quae ob partium densitatem ac varietatem lumen Solis excipiat non aequaliter, ita tamen ut stellae ibi frequentissimae ob partium densitatem appareant: quin si has caeli sive lactaei circuli partes stellas dixeris, ac propterea in eo circulo sive in ea caeli parte plurimas stellas sese obiicere, non aberrav<er>is. Nam conspicilio nuper invento frequentissimae illae quidem sed utcunque inter se distinctae cernuntur [...]. Ita quidem tum superiorem scopulum sustuli in quem impegisse visus erat noster Cicero, et Aristotelem utcunque perpurgassem, qui Ptolomaeo, Manilio, Proclo atque optimis astrologis repugnantibus, galaxiam in aere collocavit".

62 For a detailed analysis of Beni's Platonic cosmology and theory of matter, conducted in the light of Galileo's discoveries of 1609-10, see B. BARTOCCI, "Paolo Beni and Galileo Galilei: The Classical Tradition and the Reception of the Astronomical Revolution", in *Rivista di Storia della Filosofia*, 71 (2016), pp. 423-452.

63 BENI, *In Platonis Timaeum*, p. 619.

sensu percipimus, non veras esse, sed imagines quasdam verarum. [...] Ob id etiam vult fuisse ante naturam, nullamque in natura aut puchritudinem, aut veritatem, aut constantiam reperiri: sed in ideis ens contineri. Numeris, figuris aliisque huiusmodi abstrusum in modum accomodat eas. Easdemque facit rerum divino consilio gerendarum semina et exemplaria, ita ut in eas inspexerit procreator rerum Deus, atque ad illarum exemplum constituerit quae sub aspectum cadunt, immo vero mundum universum. [...] mea quidem sententia, dissideant hac in re Plato et Aristoteles: praesertim quod Aristoteles mundum efficit sempiternum atque infectum esse decrevit, ita ut ideis illis locum praecluserit quem sibi aperuerat Plato dum mundum conderet. Qui igitur hac in re [*scil.* universalis et ideae] Aristotelem cum Platone conciliare nituntur, hi sine dubio aberrant[64].

As Beni pointed out, Platonic epistemology rested on three prerequisites about epistemic objects (the Ideas) and agents (the human souls). The first requirement was the substantiality and separate existence of some kinds of universals, namely the Ideas which, being the stable reality underpinning the phenomenal realm, grounded and warranted true knowledge. The second was the ontological and chronological priority of the soul over the body and their independence. The third was the epistemological autonomy of the soul: it should be capable of performing independently its specific cognitive actions, such as the contemplation and understanding of the Ideas[65]. While the first requirement could be, and indeed had been, easily accepted by Christian thinkers, the other two were more problematic since both excessively downgraded the body, in which Christians saw much value. Beni had to resort to various hermeneutic artifices to bring these claims into line with Christian doctrine[66].

Normally, in their embodied state men could only speculate about eternal beings and, accordingly, could only have mere belief rather than certain knowledge about them. The theoretical inquiry into the incorporeal realm was the business of dialectic which, Beni points out, coincided for Plato with metaphysics — while for Aristotle dialectic was a methodological tool used for producing plausible arguments. Applying the diairetic procedure, the Platonic dialectician could arrive at the definitions of corporeal beings, namely at comprehending their natures and distinguishing them from their non-essential properties ("Dialecticus [...] est apud Platonem qui humana divinaque omnia et novit et definire potest et explicare [...] Plato ad ideas illum evehit contemplandas unde sapientia excellat"[67]).

---

64 BENI, *In Platonis Euthyphronem*, ASV, ABII, MS 116, f. 4v-5r.
65 BENI, *In Platonis Timaeum*, pp. 619-620.
66 *Ibid.*, pp. 619-620.
67 BENI, *Beniana Biblioteca*, f. 60v-61r: "Platoni enim is est dialecticus qui de unaquaque re intelligenter disputat, quique dividere ac definire optime novit, et quicquid occurrat subtiliter declarare. Itaque dialecticus is plane est apud Platonem qui humana divinaque omnia et novit et definire potest et explicare; ita ut dialectica primae Aristotelis philosophiae dialecticus divino philosopho seu metaphysico respondeat. Illud unum differunt quod Plato ad ideas illum

Although men seemed unable to achieve true knowledge of the incorporeal realm in this life, they could however have certainty about some truths concerning the phenomenal realm, such as analytic propositions like "The whole is greater than its parts", and synthetic propositions like "Fire causes heat"[68].

Aristotle's psychology had always been extremely problematic for his Christian followers. As we have seen, the doctrine of the eternity of matter and world implied the thesis of the mortality of the soul, which had not only problematic repercussions on ethics but, what is more, was completely incompatible with Christian religion. In contrast, Beni argues, Platonism offered a psychological theory which fitted perfectly with religious dogmas and beliefs, because it clearly promoted the immortality of the soul, provided that its philosophical message was unwrapped and the poetical fictions, like that of metempsychosis, were stripped away: "Sunt quaedam apud eum quae, si spolientur poeticis involucris [...] et ad philosophiae normam aestimentur, nihil plane continent impium atque absurdum, immo quaedam primigeniae veritatis speciem referunt; multa quoque per calumniam tribuuntur illi [*scil.* Platoni] ab Aristotele et Peripateticis"[69]. As a consequence of his psychological and ontological views, Plato's ethical ideas could also be easily harmonized with Christian religion. Indeed, even if he held a eudaemonist virtue ethics like Aristotle, Plato elaborated a more comprehensive theory of happiness that included the earthly, or imperfect, happiness and the celestial, or perfect, happiness[70]. Of course, Beni was not the first to mention this difference between the imperfect Aristotelian and the perfect Platonic conceptions of happiness: as seen in Chapter I, other thinkers before him, like the Dominican Chrysostomus Javelli, pointed it out[71]. Earthly happiness had a

---

evehit contemplandas unde sapientia excellat; Aristoteles, ideis spretis, rerum humanarum ad divinarum detinet contemplatione".

68 BENI, *In Platonis Timaeum*, pp. 603 and 621.
69 *Ibid.*, p. 109; cf. with BENI, *In Somnium Scipionis commentarii*, ASV, ABII, Ms. 115, f. 14r: "Totum vero hoc de humanis animis decretum [*scil.* animi immortalitatem] habetur a Platone in *Timaeo*, ubi mundi fabricator et animorum procreator Deus astris singulis singulos inserit animos, qui sint ex mundi anima delibati, et in eodem cratere temperati. Quae sane nisi commode explicentur vel accipiantur, falsa sunt, ac fabulae referunt speciem. De qua re nos in Platonis *Timaeo*"; and BENI, *Academica Disputatio habita in Parthenia, dum locus quidam ex Tusculanis Disputationibus esset explicandus*, ASV, ABII, Ms. 71, f. 8r-9v: "Cicero acerrimus semper fuit Platonis imitator, ac praecipue quae hoc in loco de animi immortalitate disserit, ex eius fontibus hausit [...] Cicero Platonem in *Phaedro* secutus, profitetur animum movere se ipsum ac propterea esse immortalem".
70 BENI, *In Platonis Timaeum*, p. 24: "Plato splendide de eo foelicitatis genere locutus est, quod sanctis viris post huius vitae curriculum reservatur, tamen asseveranter docuit in supremum coeli verticem pios animos evolare, ibidemque veritatis contemplatione summoque bono fruentes, beatissimam vitam degere".
71 C. JAVELLI, *Epitome in Ethicen, hoc est, moralem Platonis philosophiam*, Venice, in officina Aurelii Pincii, 1536, f. 71v: "Aristoteles [...] aliam non tribuit homini foelicitatem nisi pro hac vita, ita quod putat hominem foelicem qui dum anima corpori coniuncta est, divinorum entium speculationem assequitur. De foelicitate autem et miseria alterius vitae nullum penitus verbum

practical and a theoretical aspect: men could attain happiness either by acting virtuously in their public and private lives or through contemplation. Earthly theoretical happiness seemed to be reserved to the Platonic dialectician who could reach some comprehension of the Ideas and, consequently, of the phenomenal world in which she lived. Thus, the dialectician has an anticipation of the perfect happiness to come, namely the immediate knowledge of the Ideas after death[72]:

> Due sorti di felicità ci propose Platone, l'una delle quali volse che convenisse all'animo nostro, mentre dal corpo si ritrova disgiunto; l'altra giudicò potersi acquistare in questo mortale stato: e questa anche riputolla di due maniere: stimando che ad una si pervenga per via di contemplazione et all'altra colle attioni tanto pubbliche, e quanto famigliari, et private. E di ciascuna di queste sorti di felicità intendo di ragionarti: riducendo insieme e dichiarandoti tutto ciò che, in varii luoghi delle sue belle scritture, ce n'ha lasciato scritto[73].

Plato's ethics had the further advantage of accommodating Christian belief in the afterlife and, consequently, of making it possible to avoid civil disorder. For men's (natural) desire for salvation, along with the hope of afterlife rewards for good conduct on earth as well as the fear of eternal punishment for sinning in this life were powerful incentives to act virtuously and, consequently, to abide by the laws. The preservation of social and political stability is a recurring theme in the works of Beni who, when dealing with the topic, did not hesitate to criticize some unspecified "European" politicians of his time. In his view, they were guilty of having established governments that were intrinsically impious, morally corrupt and unstable since they were not modelled on the *politeia*, the ideal form of government outlined by Plato. A government based on the firm and sacred principles of the *politeia*, Beni argued, would be greatly beneficial to individual states and to Christian religion and human society in general ("cum magno Christianae Religionis ac totius humanae societatis bono"[74]). This last remark allows us to speculate on the true extent of Beni's project of shifting away from Aristotelianism towards Platonism, and more specifically on the political implications of this shift. For Beni, Platonism had contributions to make in many spheres, from philosophy

---

fecit. At Plato [...] non contentatus hac debili ac imperfectissima felicitate animae separatae perfectam assignat beatitudinem". I wish to warmly thank Maude Vanhaelen for pointing my attention to Javelli's view on Platonic happiness and for providing me with bibliographical references.

72 BENI, *In Platonis Eutyphronem*, ASV, ABII, MS.116, f. 5r: "Plato addit idearum notitiam non esse huius vitae, sed animi ab huius corporis contagione separati ac propterea si quis forte eam assequatur in hac vita, summo quodam Dei beneficio contingere".

73 BENI, *Sulle bellezze della filosofia*, ASV, ABII, MS 128, f. 9r-v. *Sulle bellezze della filosofia*, which was written in Beni's youth (probably when he was in Bologna) is an unfinished dialogue in which Beni touches upon various ethical topics among which Plato's conception of happiness; for earthly happiness Beni refers to Plato's *Seventh Letter*, *Euthydemus*, Book I of the *Laws*, *Theaetetus*, *Gorgias* and *Menexenus*.

74 BENI, *In Platonis Timaeum*, p. 147.

to religion and politics, and was better suited to address old and new challenges. It could serve as the theoretical and conceptual framework for a new philosophy, capable of including scientific innovations and providing new methodological tools that would serve the establishment of a renewed religion in the context of the Catholic Reformation. In that respect, Beni's project echoes Patrizi's call for a new philosophy centred upon Platonism, in the context of contemporary political debates held in the Accademia Aldobrandini[75]. In other words, the kind of political institutions delineated by Plato were needed, according to Beni, for peace, stability and prosperity to flourish in Europe after decades of ruinous wars whose remote causes, for Beni, were the political theories inspired by Aristotle and, plausibly, by his modern imitators like Machiavelli.

Conclusion

Beni's activity as professor of humanities and commentator of ancient philosophy testifies to his willingness to shift away from the Aristotelian model of philosophy toward a new model centred upon Platonism. In teaching and commenting upon Plato, Aristotle and Cicero Beni introduced long comparisons between Plato and Aristotle's thought which aimed at showing, first, the flaws and errors of Aristotelianism, all originating from the doctrine of the eternity of the world; and second, that Plato did not make the same mistakes as Aristotle. Beni concluded that Platonism was better suited to Christian religion than Aristotelianism, so it was the best starting point to develop the new philosophy that would replace the old one based on Aristotelianism. The best (and perhaps the only) way to bring to fruition that project was to replace Aristotle with Plato in university curricula, but this required that the Platonic dialogues and their content be reshaped and arranged as a doctrinally systematic and coherent whole apt to be taught. Thus, Beni attempted to show — like Javelli before him — the systematic dimension of Platonic philosophy and to distill Plato's view on metaphysics, ethics, rhetoric, poetics and history by collecting and synthesising the ideas that Plato had scattered in his various dialogues, and then elucidating the 'authentic' meaning of Plato's dialogues, by means of running commentaries (on the *Timaeus* and *Euthyphro*) and of a précis of Platonic philosophy.

Beni seems to have been persuaded of the need for such change by the difficult religious and political circumstances of his time caused, according to him, by Aristotelian philosophy. Hence the philosophical, religious and political dimensions of his project are inextricably intertwined. He argued that the Platonically oriented philosophy that he tried to create was superior to the Aristotelian one in all the branches of philosophy and, furthermore, it accommodated scientific discoveries

---

75 On the political aims of the Accademia Aldobrandini see BALDINI, "Ragion di stato e platonismo nel dibattito politico italiano di fine Cinquecento"; *Id.*, "Aristotelismo e platonismo nelle dispute romane sulla ragion di stato di fine Cinquecento".

that were not easily compatible with Aristotle's system. This shows that Schmitt's idea about eclectic Aristotelianism and scientific discoveries needs to be nuanced, for not only eclectic Aristotelianism, but also Platonism offered responses to the challenges resulting from late Renaissance observational evidence. In addition, Beni acknowledged that the new philosophy had an essential role in facilitating peace and stability in Europe, by helping to restore the unity among the Reformed and Catholic Churches, and in establishing new, stable and human political systems. By emphasizing the political role of Platonism Beni sided with those intellectuals, like Patrizi, who assigned a political function to Plato's philosophy in the political debates reconstructed by Baldini, which were held in Italian intellectual circles, such as the Accademia Aldobrandini, at the end of the sixteenth century.

EVA DEL SOLDATO

Plato between Pavia and Milan in the Sixteenth Century[*]

The official introduction of Plato into university curricula was a complicated business in sixteenth-century Italy. As seen in other chapters of this book, this was true even in places traditionally labelled Platonic strongholds, like Ferrara and Pisa, not to mention the controversy over the chair of Platonism at the University of Rome. Another institutionalized teaching of Plato, *in die festivo*, typically relegated to footnotes, was introduced in Pavia, in 1606. But this addition to the curriculum in a way constituted an acknowledgement of the varied forms of engagement with Platonic philosophy that were characteristic in the teaching of professors in the *Studium Ticinense* since the beginning of the sixteenth century. This engagement left its mark also on alumni of the University, who pursued careers elsewhere, for example in Paris or in nearby Milan, and were perceivable in the activity of the Accademia degli Affidati, a sort of satellite to the *Studium*. This article explores the complex pedagogical role ascribed to Plato in sixteenth-century universities, and sheds new light on the presence of Platonism in the *milieu* of the University of Pavia and at the Scuole Cannobiane in Milan.

From Agrippa to Camuzio

In 1511 Henricus Cornelius Agrippa of Nettesheim (1486-1535) arrived in Italy and took part in the Milanese session of the schismatic Council of Pisa. According

---

[*] Research for this article had largely been conducted at the Biblioteca Ambrosiana in Milan, during the period I had the privilege to spend as a Senior Visiting Professor in the Philosophy Department at the Università Statale in Milan, in May-June 2019. I wish to thank the faculty and the doctoral students in the Department for their generous hospitality. I am grateful to Maude Vanhaelen for her precious comments on an advanced draft of this article.

Eva Del Soldato • University of Pennsylvania

Teaching Plato in Italian Renaissance Universities, ed. by Eva Del Soldato and Maude Vanhaelen, Studia Artistarum, 51 (Turnhout: Brepols, 2024), pp. 119–148
BREPOLS PUBLISHERS   10.1484/M.SA-EB.5.136097

to his own testimony, he was offered a chair in theology in Pavia in 1515[1]. But in 1512, before the Swiss invasion shut down the university, his name already appeared in the academic records "ad lecturam Philosophiae" [2]. It was possibly then that Agrippa lectured on Plato's *Symposium* in Pavia. Of that course only the prolusion survives, and it is accompanied — at least in the *Opera* edition — by a direct reference to Pavia as the place where it was held ("in Ticinensi Gymnasio")[3]. Appropriately so, considering its purpose, the prolusion is not particularly dense from a theoretical point of view, but is replete with references to biblical, literary, and political examples, in large part modeled on the popular book on love by Mario Equicola, with several silent borrowings from Marsilio Ficino[4]. Agrippa defined love as a process of assimilation with God, driven by a desire for beauty. Though he primarily attributed this definition to Plato, Agrippa claimed that it was shared by the greatest theologians and thinkers, including Aristotle[5]. Thus, it seems Agrippa was well aware of the novelty of the subject of his course, and accordingly opted for a more traditional framing, by strategically referring to the author who was normally at the core of the university curriculum.

The turbulent circumstances of the Italian Wars brought yet another Platonic sympathizer to Pavia. In October 1515, the College of Doctors at the University of Pavia approved the aggregation of the physician Symphorien Champier

---

1 See H. C. AGRIPPA, *De beatissimae Annae monogamia ac unico puerperio propositiones. Defensio propositionum praenarraturum*, s.n. l., 1534, f. BViv: "Tandem Papiae Ticinensi famoso Gymnasio Theologicam cathedram in publicis scholis ascendi".
2 *Memorie e documenti per la storia dell'Università di Pavia, e degli uomini più illustri che v'insegnarono*, Pavia, Successori Bizzoni, 1878, p. 169. See also C. B. SCHMITT, "L'introduction de la philosophie platonicienne dans l'enseignement des universités de la Renaissance", in M. DE GANDILLAC and J.-C. MARGOLIN (eds), *Platon et Aristote à la Renaissance*, Paris, Vrin, 1976, pp. 93-104: 99.
3 See H. C. AGRIPPA, *Opera in duos tomos concinne digesta*, 2 vols, [Lyon, Bering?], sd, I, sp (the reference to Pavia does not appear in the first edition of the prolusion: Id., *Orationes X quorum catalogum uersa exhibebit pagella*, Cologne, Ioannes Soter, 1535, f. A2r-B3r). H. MORLEY, *Cornelius Agrippa. The Life of Henry Cornelius Agrippa von Nettesheim, Doctor and Knight, Commonly Known as a Magician*, 2 vols, London, Chapman and Hall, 1856, I, p. 261, and M. VAN DER POEL, *Cornelius Agrippa, the Humanist Theologian and His Declamations*, Leiden, Brill, 1997, p. 22 both support the idea that Agrippa offered the course on the *Symposium* in Pavia in 1512. For a different opinion see A. PROST, *Les sciences et les arts occultes au XVIe siècle. Corneille Agrippa: Sa vie et ses oeuvres*, 2 vols, Paris, Champion, 1881-1882, I, pp. 262-263.
4 On the work, see also G. MCDONALD, "Cornelius Agrippa's School of Love: Teaching Plato's *Symposium* in the Renaissance", in P. SHERLOCK and M. CASSIDY-WELCH (eds), *Practices of Gender in Late-Medieval and Early Modern Europe*, Turnhout, Brepols, 2008, pp. 151-175 and now Id., *Marsilio Ficino in Germany from Renaissance to Enlightenment. A Reception History*, Geneva, Droz, 2022, pp. 498-508, where he shows similar borrowings from Ficino in the other oration (on the Hermetic corpus) he delivered in Pavia, *In praelectione Hermetis Trismegisti*; D. GIOVANNOZZI, "*Amoris fulgoribus ego accensus, amorem vobis praedico*. L'*Oratio in Convivium Platonis* di Cornelio Agrippa", in *Bruniana & Campanelliana*, 21 (2015), pp. 347-361.
5 AGRIPPA, *Opera*, p. 1062.

(1471-1538), who was part of the French military campaign. A committed *Ficinista* and staunch defender of the Platonic cause, even within the philo-Aristotelian circle of his friend Jacques Lefèvre d'Étaples, Champier published in 1516 a *Symphonia Platonis cum Aristotele et Hippocratis cum Galeno*, wherein he intertwined his philosophical, theological, and medical preferences. By this time, he was already back in France. Though Champier spent little time in Pavia, he managed to cultivate a network of intellectual exchanges, both at the university and in the city. Evidence of this networking is provided by the extensive list of colleagues at the University of Pavia to whom he dedicated his edition of a commentary by Giovanni d'Arcolo (1518). In 1522, along with one of these colleagues, the professor of medicine Pietro Antonio Rustico, Champier edited Avicenna and entertained a long epistolary exchange that occasionally involved their mutual friend, the Augustinian Girolamo Fornari of Pavia[6]. In 1519 Fornari — with whom Champier had debated that same year about French intellectual prerogatives, in the name of his Pseudo-Dionysian Platonism — was involved in the Pomponazzi affair, and composed a treatise in defense of the immortality of the soul[7]. But aside from these suggestive personal connections, Champier's interactions with Pavia professors and theologians were not, apparently, focused on his Platonic predilections.

Yet, by the 1530s, it seemed impossible to ignore the presence of Platonism at the University of Pavia. For the academic year 1536/1537 the Franciscan Cornelio Musso (1511-1574) was, in fact, listed in the *ruoli* as the instructor of Metaphysics, and official documentation clearly refers to him as "platonicus". The same adjective was used to describe another teacher from Piacenza, Giulio Ferrari, whose name was put forward by the rector Nicolaus de Augustis to teach moral philosophy that very same year[8]. Ferrari's application was ultimately rejected, and it is unclear how he deserved those Platonic credentials. This is not the case with Musso, as we can gather at least from his religious sermons, which are brimming with praise for Plato. Plato's elaborate way of writing philosophy represented a model for Musso, who celebrated the ancient thinker for his compatibility with

---

6 B. P. COPENHAVER, *Symphorien Champier and the Reception of the Occultist Tradition in Renaissance France*, The Hague-Paris-New York, Mouton, 1978, pp. 60-62, 68; N. SIRAISI, *Avicenna in Renaissance Italy: The Canon and Medical Teaching in Italian Universities After 1500*, Princeton, Princeton University Press, 1987, pp. 188-189.
7 See S. CHAMPIER, *Duellum epistolare Galliae et Italiae antiquitates complectens*, [Lyon], Impressum per Ioannem Phiroben & Ioannem Diuineur sumptibus Iacobi Francisci De Ionta, 1519. The treatise against Pomponazzi is G. FORNARI, *De anime humane immortalitate examen perspicacissimum totius disceptationis inter Augustinum Suessanum et Petrum Pomponatium Mantuanum vertentis circa anime immortalitatem*, Bologna, per Iustinianum Ruber, 1519.
8 See the documents published by S. FAZZO, "Girolamo Cardano e lo Studio di Pavia", in M. BALDI and G. CANZIANI (eds), *Girolamo Cardano. Le opere, le fonti, la vita*, Milan, Franco Angeli, 1999, pp. 521-574: 544-546 that supplements D.A. LINES, *Aristotle's Ethics in the Italian Renaissance (ca. 1300-1650): The Universities and the Problem of Moral Education*, Leiden, Brill, 2002, p. 450.

Christianity[9]. Conversely, in the same sermons, Musso showed himself hostile towards Aristotle and his followers, not only when discussing the immortality of the soul, but also in matters of ethics.

We have no extant record of Musso's teaching in Pavia that would allow us to evaluate if, and how, he incorporated Platonic readings into his lectures. However, we can assume that 1536 was a particularly vibrant year for Platonism in Pavia. It was around that year that the young Andrea Camuzio (c. 1512-1587) held a public dispute on the agreement between Plato and Aristotle[10]. Camuzio was at the beginning of his career at the University of Pavia where, for years, he would teach logic, philosophy and, finally, *medicina theorica*, in competition with Girolamo Cardano. That dispute was no doubt used by the young physician for self-promotion, and to cultivate a persona *à la* Pico. But the practice of holding public disputes on Plato and Aristotle became a sort of trademark for Camuzio, since he held at least three more, in 1539, 1540, and 1541. For the 1539 and 1540 disputes, Maude Vanhaelen has recently found the public announcements, both printed in Pavia, at the University Library of Marburg[11]. The disputes had different purposes and advertised different degrees of commitment to Platonism. While in 1536 Camuzio was — as said — interested in reconciling Plato and Aristotle, in 1539 he appeared to have abandoned this project in favor of exclusive loyalty to Plato. Not only did he conclude the 1539 dispute claiming "quicquid dixit Plato, bene dixit", but, more importantly, this determination was reached by defending one-hundred-eighty-five conclusions "in quibus divinus Plato peripatheticae sectae adversatur"[12]. As Camuzio explained, in his address to the Milanese senator Filippo Castiglioni, Plato's philosophy was the closest to Christianity. Yet, he argued, it was neglected by their contemporaries for several reasons, including the tendentious ways in which Aristotle presented his teacher's doctrine, and the stubborn reliance on Averroes and other commentators, with no easy access to Plato's original texts. According to Camuzio, Averroes was an

---

9 See, e.g., C. Musso, *Prediche*, Venice, appresso Gabriel Giolito de' Ferrari, 1556, and especially the sermons *Della cognitione di se stesso*, p. 49, and *Dell'imitatione di Christo nostro Signore*, p. 474; see also Id., *Prediche sopra il Simbolo degli Apostoli*, Venice, nella stamperia de' Giunti, 1590, p. 62. In the context of a peculiar praise of Marsilio Ficino, for not having confused Platonism and Christianity, Botero also mentioned Musso: see G. Botero, *Detti memorabili di personaggi illustri*, Turin, per Gio. Domenico Tarino, 1614, p. 553.
10 C. B. Schmitt, "Andreas Camutius on the Concord of Plato and Aristotle with Scripture", in D. J. O'Meara (ed.), *Neoplatonism and Christian Thought*, Norfolk, SUNY Press, 1982, pp. 178-184. We can date the dispute to 1536 since, in A. Camuzio, *In sacrarum literarum cum Aristotele & Platone concordiam, praefatio*, Pavia, Io. Maria Simoneta, 1541, f. Ciiir-v., Camuzio said he was almost twenty-four years of age when it first happened. The same text also suggests that Camuzio held disputes on the same topic not only in Pavia, but also in Bologna and Padua.
11 Maude Vanhaelen will focus in depth on this material (UBM, MS 15, III, f. 61v-63v) in her forthcoming monograph, *Plato in the Place of Aristotle. The Reception of Plato's Dialogues in Sixteenth-Century Italy*. I thank her for generously sharing these texts with me in advance.
12 UBM, MS 15, III, f. 62r.

especially dangerous obstacle, because of his doctrine of intellectual happiness, which made it impossible to appreciate the Platonic mysteries. In concluding his 1539 dedication to Castiglioni, Camuzio added that sometimes Plato clashes with Galen, but is constantly in conflict with Aristotle and his followers. In June 1540 Camuzio appeared to have reconsidered this statement. He proposed a new dispute, which was somewhat reminiscent of Champier, indeed another physician, at least in terms of the title: "non modo Platonem divinum in omnibus recte sentire, verumetiam neque Aristotele neque Galeni aliqua ex parte adversari"[13]. As evidenced in the dedication to Cardinal Madruzzo, a personality that we have already met in chapter III for his later association with Beni, Camuzio had not abandoned the polemical vein of the previous debate; he simply directed his attack exclusively on Aristotle's followers, who — in his opinion — were responsible for promoting the false idea that the Philosopher disagrees with his teacher Plato. After all, already in the 1539 debate, the *Peripatetici*, and not Aristotle himself, were Camuzio's main opponents. An even more significant shift in philosophical targets is offered in the 1541 dispute that Camuzio held in Milan, again addressed to Madruzzo. The topic of this dispute was specifically the agreement between Plato, Aristotle, and the Scriptures, and its contents can be discerned thanks to the prolusion Camuzio published in Pavia that very same year[14]. Not only did Camuzio argue for the harmony between Plato and Aristotle, he also reconciled them with Christian faith. He rejected the idea that philosophical truths can oppose theological truths, on the grounds that — otherwise — professors of philosophy would simply be charlatans, peddling false doctrines. Though Camuzio's palpable sympathy for Plato throughout the prolusion, he firmly maintained the harmony between Plato and Aristotle in order to argue for the compatibility of natural and theological reasons. While in his earlier disputes Camuzio seemingly hinted at tensions among professors of philosophy — such as between those like Camuzio, who were open to Plato's inclusion in the curriculum, and stubborn traditionalists — the 1541 dispute revealed a different kind of conflict. In this case, the opposition was between those who separated religion and philosophy and those who, like Camuzio, believed in their reconciliation[15]. In the prolusion, Camuzio described his opponents as a group of philosophers and theologians in Pavia.

In fact, there is proof that debates on Plato, Aristotle, and their respective utility for Christian faith took place in Pavia at the time[16]. In 1540, only one year before Camuzio's dispute, a *libellus* by the humanist Bernardino Donato

---

[13] UBM, MS 15, III, f. 61v.
[14] CAMUZIO, *Praefatio*.
[15] K. GESSNER, *Bibliotheca Universalis, sive Catalogus omnium scriptorum locupletissimus*, Zurich, apud Christophorum Froschoverum, 1545, f. 39r, acutely described Camuzio's prolusion as an "opusculum quoddam in quo philosophiam et theologiam conciliare conatur".
[16] E. DEL SOLDATO, *Early Modern Aristotle. On the Making and Unmaking of Authority*, Philadelphia, University of Pennsylvania Press, 2020, pp. 38-41 and 43-44.

(1483-1543) entitled *De Platonicae atque Aristotelicae philosophiae differentia* was printed in Venice. This booklet contains the first printed edition of Pletho's *De differentiis* (c. 1439), in its original Greek version, along with a sort of dialogic transposition of *De differentiis*, in Latin, authored by Donato himself. The intellectual program behind the booklet is obvious. In a paradoxical reversal that was embraced by other sixteenth-century writers, Pletho — who only a few decades earlier had been suspected with good reasons of being a Platonizing neo-pagan — was used by Donato to serve the cause of the Roman faith. But only to an extent. Donato agreed with Pletho that Platonic doctrines better support religious dogmas than Aristotelianism, but he resolutely proclaimed their intrinsic limitations: philosophy will always be inferior to theology. This is precisely the argument Camuzio attacked in his prolusion, and for this reason it does not come as a surprise to notice that Donato's dialogue is set in Pavia. Moreover, the main interlocutor of the dialogue is an historical character, the Augustinian Callisto Fornari of Piacenza, who often quoted Plato in his sermons and was in close contact with the intellectual world of Pavia[17].

If Camuzio was indeed reacting to these discussions with his 1541 dispute, it must be emphasized that, despite their different views on the relationship between philosophy and faith, he and his adversaries shared a predilection for Platonism on a religious basis. Consequently, one can infer that Plato had many supporters in Pavia, even if appeals to his name and his doctrines were at that point mostly made in connection to theological debates. While the attraction exercised by Platonism in theological *milieux* continued in the following decades, especially among Franciscans and Augustinians, it was not through theology that Plato found not only in Pavia a more stable presence into university teaching, but, as we will now see, through a reappraisal of his links with Aristotle.

From Rovida to Vimercato

One of the most fascinating book collections, among the many housed at the Biblioteca Ambrosiana in Milan, belonged to the Pavian professor Cesare Rovida (1549-circa 1592)[18]. An *enfant prodige* educated in Greek, Rovida taught philosophy and medicine in Padua from 1575 until his premature death[19]. Rovida did not publish anything in print during his lifetime. Among the manuscripts in the *fondo* Rovida of the Ambrosiana, however, there are two different versions of a *comparatio* between Plato and Aristotle, entitled *De dogmatibus Platonis et Aristotelis*,

---

17 E.g., he published in Pavia, precisely in 1541, his *Expositione di Ageo propheta*, Pavia, Io. Maria Simoneta.
18 On Rovida's activity as a commentator on Aristotle see C. H. LOHR, *Latin Aristotle Commentaries. II Renaissance Authors*, Florence, Olschki, 1988, pp. 391-394.
19 F. ARGELATI, *Bibliotheca scriptorum Mediolanensium*, 2 vols, Milan, In aedibus Palatinis, 1745, II.1, col. 1247-1250. On Rovida's proficiency in Greek see, e.g., BAM S89 inf.

one of which is attributed in the Ambrosiana catalog to Rovida himself[20]. The bulky text focuses on issues of natural philosophy and addresses slippery topics such as the eternity of the world. The attribution of the work to Rovida makes sense from an inductive point of view, since several pieces in the *fondo* Rovida are his own working notes. Yet we have little evidence of any serious engagement with Plato and Platonism on Rovida's part. Even a well-informed biographer such as Filippo Argelati did not mention *De dogmatibus* in his list of Rovida's works; Argelati only referenced a manuscript containing a commentary by Proclus, in Greek and Latin, to which Rovida added a few annotations[21]. In his public courses *On the Heavens* and *On the Soul*, Rovida only occasionally quoted Iamblichus, Themistius, Syrianus, and Plato's *Timaeus*[22]. More interestingly, as part of his private teaching, Rovida lectured on the commentaries on *Physics* by Simplicius in 1581[23]. He also used the composition of dialogues as an educational tool for his disciples at the Academy he hosted, the Accademia Rovidiana, an exercise that could appear *prima facie* more Platonic than Aristotelian[24]. Yet, not only were dialogues common didactic tools within the Aristotelian tradition — one can think of Jacques Lefèvre d'Étaples[25] —, but the Accademia Rovidiana itself was generally described as an Aristotelian hub. Another of Rovida's biographers, Giovan Battista Selvatico, indicated that he directed his academy "peripatetico

---

20 DEL SOLDATO, *Early Modern Aristotle*, pp. 180-181. The signatures are BAM, S169 inf. and (attributed to Rovida) S12 inf..
21 Argelati identified it as Proclus' commentary on *Phaedrus*, but this is unlikely since the work is lost. The piece referred to by Argelati could instead be a copy of Proclus' commentary on Plato's *Parmenides* now in BAM, A167 sup., introduced by a note reading "Proclus in Parmenidem Platonis emptus una cum multis aliis ab haeredibus Rovidii senatoris Mediolanensis" and which seems to be annotated by Rovida at f. 141v. Alternatively, it may be another of Proclus' commentaries, among those listed at n. 33 below, which were originally part of the library of Ottaviano Ferrari. I thank Dr. Fabio Cusimano for the help he provided during my research.
22 BAM, S72 inf. and S180 inf., f. 157r. An edition of Themistius' *Opera omnia*, annotated by Rovida, can be recognized in BBM AO. XIV. 34: see S. FAZZO, "Philology and Philosophy in the Margins of Early Printed Editions of the Ancient Greek Commentators on Aristotle, with Special Reference to Copies Held at the Biblioteca Nazionale Braidense, Milan", in C. BLACKWELL and S. KUSUKAWA (eds), *Philosophy in the Sixteenth and Seventeenth Centuries. Conversations with Aristotle*, London, Routledge, 1999, pp. 48-75: 71 and 74.
23 F. CICERI, *Epistolarum libri*, 2 vols, Milan, S. Ambrogio, 1782, II, p. 273: "[…] Simplicii ejusdem commentariis in Aristotelis *Physica*, quae ipse privatim fere quotidie interpretatur […]". A copy of Simplicius' *Physics* with Greek annotations in Rovida's hand is today in BBM, AO. XIV.25. See FAZZO, "Philology and Philosophy in the Margins", pp. 70 and 74.
24 F. CICERI, *Epistolarum libri*, pp. 273-274: "Rovidius totus erat in dialogis conscribendis, quos mox ediscendos daret adolescentibus illis, quos exercere decreverat ad disputandum in contraria partes, de utraque quaestione proposita, Logica videlicet, ac Physica".
25 L. BIANCHI, "From Lefèvre d'Étaples to Giulio Landi: Uses of the Dialogue in Renaissance Aristotelianism", in J. KRAYE and M. W. F. STONE (eds), *Humanism and Early Modern Philosophy*, London and New York, Routledge, 2000, pp. 41-58.

more", and celebrated Rovida's engagement with Alexander of Aphrodisias[26]. And, after all, Rovida's writings — both those related to his teaching in Pavia and those connected to his parallel activity at the Accademia — were largely focused on logical Aristotelian doctrines, and did not engage in conversations with other philosophical traditions, Platonism included. This is further confirmed by a *florilegium*, in Rovida's hand, which listed notable passages from the Aristotelian corpus: in it, the entries on Plato were disappointingly meager[27]. It seems hard, therefore, to reconcile this substantial absence of interest in Plato and the Platonic tradition with Rovida's alleged authorship of a work like the Ambrosiana De dogmatibus.

Though we must rule Rovida out as the author of *De dogmatibus*, the adventurous history of the *fondo* Rovida offers us answers regarding the real author of the work[28]. Rovida's library was, in fact, partially formed through the bequest of his friend Bartolomeo Capra. And, in its turn, Capra's book collection was largely comprised of pieces he inherited from his friend Ottaviano Ferrari (1518-1586), *magister* in Pavia, Padua, and Milan[29]. Rovida maintained that Ferrari wanted him to have his collection after Capra's demise[30]. Those books that Rovida received

---

26 G. B. SELVATICO, *Collegii Mediolanensium medicorum origo, antiquitas, necessitas, utilitas, dignitates, honores, privilegia, et viri illustres*, Milan, Apud Hieronymum Bordonum, Petrum Martyrem Locarnum, & Bernardinum Lantonum, 1607, p. 65.

27 BAM, S181 inf.. Another manuscript in the *fondo*, BAM, N II 5 inf., which largely focuses on the topic of *phantasia* from a Platonic perspective, is not in Rovida's hand. See U. ROZZO-R. FERRARI, "Un filosofo e bibliofilo milanese del '500: Cesare Rovida", in *Stasimon*, 3 (1984), pp. 81-115: 114.

28 See on this ROZZO-FERRARI, "Un filosofo e bibliofilo milanese del '500".

29 On Ferrari's life, see the details provided in his funeral oration composed by Francesco Ciceri and published in CICERI, *Epistolarum libri*, II, pp. 222-244.

30 See the letter Rovida wrote to Gian Vincenzo Pinelli on 14 April 1589 in BAM, S107 sup., f. 2r: "Questo mio signore mentre era in vita più volte et a me et ad altri haveva detto di volermi lasciare la sua libraria, nella quale vi è ancor quella del signor Ottaviano Ferraro, sì per l'amore che mi portava, sì ancora perchè sapeva che la volontà del signor Ottaviano era che doppo lui pervenissero in me i suoi libri, la quale sebbene non fu così dichiarata per scrittura, nondimeno dal legato che 'l signor Ottaviano gli fece, si poteva in qualche modo conoscere questa sua volontà". The library was finally obtained by Rovida in March 1590, see BAM, S107 sup., f. 9r. From the numerous exchanges Rovida had with Pinelli, we also learn that he hoped to leave the University of Pavia for Padua, and that he cultivated the idea of publishing in Italy and in Paris works left in manuscript by Ferrari. The project of printing Ferrari's works in Paris was disrupted by the ongoing wars of religion (see BAM, S106 sup., f. 12r, 18r, 50r). When discussing the possibility of having Ferrari's texts printed at f. 50r, Pinelli remarked on the superior quality of the editorial work offered in Venice by publishers like Giunti (who, unlike the French, would take good care of Ferrari's frequent use of Greek): "[…] come V.S. può sapere, [the Parisians] pensano in questi tempi travagliati ad altro che libri. Si potrebbero però stampare a Venezia, da qualche stampatore principale, come Giunti, o simile, i quali hanno correttori greci et persone intendente, come si vedrà presto dalle opere di Ippocrate greco latine che stampano. In questa maniera si fuggirebbe il pericolo di mandarli lontano s'harebbe sicurezza che [non] saranno alterati, cosa che gli oltramontani sogliono fare in cose altrui [*strikethrough in the ms.*], et se ne spererebbe miglior e più presta espeditione. (e

from Ferrari reveal that the late Ottaviano was much more engaged in the Platonic tradition than Cesare. We find Ferrari's *ex libris* in texts by Simplicius[31], various works by Plutarch[32], Proclus' commentaries on the *First Alcibiades* and the *Cratylus*[33], and Calcidius' commentary on the *Timaeus*[34]. Yet Ferrari's uses of Plato in his teaching were mainly focused on methodological and ethical issues, as will be shown, and have nothing in common with a work like *De dogmatibus*, which was fully centered on natural philosophy. Natural philosophy, combined with an interest in comparing Plato and Aristotle, was instead a trademark of one of Ferrari's dearest friends, and former student at the University of Pavia, Francesco Vimercato (d. 1569). After studying in Pavia, Vimercato moved to Paris where he taught first at the Collège Duplessis and then at the Collège Royale. He built his career during a time in which Plato was particularly appreciated at the French court, by emphasizing the importance of knowing Plato's philosophy to better understand Aristotelian texts. Vimercato first displayed this approach in his lectures at the Collège Duplessis, and then in an unfinished *comparatio* on Plato and Aristotle's natural philosophies, *De placitis* (c. 1541)[35]. He subsequently planned a series of commentaries on the works of the two ancient thinkers through the same comparative lens, but only partially accomplished his project, commenting on some Aristotelian texts. Another work by Vimercato on natural philosophy, again focused on Plato and Aristotle, *De principiis rerum naturalium*, appeared posthumously in 1598. It is precisely *De principiis* that enables us to solve the authorship issue of the Ambrosiana *De dogmatibus*[36]. In *De principiis* Vimercato made numerous references to another work of his, entitled *De dogmatibus*. The identification of this text, otherwise considered lost, with the one contained in the Ambrosiana manuscripts, is supported and confirmed by several elements. First, the content of the Ambrosiana manuscripts corresponds to Vimercato's description of *De dogmatibus* in *De principiis*. Second, S 169 inf. — one of the Ambrosiana exemplars containing *De dogmatibus*, and the only one that preserves it in its entirety — is written in Vimercato's hand, as can be easily proven by a comparison with the philosopher's other autograph manuscripts[37]. The pieces likely ended up in Rovida's possession through Ferrari's bequest. Indeed, it was to

---

poi si spargerebbono più facilmente in Italia, libri stampati in Francia da noi non arriverebbero facilmente)". Nonetheless, Pinelli suggested that the works could be eventually reprinted in France, after a first Italian edition.

31 BAM, E4 inf. and E99 sup..
32 BAM, E10 sup..
33 BAM, C9 sup. and P267 sup.. See also BAM, H18 sup..
34 BAM, D29 sup..
35 In *De placitis* (BNF, Par. lat. 6330, f. 2v), he wrote: "Neque enim fieri potest ut quid sibi velit Aristoteles multis in locis, ubi in Platone invehitur, cognoscamus, adeo breviter et concise illius opinionem ponit, nisi illam apud eundem Platonem latius fusiusque explicatam viderimus, id quod omnibus per otium non licet".
36 DEL SOLDATO, *Early Modern Aristotle*, p. 56.
37 See, e.g., BAM, N. II. 5 inf.. S12 inf. is evidently a *bella copia*, which was never completed.

his friend Ferrari that Vimercato entrusted several of his works after he returned from France, in the hope that they might be published[38]. The improbable attribution to Rovida of a *comparatio* like *De dogmatibus* can therefore be corrected, but it cannot be forgotten that, in his interest to establish a constant comparison between Plato and Aristotle, Vimercato was himself a product of the University of Pavia. To be sure, his treatment of Plato and Aristotle was very different from that of Camuzio in his disputes, or from what can be conjectured about Musso's lectures. Vimercato had little interest in metaphysical issues and was not concerned with establishing a dialogue between the two ancient philosophers and Christian theology. On the contrary, as previously mentioned, he made natural philosophy the center of his inquiry. However, this focus on natural philosophy was, in many ways, strategic and responded to specific polemical exigencies. The dimension *in puris naturalibus*, in fact, helped to highlight the philosophical merits of the *physicus* Aristotle, while downplaying those of Plato "the theologian." In many different sections of *De dogmatibus*, for example, Vimercato repeated that Aristotle "ad naturae veritatem propius accessisse sententiamque suam firmioribus ac magis cogentibus rationibus confirmasse docuimus"[39]. And while exposing the limits of Plato's natural philosophy, he also took good care to reject Christianizing readings of his thought, precisely because Plato's doctrines occupied — in his view — "medium quodammodo locum inter naturae ac religionis veritatem"[40].

And this perspective was necessary for defusing the attacks Vimercato's colleague, Petrus Ramus (1515-1572), was making against Aristotle, in his attempt to renew the university curriculum. Ramus often justified his attacks by describing Aristotle as an impious man, and — conversely — conveniently celebrating Plato and Platonism. Along with other professors of the Collège, including Léger Duchesne, Pierre Galland and Adrien Turnèbe, Vimercato contributed to the first condemnation of the writings of Ramus in 1544, and a few years later he was

---

38 See CICERI, *Epistolarum libri*, II, p. 235 ("Porro Franciscus Vimercatus Mediolanensis, qui Lutetiae, velut aetherius sol, universam naturam cum omnium auditorum ex tota Europa eo confluentium admiratione illuminavit, non ita multis annis ante Taurini moriens, tantam fidem Octaviano Ferrario habuit ut testamento illi omnia sua scripta, quae nondum vulgarat, emendanda primum ab ipso, deinde in lucem proferenda, legaverit") and ARGELATI, *Bibliotheca scriptorum Mediolanensium*, col. 610 (he said that Vimercato, once back to Italy, "eruditis universis posthabitis, unum Octavianum elegerit, cui edendorum operum suorum provinciam demandaret"). On Ferrari's books see C. PASINI, "Giovanni Donato Ferrari e i manoscritti greci dell'Ambrosiana", in *Νέα ' Ρώμη. Rivista di ricerche bizantinistiche*, 1 (2004), pp. 351-386: 354-356.
39 BAM, S169 inf., f. 199r (in S12 inf., f. 105r).
40 See, e.g., BAM, S169 inf., f. 485r (S12 inf., f. 36v-37r): "Sed illud primus explicabitur, Platonem quamque cum Mosi et religionis nostrae dogmate magis quam Aristoteles consenserit, non plane tamen consensisse, imo utraque in quaestionis parte non parum discordasse, ut medium quodammodo locum inter naturae ac religionis veritatem dogma illius habere videatur".

likely involved in an anti-Ramist editorial project directed by Ramus's archenemy, Jacques Charpentier[41].

The conflict with Ramus led Vimercato to progressively radicalize his position, especially in terms of his attitude toward Plato. Indeed, in his first *comparatio*, the above-mentioned *De placitis*, which was written before the quarrel with Ramus, Vimercato at times seemed even more sympathetic toward Plato than toward Aristotle, while defending their substantial agreement. One can wonder if this initial fondness for Plato and defense of his harmony with Aristotle were dictated by considerations about his career within the French context, or whether they should be considered a legacy of the Platonic debates he witnessed while studying in Pavia. At any rate, after the conflict with Ramus, Vimercato's Plato was mostly described as a clumsy natural philosopher and a poor theologian. Yet the conflict did not change Vimercato's mind about the utility of Plato as a didactic tool for better understanding Aristotle. And this practice was destined to find several followers among his fellow Aristotelians in Pavia and Milan.

Ottaviano Ferrari and the Scuole Cannobiane in Milan

Even if Rovida and Vimercato were both committed Aristotelians, their respective attitudes toward the pedagogical use of Plato were certainly diverging. Considering the teaching activity of the individual who represented a link between Rovida and Vimercato — Ottaviano Ferrari — seems to suggest that the "odd one" in the trio was actually Rovida, who did not bring Plato in his teaching. Ferrari's work represents, indeed, an interesting and seldom studied chapter in the history of the use of Platonic doctrines and texts within didactic settings.

After having studied in different cities — Pavia, Padua, and Pisa — the Milanese Ferrari taught logic and philosophy in Pavia from 1545 to 1557. In 1557, he moved back to Milan to teach at the Scuole Cannobiane, named after their founder, the nobleman Paolo da Cannobio (d. 1557)[42]. The Scuole were a public institution, aimed at providing pre-university training. Whereas teachers in the Milanese public schools were typically clergymen, Paolo da Cannobio explicitly stated in his will that the instructors at the Scuole be laymen[43]. In fact,

---

41 See P. SHARRATT, "Nicolaus Nancelius, 'Petri Rami Vita'. Edited with an English Translation", in *Humanistica Lovaniensia*, 24 (1975), pp. 161-277: 254-256. On Charpentier's project see E. DEL SOLDATO, "Sulle tracce di Bessarione: la fortuna cinquecentesca dell'*In calumniatorem Platonis*," in *Rinascimento*, 2nd s., 50, 2010, pp. 321-342. On Ramus's anti-Aristotelian agenda see at least S. MATTON, "Le face à face Charpentier-La Ramée. À propos d'Aristote", *Revue des sciences philosophiques et théologiques*, 70 (1986), pp. 67-86; M.-D. COUZINET, *Pierre Ramus et la critique du pédantisme: philosophie, humanisme et culture scolaire au XVIe siècle*, Paris, Champion, 2015.
42 He taught at the Scuole for twenty-two years. See CICERI, *Epistolarum libri*, II, p. 229.
43 See P. BOSSI, "Le Scuole Cannobiane 'celebrius inter alia publica gymnasia', nel panorama delle scuole pubbliche milanesi in età moderna", in B. AZZARO (ed.), *L'università di Roma La Sapienza e le università italiane*, Rome, Gangemi, 2008, pp. 133-146. See also C. MARCORA,

the three subjects taught at his Scuole were specifically chosen to prepare students for public life, including logic (taught by a poorly-paid instructor) and, more importantly, ethics and politics (taught instead by a well-paid *magister*)[44]. In his will, Cannobio provided a detailed job description for the position of professor of ethics and politics, which perfectly matched Ferrari's profile. The ideal teacher should have been a mature, respectable man, with previous experience in a major university like Padua, Pavia, Bologna, or Paris, and well educated in Latin and Greek. This individual should have taught Aristotle's ethics and politics, always according to the same order, and maintaining the same lectures in future iterations of his teaching.[45] For the lectures on the *Ethics*, Cannobio recommended the use of Eustratius's commentary. However, he left to the *magister* the discretion to exclude — at least initially — parts of the texts that have been too difficult or not useful for his students; he cited, as an example, the section devoted to Aristotle's discussion of the Platonic Ideas in Book I of the *Nicomachean Ethics* and other unspecified parts of the *Politics*[46]. Cannobio acknowledged therefore that the text of the *Ethics* and the *Politics* could be approached selectively, by highlighting those parts that provide guidance in concrete matters. Cannobio's specific guidelines about the Aristotelian passage on Plato's theory of the Ideas in the *Ethics* could certainly be related to his recommendation of using Eustratius's commentary, which devoted a large section to the issue[47]. Yet, Cannobio's recommendations

---

"La chiesa milanese nel decennio 1550-1560", in *Memorie Storiche della Diocesi di Milano*, 7 (1960), pp. 254-501: 286.

44 Cannobio stated that logic must be a bridge toward ethics and politics, not a tool to become a worker or a merchant. Cannobio's will was printed in the *Letture instituite dal Sig. Paolo Canobio, gentil'huomo milanese*, Milan, appresso Pacifico Pontio, 1575 (the Ambrosiana exemplar bears the signature S. I. L. IV 23, 2; there also exists a 1581 edition). This brings to mind the almost contemporary pedagogical project suggested for his ideal academy by B. TAEGIO, *Il Liceo, dove si ragiona dell'ordine delle accademie*, Milan, appresso Girardo di Comaschi, 1572. For the teaching of politics, Taegio's curriculum (f. 18r) included both Aristotle (*Politics*) and Plato (sections of the *Republic*). As a member of the Collegio dei Giureconsulti, Taegio was among those who oversaw the Scuole Cannobiane.

45 The possibility of suspending the teaching of politics was taken into consideration, probably out of concern for social unrest: see the *Ritrattazione* published in *Decreta Ill.mi Collegii DD. J. PP. Mediolani Judicum, Comitum Et Equitum*, Milan, ex typographia Petri Francisci Navae, 1723, p. 76. More generally, on the priority traditionally given to ethics over politics in moral teaching, see LINES, *Aristotle's Ethics in the Italian Renaissance*, pp. 125-127, 145-148, 205.

46 Any omission, however, needed to be approved by the Protettori of the Scuole: "Al quale sia ancora lecito lasciare di leggere alcune parti di detti libri, come forse ove si parla delle Idee di Platone nel primo della *Ethica*, et similmente alcune della *Politica*, se alcune d'esse giudicherà dovere essere più faticose, o meno utili del bisogno a quelli auditori, che i tempi gli concederanno, finchè a tal trattatione non siano più idonei et più eruditi, la qual omissione intendo non doversi fare senza participatione, et consenso di quelli ch'io advocarò per Protettori circa il fine di questa institutione" (*Letture instituite dal Sig. Paolo Canobio*, np).

47 In the long section on the Ideas in his influential commentary, Eustratius defended Plato from Aristotle's criticism. See L. BIANCHI, "Un commento 'umanistico' ad Aristotele: l'*Expositio super*

also suggest — similarly to a context we have already encountered in Chapter I of this volume — that Platonic interludes were typical in the teaching of Aristotelian texts, and on the other hand that they could also be flagged as diversions from the main purpose of the text, especially within the pragmatic context of the Scuole.

The *reportationes* of Ferrari's lectures on the *Ethics* and the *Politics* allow us to evaluate the extent to which Plato was present within his teaching[48]. They reveal that Ferrari was keen to bring Platonic counterpoints into his classroom to gain a better understanding of Aristotle's own positions, when the Philosopher takes issue with his former teacher. Like Vimercato, and in line with the philological trend described in Chapter I, Ferrari looked into Plato's texts to verify Aristotle's statements, even if he unfailingly ended up to side with the Philosopher[49].

The passage on the Ideas, in the opening book of the *Nicomachean Ethics*, was no exception and occupied — in spite of Cannobio's suggestions — a significant section in Ferrari's lectures. The issue, however, was framed in larger terms. Ferrari began by commenting on lines 1096a11-16, often synthetized as "amicus Plato, sed magis amica veritas".[50] Though here Aristotle was speaking of friends in vague terms, he was clearly alluding to Plato alone — Ferrari claimed, reelaborating on the use of a *topos* we already encountered in Chapter I of this volume in relation to Valier's lectures — because without having had Plato as a teacher for

---

libros Ethicorum di Donato Acciaiuoli", in *Id., Studi sull'Aristotelismo del Rinascimento*, Padua, Il Poligrafo, 2003, 11-39: 23-24.

48 Again, these pieces are part of the elusive *fondo* Rovida and, in some cases, are erroneously attributed to Rovida. They are certainly to be connected with Ferrari's teaching in the Scuole Cannobiane on the basis of several internal elements, including the mention of Ferrari's printed works; the reference to other manuscripts he possessed (see below); and the mention of personal interactions with scholars, which Rovida could not have met for chronological reasons (e.g., Lazzaro Buonamico, who Ferrari met and befriended in Padua, see BAM, B8 inf., f. 230v). See LOHR, *Latin Aristotle Commentaries II*, p. 147. On Buonamico and Ferrari see CICERI, *Epistolarum libri*, II, p. 226. See also the third volume of the Aldine Greek Aristotle (*De animalibus*) densely annotated by Ferrari, for sale on the Sokol Books: *For Aldus. Ad multos annos* catalogue (permanent link https://sokol.co.uk/wp-content/uploads/2015/06/Sokol-Books-Aldine-Catalogue-2015.pdf [last accessed September 7, 2023]): an annotator – again, likely, Ferrari – wrote in the final leaf that he used, among others, a codex owned by Buonamico.

49 Another *magister* from Pavia, Lucilio Filalteo (d. 1578) was among those who, in spite of not endorsing Plato's doctrines, demonstrated nonetheless a remarkable familiarity with his dialogues. See C. MARTIN, "Interpreting Plato's Geometrical Elements in Renaissance Aristotle Commentaries", in A. CORRIAS and E. DEL SOLDATO, *Harmony and Contrast: Plato and Aristotle in the Early Modern Period*, Oxford, Oxford University Press, 2022, pp. 149-171: 160-164.

50 H. GUERLAC, "Amicus Plato and Other Friends", in *Journal of the History of Ideas*, 39 (1978), pp. 627-633; L. TARÁN, "*Amicus Plato sed magis amica veritas*: From Plato and Aristotle to Cervantes", in *Antike und Abendland*, 30 (1984), pp. 93-124.

twenty years, the Philosopher would never have reached his level of excellence[51]. Anticipating a discussion that occurs later in the *Nicomachean Ethics* (book VIII), Ferrari copiously demonstrated that the friendship that united Plato and Aristotle was based on virtue, and not on pleasure, or utility[52]. After this introductory discussion, Ferrari delved into the issue of the Ideas. He repeatedly rejected the interpretation Eustratius offered of this section in his commentary, and referred to the *Metaphysics* (987a32-987b10) to explain that Plato concocted the Ideas as a reaction to Heraclitus' flowing reality. But by recognizing that only what perpetually persists is the object of knowledge, Plato denied that one could know individual objects. Ferrari vigorously criticized Plato's theory of the Ideas, on the ground that the existence of a separate nature would lead one to despair about the possibility of grasping any form of truth[53].

Ferrari had previously used the reference to "amicus Plato" also as a proof against those who, like Mario Nizolio, contested the authorship of the *Nicomachean Ethics*, and attributed it to Aristotle's son, Nicomachus[54]. Another issue of attribution of Aristotelian works notably resurfaced when he discussed the Platonic Ideas. Ferrari noticed that there would be inconsistencies in the position Aristotle held on the topic between the *Nicomachean Ethics* and *Eudemian Ethics*. His solution to the issue was refusing to recognize the *Eudemian* as genuinely Aristotelian. In another writing, the *Quaestio de scientiae naturalis utilitate et de generatione virtutum moralium*, Ferrari indeed offered a more detailed rejection of the Aristotelian authorship of the *Eudemian Ethics*, by claiming that Aristotle would never falsely attribute opinions to Plato or Socrates, like he believed to recognize in the *Eudemian* (at 1216b3 ff.)[55]. In both instances, Ferrari had no

---

51 This is stated in DIOGENES LAERTIUS, *Vitae philosophorum*, V.1, but is also mentioned by BESSARION in his *In calumniatorem Platonis* (I.3.5, ed. MOHLER), a text Ferrari perused in his lectures (see below).

52 BAM, D382 inf., f. 50v.

53 BAM, D382 inf., f. 52r: "Possemus enim sic argumentari, si quae per se sunt cognosci nequeunt, ergo nec definitio, si definitio igitur neque scientia. Igitur nulla erit rerum scientia, sed tantum opinio quae sane perabsurdum est, nam omnino de veritate desperandum esset" and f. 58v: "Probat nunc Aristoteles ideam esse prorsus inutilem, nam aut est universalis aut singularis. Si universalis, non cadet sub actione, nam actio est singularium [...] At nos quaerimus bonum, quod sub actione cadat. Si vero sit singularis, sed separata ut volebat Plato a singularibus quorum est Idea, neque eam umquam assequemur, at nos inquit quaerimus bonum parabile, itaque omnino inutilis".

54 On the debate on the attribution of the work see J. KRAYE, "Like Father, Like Son: Aristotle, Nicomachus and the *Nicomachean Ethics*", in R. IMBACH, F. DOMINGUEZ, T. PINDL-BÜCHEL, P. WALTER (eds), *Aristotelica et Lulliana magistro doctissimo Charles H. Lohr septuagesimum annum feliciter agenti dedicata*, Turnhout, Brepols, 1995, pp. 155-180.

55 For the *quaestio* see BAM, C14 suss., f. 22v-25v: "Patebit enim qua in re ille author ab Aristotele differat, simulque falso iniusta Platoni calumnia tolletur. Ait igitur ille author Σωκράτης μὲν οὖν ὁ πρεσβύτης, percurramus verba, ut pateat falso insimulari Platonem ab hoc authore, dum quaedam ab eo reprehenduntur, quae neque sensit Plato, neque scripsit. Hoc autem numquam ab Aristotele factum quisquam probabit, licet de Socrate et Platone passim multa dixerit".

doubts about the reliability of Aristotle in reporting Plato's doctrines, after all he had highlighted that the Philosopher was Plato's student for years, and being unable to identify in the Platonic corpus the references present in the *Eudemian Ethics*, he concluded that the text had to be the work of a different author. What is notable here in Ferrari's reasoning, aside from the devotion to Aristotle, is its resorting to Platonic works, to show that they did not correspond to what was reported in the *Eudemian*. The integrity of the *corpus Aristotelicum*, according to Ferrari, could also be defended and appreciated thanks to the knowledge of Plato's works.

In the closing part of the lecture, Ferrari discussed the problem of the Ideas within the framework of the Aristotelian doctrine of demonstration, as described in the *Posterior Analytics*. As they are separate, Platonic Ideas go against Aristotle's statement according to which "illud autem quod demonstratur est coniunctum cum eo de quo demonstratur". It is therefore possible that Cannobio would have been pleased with Ferrari's lecture on *Nicomachean Ethics* I.8, despite his reservations about devoting time to the doctrine of the Ideas. Ferrari took the opportunity to intertwine erudite matters (including the authorship of several works in the Aristotelian corpus) with his interest in methodological issues, from a clearly pedagogical perspective, which somehow underplayed the metaphysical aspects of the subject.

A similar attitude can be observed in the "Platonic" sections of his course on *Politics* (now in BAM B8 inf.). I am here referring to Ferrari's lectures on the community of women, a Platonic doctrine heavily criticized by Aristotle (1260b25 ff.), and which was often discussed in university settings, as seen in Chapter I[56]. It is fascinating that Ferrari coped with the issue mostly "by proxy," by presenting the Platonic doctrines as espoused in Bessarion's *In calumniatorem Platonis*[57]. The work, published for the first time in 1469, and subsequently reprinted by Manutius in 1503 and 1516, had a solid reputation in the Aristotelian

---

Ferrari owned a Greek manuscript containing the *Eudemian Ethics* (BAM, E40 sup.). The Aristotelian paternity of the *Eud. Eth.* is not disputed today, though the attitude of Aristotle toward Plato in the text is. See, e.g., L. JOST, "The *Eudemian Ethics* and Its Controversial Relationship to the *Nicomachean Ethics*", in R. POLONSKY (ed.), *The Cambridge Companion to Aristotle's* Nicomachean Ethics, Cambridge, Cambridge University Press, 2014, pp. 410-427.

56 On this issue and its discussion in the fifteenth century see also J. HANKINS, *Plato in the Italian Renaissance*, 2 vols, Leiden, Brill, 1991, *passim*.

57 Ferrari also used the *In calumniatorem Platonis* in his lectures on *Ethics*, e.g., with reference to the rendition of the Greek term *tagaton* (BAM, D382 inf., f. 10v: *In calumniatorem*, III.19, ed. MOHLER), and the debate on the deliberation of nature (BAM, D382 inf, f. 99v: *In calumniatorem* VI). In a different manuscript (BAM, D381 inf., f. 93r), possibly related to a different course on the *Politics*, Ferrari briefly discussed the issue of the community of women and attacked Donato Acciaiuoli's exegesis (Ferrari could have read it in D. ACCIAIUOLI, *In Aristotelis libros octo Politicorum commentarii*, Venice, apud Vincentium Valgrisium, 1566), by claiming that the Florentine did not accurately read the *Republic* when contending that Plato spoke metaphorically ("ipsum non recte legisse quae scribuntur ab Platone").

milieu, for advancing an interpretation *in puris naturalibus* of the Philosopher[58]. In his lectures Ferrari focused on the exegetical keys Bessarion suggested for reading Plato's *Republic*. In Ferrari's opinion, Bessarion did not faithfully report Plato's position and did not succeed in confuting the arguments presented by Aristotle against the communion of women. Yet Bessarion also tried to minimize the conflict between Plato and Aristotle, by claiming that they ultimately agreed on the issue of the unity of the state, "sed alter intensius..., alter remissius"[59]. Ferrari conceded this much, but objected that this did not necessarily make Plato better than Aristotle. Bessarion, however, accounted for the different intensities with which Plato and Aristotle presented their doctrines and argued, based on Simplicius, that the *physicus* Aristotle employed an easier way of speaking, "sensui nostro propinquior", while Plato instead appealed to the nobler part of man, the intellect[60]. Ferrari reacted by quoting *On the Soul* and *Posterior Analytics*, endorsing the superiority of sense. We find the same fondness for Aristotle's approach in another *reportatio* of Ferrari's on the first two books of the *Politics*, where he rejected the idea that Plato could be seen as a natural philosopher:

> Non est mirandum quod Aristoteles tam diligenter vitae species ac differentias sit persecutus. Nam ex his species etiam rerum publicarum diversas investigabit; ex diversis enim vitae generibus diversi populi fiunt, ex diversis populis diversae civitates, ex diversis civitatibus diversae item existunt res publicae, quod Plato non vidit, ut qui rerum naturalium non ita peritus fuerit [...][61].

A call for an "empirical and sectorial instruction" was essential in Ferrari's methodological writings like *De disciplina encyclio* and *De sermonibus exotericis*, which were closely connected to his teaching experience at the Scuole Cannobiane[62]. The dialogue with Plato allowed Ferrari to define and highlight the

---

58 E. DEL SOLDATO, "Bessarion as an Aristotelian, Bessarion among the Aristotelians", in S. MARIEV (ed.), *Editing, Translating and Interpreting Bessarion's Literary Heritage*, Berlin, De Gruyter, 2020, pp. 93-109. The precise references in Ferrari's lectures made clear that he was in possession of an Aldine edition: see, e.g., BAM, B8 inf., f. 110v, with a reference to "charta 63" for the second chapter of the fourth book of the *In calumniatorem Platonis*.

59 BAM, B8 inf., f. 118v.

60 Ferrari was not particularly fond of Simplicius, whom he criticized not only in these lectures (see appendix I) but also in other works. See, e.g., the *Quaestio de scientiae naturalis utilitate et de generatione virtutum moralium* in BAM, C14 suss..

61 BAM, D381 inf., f. 54r. For another instance in which Ferrari reused the *topos* Plato *divinus*/Aristotle *physicus*, see his lectures *On the Soul*, held in Pavia in 1552 (BAM, A48 inf., f. 202r and f. 396r).

62 O. FERRARI, *De disciplina encyclio*, Venice, apud Paulum Manutium, 1560, is quoted, e.g., in the margins of BAM, B8 inf., f. 26v; Ferrari's *De sermonibus exotericis* was first printed in Venice (apud Aldum) in 1575 (Ferrari discussed the meaning of the term "exotericus" in his lectures on the *Ethics*, see BAM, D381 inf., f. 70v). On all these writings by Ferrari see D. FACCA,

epistemological merits of Aristotelian philosophy, from a practical perspective, which was central to the mission of the Scuole.

To further show Bessarion's vulnerabilities, Ferrari concluded the lecture on the community of women by invoking Theodore Gaza who, though a great friend of the cardinal, occasionally disagreed with him, including on this topic. The mention of Gaza clearly displays Ferrari's bibliophilia and passion for rare sources, by making reference to Gaza's *Adversus Plethonem de substantia*, a work he personally possessed in manuscript[63]. Yet, despite this final thrust, Ferrari acknowledged that Bessarion was the only competent sparring partner on the issue and claimed that the arguments of other Latin philosophers on Plato were pointless to discuss. Though Ferrari did not identify these Latin philosophers, they may have included Donato Acciaiuoli (see n. 57) and even a Platonist like Marsilio Ficino — whom he openly attacked in other passages[64].

Ferrari brought his philological skills to the Scuole Cannobiane and challenged his students, not only by relying on rare works and interpreters but also, it seems, by using the original Greek text in his lectures[65]. His use of Plato and Platonic doctrines was largely instrumental in emphasizing Aristotle's merits and fully appreciating important sections of the Aristotelian corpus. But this did not lack interest because of the coherent pedagogical program in which he situated it.

While Plato occupied a more visible role in other Milanese institutions, such as paradoxically — in the case of Paolo Beni — the Jesuit College, the Scuole Cannobiane displayed a strong Aristotelian identity since their inception[66]. Yet Ferrari proved that expertise in Plato was a crucial, if not obvious, qualification for teaching Aristotle.

Teaching Federico: Flaminio Papazzoni

Thus far, we have focused on the presence of Plato in public teaching, in Pavia and Milan. The case of Flaminio Papazzoni (d. 1614) instead offers invaluable insight into the presence of Platonic doctrines within a private teaching setting. Papazzoni was the philosophy tutor of a very special student, the future cardinal

---

Early Modern Aristotelianism and the Making of Philosophical Disciplines, Bloomsbury, London, 2020, pp. 13-25 (the quotation at p. 18).

[63] I have been able to identify the manuscript owned by Ferrari in the Ambrosiana collection: it is BAM, F88 sup.. Ferrari also quotes the work in his lectures on *Ethics*, BAM, D383 inf., f. 68r.

[64] See, e.g., BAM, D383 inf., f. 310v.

[65] See CICERI, *Epistolarum libri*, II, p. 231 ("Primum, omnium verba Aristotelis constabilire, graeca cum latinis conferre, adhibitis veteribus libris novos emendare; nihil denique, quod non vulgarem interpretem deceret, non facere solebat"), and 237 ("ita bene graece loquebatur, ac scribebat, ac si Athenis et natus, et enutrititus fuisset"); see also pp. 238 and 244. Ferrari often discussed textual emendations with Pietro Vettori: see, e.g., the manuscript notes of Rovida in Ferrari's exemplar of *De sermonibus* (BAM, S Q D VII 37).

[66] On Beni, see chapter III in this volume.

Federico Borromeo (1564-1631). Federico was sent to Bologna in 1579, where he studied logic under the guidance of the young Papazzoni. The following year, when Federico moved to the newly opened Collegio Borromeo in Pavia, his teacher accompanied him, and remained in the city until 1588. Through his uncle Carlo, Federico obtained a chair for Papazzoni at the University of Pavia. This arrangement did not, however, disrupt their private lessons, and Papazzoni maintained a constant connection with his former patron even after leaving Pavia[67].

Yet again, the Ambrosiana collections help to better understand the content of Papazzoni's private teaching, since they house several of his lectures for Federico. Many of these lectures focused on logic, the subject of Federico's early studies, while others dealt with metaphysics, physics, the soul, and the nature of heavens. The structure of this curriculum was centered on Aristotle, yet Papazzoni opened his *Praelectiones philosophicae* by questioning the authority of the Philosopher:

> Ego non eius cogitationis sum, ut Aristotelis amore captus Platonem damnandus putem. Sed rem ipsam spectemus: si Platonis scripta perlego, suavissimus huic inest loquendi modus, argutissima disputandi ratio, ac protervis redarguendi, ac omnia confuse tradit. Vix probabilem rationem attingit, remotis a rei natura principiis ut plurimum utitur. Naturalia ac divina per res mathematicas, quatenus sunt illis posteriores, docet. Aristoteles ex adverso arcto quodam dicendi modo usus summo ordine res pertractat, maxima inventione pollet, iuditiii gravitate praestat, solidissimisque demonstrationibus, quantum et rei natura patitur, et vis ingenii nostri suffert, veritatem indagat, ita ut quemadmodum illis prioribus gratias habendas ducimus, quod aditum philosophiae patefecerunt, sic huic quod ipsi extremamque manum imposuerit. Hoc dixi quod cum Aristotelem auditis, non oraculum propterea eum fuisse putetis, nec mirum vobis videri debet, si quandoquidem qui vere pie sancteque philosophantur, ubi Aristotelis sententiam circa res obscurissimas aperuerunt, quid verae phylosophiae principia postulent et praescribant praecipientis, ab Aristotile deficiunt. Quam vero sint horum duorum Phylosophorum sententiae inter se diversae, quam alieni modi phylosophandi qui in utrisque fuerit optime versatus facile iudicabit. Unus scire nostrum reminisci vocat, ac determinat, alter expertem esse prorsus mentem hominis omnis cogitationis existimat. Unus formas induci, alter educi putavit, loquor de materialibus. Unus nihil se ipsum movere putavit, in quo non adsit quis movens, et pars mota, alter idem simpliciter movens et motum esse posse voluit, et in aliis multis discreparunt

---

[67] A fuller reconstruction of the relationship between Papazzoni and Federico is in M. CAMEROTA, "Flaminio Papazzoni: Un aristotelico bolognese maestro di Federico Borromeo e corrispondente di Galileo", in D. A. DI LISCIA, E. KESSLER, and C. METHUEN (eds), *Method and Order in Renaissance Philosophy of Nature: The Aristotle Commentary Tradition*, Aldershot, Ashgate, 1997, pp. 271-300. On Federico as a student see also R. MAIOCCHI and A. MOIRAGHI, *L'almo Collegio Borromeo. Federico Borromeo studente e gli inizi del Collegio*, Pavia, Scuola tipografica Artigianelli, 1916.

> quae longum esset recensere, in quibus multi operam navarunt ut eos inter se conciliarent. Omisso ergo Platone, Aristotelem sequamur, non ut in eo finem studiorum nostrorum referamus, sed tanquam in viam, quia maiora suscipiamus [...][68].

Papazzoni claimed that he was not in love with Aristotle to the extent of condemning Plato, a sentence echoing Bessarion's preface to his *In calumniatorem* (I.1), in which the cardinal claimed the same about his love for Plato. Papazzoni then briefly evaluated the Platonic perspective and, though ultimately preferring Aristotle's clarity, felt the need to justify this preference[69]. Reusing a traditional *topos*, Papazzoni argued that Plato is pleasant and clever, but terribly confused. He went on to say that Plato's arguments were barely probable, his principles were remote from the natural world, and that he indefensibly used mathematics — which is *a posteriori* — to investigate natural and divine realities. Papazzoni admitted that Aristotle is not an oracle and cannot always be reconciled with Christian theology, but he praised him for having perfected the philosophy of his predecessors, including therefore that of Plato. Plato and Aristotle's philosophies were incommensurable, they differed from one another both in terms of content and style, and the wisest course — according to Papazzoni — was to set Plato aside, while embracing Aristotle at least from a methodological perspective. Papazzoni was probably influenced by the recent debates on philosophical method, in which one of his most beloved teachers, Federico Pendasio (d. 1603), supported the Aristotelian side[70]. Notwithstanding his preferences for Aristotle, Pendasio was also well versed in Platonism and discussed Plato in his commentaries and lectures, as seen in Chapter I[71]. Papazzoni followed his teacher to some degree also in this regard. The contents of Papazzoni's lessons for Federico were, in fact, more polyphonic than this introduction would lead to believe. In the lectures on the question of the soul, for example, Papazzoni dedicated entire sections to Platonic interpreters (Ficino, but also Plotinus and Proclus), especially when discussing the crucial issue of immortality[72].

---

[68] BAM, B221 suss., f. 5r-v. The complete title of the work is *Praelectiones philosophicae Flaminii Papazzonii ad Federicum comitem Borromeum*.

[69] A concept repeated in BAM, B222 suss., f. 1r, wherein Aristotle is described as the one "qui alios omnes philosophos ordine ipso ac vi demonstrationis superavit [...]".

[70] On Pendasio see F. PURNELL JR., "Iacopo Mazzoni as a Student of Philosophy at Padua", in *Quaderni per la storia dell'Università di Padova*, 7 (1974), pp. 17-26; DEL SOLDATO, *Early Modern Aristotle*, pp. 66-67.

[71] See also S. FELLINA, "Le fonti platoniche di Federico Pendasio: note sulla diffusione nel '500 degli *scholia* al *Fedro* di Ermia Alessandrino e dei commenti al *Fedone* e al *Filebo* di Olimpiodoro e Damascio", in *Noctua*, 9 (2022), pp. 188-221.

[72] BAM, B222 suss., f. 84rff.

To be sure, Borromeo, whose Platonizing tendencies have often been highlighted by scholars, enjoyed the approach of his teacher[73]. In 1588, in fact, the Bolognese ambassador in Rome Camillo Paleotti discussed the possibility of establishing a chair of Platonism in Bologna together with Federico Borromeo and his friend Agostino Valier, who at that date were both cardinals. As seen in Chapter I, Valier had lectured on Plato in Venice, so this effort was clearly part of a Platonic alliance which also lobbied — with ephemeral success — for the institution of a Platonic chair in Rome, which would be initially assigned to Francesco Patrizi (1529-1597), another of Cardinal Federico's associates[74]. Borromeo and Valier suggested to Paleotti that the Bolognese chair of Platonism be given to Papazzoni, who wanted to return to his hometown[75]. The second candidate they proposed was another protégé of theirs, Giovan Paolo Muzzoli (d. 1594)[76]; their suggestion, in case of Muzzoli's success, was that Papazzoni would inherit the *lettura* previously occupied by Muzzoli. In any case, they considered both candidates equally good for the position. Unfortunately, despite the notable support of Borromeo and Valier, and Paleotti's diplomatic recommendation, the chair was considered by the Bolognese authorities to be "more of a frill than a necessity"[77], and the plan was ultimately abandoned. Papazzoni's personal connection to Federico Borromeo was certainly instrumental in his candidacy

---

73 On Borromeo's Platonism see P. PRODI, "Borromeo, Federico", in *Dizionario Biografico degli Italiani*, 13 (1971), permanent link at https://www.treccani.it/enciclopedia/federico-borromeo_(Dizionario-Biografico) [last accessed December 13, 2021]; more on this, and on Borromeo's related Pythagorean interests, in C. MARCORA (ed.), *Catalogo dei manoscritti del card. Federico Borromeo nella biblioteca Ambrosiana*, Milan, Biblioteca Ambrosiana, 1988, p. 42.

74 Francesco Patrizi addressed several works of his to Federico, including *De l'ordine de' libri di Platone* and *De numerorum mysteriis*. Upon Patrizi's death, Borromeo bought Patrizi's extant library. On the Roman chair see the bibliography in n. 89 below.

75 On the Bolognese chair of Platonism see E. COSTA, *Ulisse Aldrovandi e lo Studio bolognese nella seconda metà del secolo XVI*, Bologna, Stabilimento Poligrafico Emiliano, 1907, p. 90; P. O. KRISTELLER, "The European Significance of Florentine Platonism", in *Id., Studies in Renaissance Thought and Letters III*, Rome, Edizioni di Storia e Letteratura, 1993, pp. 49-68: 55. On Papazzoni's nomination, see a letter written by Camillo Paleotti (June 11, 1588), ASB, Assunteria di Studio, b. 79, Lettere di diversi all'Assunteria, 1575-1691, np. The letter is published in appendix to this chapter. P. F. GRENDLER, *The Universities of the Italian Renaissance*, Baltimore and London, Johns Hopkins University Press, 2001, p. 307, makes mention of the letter. On Papazzoni's teaching in Bologna, see D. A. LINES, "Natural Philosophy in Renaissance Italy: The University of Bologna and the Beginnings of Specialization", in *Early Science and Medicine*, 6 (2001), pp. 267-323: 317; CAMEROTA, "Flaminio Papazzoni", pp. 284-285.

76 Hints of Muzzoli's interest for Plato can be found in his only printed works, the orations he delivered when joining and then leaving the *Studium Ticinense*. See G. P. MUZZOLI, *Sermo habitus in ingressu suarum scholarum*, Pavia, apud haeredes Hieronymi Bartoli, 1593; *Id., Sermo habitus in egressu scholarum*, Pavia, apud haeredes Hieronymi Bartoli, 1594. On Muzzoli in Bologna see also LINES, "Natural Philosophy in Renaissance Italy", p. 316.

77 COSTA, *Ulisse Aldrovandi e lo Studio bolognese*, p. 90, and GRENDLER, *The Universities of the Italian Renaissance*, p. 307.

for the Bolognese chair of Platonism, and the *magister* managed nonetheless to obtain a position at his *alma mater* the following year, in 1589, teaching "the standard Aristotelian texts"[78]. It should not be surprising, however, that someone "riputato gran Peripatetico", as Papazzoni would be defined a few years later, was considered for the Platonic position[79]. A commitment to Platonic philosophy, like those exhibited by contemporaries including de' Vieri in Pisa and Patrizi in Ferrara and Rome, was not a requirement for being considered for a chair of Platonism[80]. Papazzoni, who included Plato in his lectures not out of personal engagement with his method and doctrines, but in order to properly explain and navigate the *corpus Aristotelicum*, had given the young Borromeo enough proof of being perfectly suited to hold the chair of Platonism.

The Affidati and Leone Maurizi: An Epilogue

In Pavia there was no shortage of *Accademie*, and each had its own identity. While, as we have seen, the Accademia Rovidiana was resolutely Aristotelian, the Accademia degli Affidati had a much more varied agenda[81]. *In die festivo* the Affidati held public lectures (in Italian) on Hebrew language, cosmography and astronomy, military art, agriculture, and many other subjects. Notably, they lectured on Aristotle's works (namely *Poetics, Rhetoric, Ethics,* and *Politics*), but also on Plato's *Symposium, Timaeus,* and *Republic*[82]. The most noteworthy of the Platonic works discussed by the Affidati was certainly the *Timaeus* which, as we know, played an important role in medieval and Renaissance teaching contexts. The *Symposium* offered a discussion on love otherwise absent in Aristotelian works and was often debated within academies, while the *Republic* could be engaged in direct conversation with Aristotle's *Politics* (as seen in the case of Ferrari). But by selecting the *Timaeus*, the Affidati were somehow endorsing Plato as a natural philosopher, following a trend we already saw in Chapter I of this volume, regardless of the open rejection of his treatment of the subject expressed by *magistri* like Vimercato and Papazzoni. More importantly, it is possible that, by reading the *Timaeus*, the Affidati were trying to fill a gap they perceived in the curriculum of the *Studium* in Pavia, an institution with which the Accademia was

---

78 GRENDLER, *The Universities of the Italian Renaissance*, p. 307.
79 Letter of Giovanni Ciampoli to Galileo, September 1, 1621, in *Le opere di Galileo Galilei. Edizione Nazionale*, ed. A. FAVARO, 20 vols, Florence, Barbera, 1901, XI, p. 390.
80 DEL SOLDATO, *Early Modern Aristotle*, pp. 68-76.
81 On the Affidati see, for instance, P. PISSAVINO, "Politica e accademie nella Lombardia spagnola", in D. S. CHAMBERS and F. QUIVIGER (eds), *Italian Academies of the Sixteenth Century*, London, Warburg Institute, 1995, pp. 91-103; Id., "Università e Accademie", in D. MANTOVANI (ed.), *Almum Studium Papiense I.2*, Pavia, Cisalpino, 2013, pp. 1223-1258.
82 S. BREVENTANO, *Istoria della antichità, nobiltà, et delle cose notabili della città di Pavia*, Pavia, appresso Hieronimo Bartholi, 1570, f. 13r.

more than closely connected. Many Affidati were in fact professors at the *Studium*, including Girolamo Cardano — who enjoyed teaching relief because of his participation in the life of the Academy —, but also his friend and colleague Giovan Pietro Albuzio (1507-1583)[83]. Albuzio, a physician, was the one who lectured on the *Symposium* at the Affidati academy. And one can reasonably assume that, because of his expertise, Albuzio's lectures were very different from those offered on the same topic by Agrippa at the beginning of the century, which were more theologically inclined. It is also conceivable that precisely an association between medicine and Platonism played a role in the Affidati's interest in the *Timaeus*. It was because of that dialogue, which was so central in Galen's discussion of philosophy, that some Paduan professors had heralded the advantages of the Platonic method[84]. Platonizing tendencies were also evident among other members of the Accademia, who were active within the University, including the student Alessandro Farra (d. *post* 1577), and the jurist Sforza Alemanni (d. 1639)[85]. It is therefore unsurprising that the individual called to the teaching post of Platonism *in die festivo* at the University of Pavia was himself a member of the Academy. This feast-day teaching was offered, between 1606 and 1611, by Leone Maurizi from Arezzo, who also taught at Pavia "traditional" Aristotelian courses (1601-1614). We know very little about Maurizi's lectures on Plato, but the fact that he had been a student of Francesco de' Vieri in Pisa, where he also taught and had exchanges with Jacopo Mazzoni, is certainly significant[86]. The short life of the Platonic chair in Pavia is not surprising given the equally ephemeral experiences in Ferrara and Rome[87]. And, after all, the Pavian teaching of Platonism blossomed late when compared to them. At that point — on the one hand — lectures on the Aristotelian corpus typically included as a didactic practice sections on Platonic

---

[83] On Albuzio, see G. M. MAZZUCCHELLI, *Gli scrittori d'Italia*, Brescia, presso a Giambattista Bossini, 1753, I.1, p. 350. On Cardano and the Affidati see PISSAVINO, "Università e Accademie", p. 1241. Andrea Camuzio was also a member of the Affidati (see again PISSAVINO, "Università e Accademie", p. 1239).

[84] See M. VANHAELEN, "What Is the Best Method to Study Philosophy? Sebastiano Erizzo and the 'Revival' of Plato in Sixteenth-Century Venice", in *Italian Studies*, 71 (2016), pp. 311-334.

[85] See P. PISSAVINO, "Il capitano neoplatonico", in M. RIZZO and G. MAZZOCCHI (eds), *La espada y la pluma. Il mondo militare nella Lombardia spagnola cinquecentesca*, Baroni, Viareggio, 2000, pp. 131-149.

[86] Maurizi was a doctor in philosophy and medicine. He obtained a position as teacher of logic in Pisa in 1586, upon the recommendation of Eleonora Habsburg-Gonzaga, sister-in-law of Francesco de' Medici (see ASF, Mediceo del Principato 269, f. 163r). In 1593 he quarreled with a colleague, Giulio Libri, and left Pisa in 1595 (see J. DAVIES, *Culture and Power. Tuscany and Its Universities 1537-1609*, Leiden, Brill, 2009, p. 172). He moved to Genoa (see PISSAVINO, "Il capitano neoplatonico", p. 143), and then taught in Perugia for a very generous salary until 1601 (O. SCALVANTI, *Inventario-regesto dell'Archivio Universitario di Perugia*, Perugia, Unione Tipográfica Cooperativa, p. 177).

[87] See, on this, the introduction and n. 89 below.

doctrines, in order to better understand Aristotle's texts[88]; on the other, in the final decades of the sixteenth century, Plato had started to be looked upon with suspicion by ecclesiastical authorities, especially because of the opposition of the Jesuits who preferred the patent impiety of Aristotle to the slippery piety of Plato. That, they perceived as a potential source of heresy (indeed, the misadventures of Patrizi and then the short life of the Roman chair of Platonism were largely a consequence of the Jesuit's anti-Platonic stance)[89].

**

This review of Platonic experiences in the closely connected contexts of Pavia and Milan can be seen as a collection of episodes and isolated experiments. Nevertheless, one can at the same time discern clear patterns and tendencies that should not be overlooked. Whereas during the first four decades of the sixteenth century, the engagement with Plato's philosophy was normally intertwined with the discussion of theological issues — as the cases of Agrippa, Musso and Camuzio seem to highlight — in subsequent years an exegetical and pedagogical approach prevailed, as the examples of Vimercato, and then of Ferrari and Papazzoni clearly attest. These latter authors were not Platonists, and were even highly critical of Plato, especially as a natural philosopher. However, they were aware that they had to engage with Plato and his works in order to grasp a better understanding of the *corpus Aristotelicum*, in which the Platonic doctrines were so often discussed. Even if in the role of sparring partner, Plato became for this reason a staple of their Aristotelian teaching. An exception could be the curriculum offered by the Affidati, which seemed instead more favorably oriented in the direction of Platonic natural philosophy, and possibly influenced the content of Maurizi's teaching at the *Studium*.

---

88 Even in "Aristotelian strongholds" like Padua. See the remarkable praise of Cesare Cremonini in A. PORTENARI, *Della felicità di Padova*, Padua, per Pietro Paolo Tozzi, 1623, p. 234: "Questo hoggidì é il più famoso Filosofo di Europa, eruditissimo non meno nella dottrina Platonica che nella Aristotelica [...]". On later attempts to formalize the presence of Plato in the University curriculum see E. DEL SOLDATO, "Between Past and Present: Paganino Gaudenzi (1595-1649) and the *comparatio* Tradition", in A. CORRIAS and E. DEL SOLDATO (eds), *Harmony and Contrast. Plato and Aristotle in the Early Modern Period*, Oxford, Oxford University Press, 2022, pp. 172-188.
89 See A. ROTONDÒ, "Cultura umanistica e difficoltà di censori: Censura ecclesiastica e discussioni cinquecentesche sul platonismo", in J. GUIDI (ed.), *Le pouvoir et la plume: Incitation, contrôle et répression dans l'Italie du XVI*ᵉ *siècle*, Paris, Université de la Sorbonne Nouvelle, 1982, pp. 15-50; M. MUCCILLO, "Il platonismo all'Università di Roma: Francesco Patrizi", in P. CHERUBINI (ed.), *Roma e lo Studium Urbis: Spazio urbano e cultura dal quattro al seicento*, Rome, Ministero per i beni culturali e ambientali, 1992, pp. 200-236; A. E. BALDINI, "Aristotelismo e platonismo nelle dispute romane sulla ragion di stato di fine cinquecento", in *Id.* (ed.), *Aristotelismo politico e ragion di stato. Atti del convegno internazionale di Torino, 11-13 febbraio 1993*, Florence, Olschki, 1995, pp. 201-226; DEL SOLDATO, *Early Modern Aristotle*, pp. 47-48, 62.

Benefitting from the mobility and receptivity to new suggestions of its *magistri* and patrons, Pavia offers a fascinating case study in the history of Plato in the University, which shows the varied ways and perspectives by which "Aristotelians" could import Plato in their teaching, both in public and private settings, both in universities and academies. The Platonic chair, albeit short-lived, was mostly the proof of an engagement with Plato that over a century took disparate and even divergent forms.

Appendix

I.

Biblioteca Ambrosiana, Milan, ms. *B8 inf.*, f. 113v-120r

I offer here a diplomatic transcription of Ferrari's lecture on *Politics* 1262b22 ff. I have limited my interventions to standardizing the punctuation and the italicization of works' titles.

/113v/ Lectio Xxxvi

Proposuimus in superiore lectione nos velle ea diligenter perpendere, quae a Platonicis adversus Aristotelis reprehensionem dicebantur, ut diligentius quae de communi mulierum usu ab utroque dicebantur percipiantur. Itaque cum primo occurrat doctissimi et eruditissimi Bessarionis cardinalis defensio, eam primo examinemus. Unde vero est exorta Bessarionis defensio? Ex eo sane maledicentissimo Trapezuntii libro, quem contra Platonem scripsit, quo in loco reprehendit Platonem, qui communem mulierum usum in sua Republica esse voluisset. Bessarion igitur cum ad eum locum accessisset multa verba facit de Platonis opinione, eumque conatur tueri, et excusare. Nos tripartito eius longam orationem dividemus, atque de singulis partibus ex Aristotelis verba faciemus. Trapezuntius /114r/ reprehendebat Platonem hac ratione, "nam si communes erunt mulieres et filii, negotia, inquit, publica necesse esse negligantur, caritas et amor extinguatur, tollatur officium quod a filiis parentibus debetur"[90]. Hoc argumentum ex Aristotele sumptum ait Bessarion. Ego arbitror ex his Aristotelis verbis sumpsisse, δύο γάρ ἐστιν ἃ μάλιστα ποιεῖ κήδεσθαι τοὺς ἀνθρώπους καὶ φιλεῖν, τό τε ἴδιον καὶ τὸ ἀγαπητόν[91]. Antequam igitur Platonem a Trapezuntii argumento defendat, cum iam concesserit ex Aristotele esse sumptum, reperit Platonis sententiam causamque, cur hanc civitatis unionem induxerit. Quoniam inquit inter homines constat nihil, vel melius in Republica esse, quam quod homines coniungit et unit, nihilque peius quam quod distrahit, et animo vario ac diversa voluntate multiplicat, alterum enim meum, et non meum exitiosum illud in Republica peculiare, summamque discordiam civium facit, alterum commune omnium commodum, et summam concordiam ponit. Hanc autem coniunctionem et quasi unionem effici non posse Plato existimabat, nisi una cum ceteris rebus uxores etiam, et filii sint communes. Idcirco rem uxoriam communem esse voluit, putavitque ita fore ut cives omnes ex eiusdem rebus voluptatem, moeroremque perciperent. Idemque omnium esset vel proprium, vel alienum, unoque animo omnes omnia agerent, et /114v/ cogitarent, his deinde adiungit, hoc quidem esse difficile admodum, et laboriosum esse, tamen fieri posse ait modo plures illi viri ita eruditione, virtuteque instituti essent, ut omnes quasi unus eadem bona et vellent, et exercerent, virtutis enim talis est vis, ut et si non sine difficultate efficere tamen possit, ut plures homines idem sentiant, idem volint, ita denique vivant,

---

90 BESSARION, *In calumniatorem Platonis*, IV.3.iii (ed. MOHLER).
91 ARISTOTLE, *Pol.* 1262b22-24.

ut qui plures sint, quasi unus secum vivere consentiens, constans, placidus videatur[92]. Facta hac sententiae Platonis expositione, respondet argumento Trapezuntii, docetque ex hac unione non negligi negotia publica, non tolli officium et charitatem, nam cum cives ita sint virtute, doctrina, litteris educati, instituti et eruditi, officium vero virtutis sit coniungere, fiet ut tamquam unus homo sibi constans idem vellent cives, idem nollent, iisdem rebus gauderent, iisdem moererent; quo constituto, quid est quod vereamur negotia publica negligi, quando plures cives quasi unus rem suam, hoc est, communem curent et tueantur[93]? Ad Aristotelis vero argumenta inquit levia et vana (quod pace Aristotelis inquit dictum sit) ac nihil contra Platonis rationes momenti habere, addit praeterea quaedam quae ad historiam pertinent, docetque nulla alia de causa plurimas /115r/ republicae eversas fuisse, nisi quod cives relicta publicarum rerum cura, propriis negotiis nimium indulserint, atque id exemplo Lacedemoniorum, quorum etiam meminit Xenophon, et Plutarchus in vita Lycurgi, docet etiam exemplo M. Catonis Censorii, cuius etiam mentionem facit idem Plutarchus in eius vita, et aliorum praeterea multorum exemplo[94]. Ad extremum tandem quoddam addit, non temere silentio praetermittendum. Dicit enim se videre causam cur a Platone descenserit Aristoteles, neque valde differre hos philosophos sibi videri, nam uterque unire civitatem vult, et unam esse. Hoc solum differunt, quod Plato intensius vult unam esse, Aristoteles vero remissius. Verum quo minus fit una, eo plura incommoda evenire necesse est. Principium namque et causa commodi unio est, et civium communitas, incommodi vero, divisio et proprietas, quod volebat Aristoteles atque huius differentiae causam esse dicit, quod in disciplinis tradendis Aristoteles et Plato differant. Aristoteles enim scribit principia sumere, quae nostro sensui propinquiora sunt, ut physicum decet, cuius personam gerit Aristoteles. Plato vero communem respicit partem enim hominis quae sensu nobilior est, mentem videlicet et intelligentiam sequitur, ob idque difficiliora semper aggreditur, sed quae mente et intelligentiae magis conveniant. / 115v/ Itaque Aristotelis sententia sensui, Platonis intelligentiae propinquior est[95]. Haec sunt igitur quae a Bessarione in Trapezuntium et Aristotelem pro Platone suo dicuntur. Eius opinionem et responsionem in tres partes dividimus, ut commodius de singula quaque parte quid nobis videatur verba faciamus. Prima pars erit de Platonis sententia. Altera erit solutio argumenti Aristotelis a Trapezuntio allati; altera erit de differentia principiorum in tradendis disciplinis inter Aristotelem et Platonem. Primum quod mihi videtur observandum est hoc, quod non mihi videtur Platonis sententiam satis diligenter referre. Dicit enim quoniam constat inter omnes nihil melius in republica esse, quam quod homines coniungit et unit, hoc recte adiecit. At quod sequitur, scilicet, quod maxime unit civitatem facit commune summum commodum, et summam concordiam parit, non recte, neque ita loquitur Plato, sed civitatem usque eo esse unam, ut proxime accedat ad naturam unius hominis, ut quemadmodum in uno homine eadem est voluptas, et idem dolor; ita et in civitate communis sit voluptas, communis dolor, iisdem rebus omnes gaudeant, iisdem etiam laetentur statuamus, igitur inquit Plato legem, quae communes coniungat voluptates,

---

92 Bessarion, *In calumniatorem Platonis*, IV.3.ii (ed. Mohler).
93 Bessarion, *In calumniatorem Platonis*, IV.3.iii (ed. Mohler).
94 Bessarion, *In calumniatorem Platonis*, IV.3.xiii (ed. Mohler).
95 Bessarion, *In calumniatorem Platonis*, IV.3.iv (ed. Mohler).

communes faciat dolores, /116r/ ita ut si filius aliquis bene rem gesserit, omnes laetentur, et gaudio efferantur. Sin contra male rem gesserit, omnes etiam doleant, et cruciantur, quae res efficiet ut omnes sint amici, sint concordes, nullae oriantur seditiones, nulla denique fiant incommoda civitati[96]. Haec Platonis sententia est satis probabilis, nam id sensu videmus, qui enim iidem rebus laetantur, et dolent, simul gaudeant re bene gesta, cruciantur simul re male gesta amicos esse necesse est, et inter se amari. At illud rogandum Bessarionem censerem, cum dicit nihil melius esse reipublicae et civitati, quam illud quod unam efficit civitatem, quo modo intellegat illud unam. Si dicit unam numero, sequuntur ea incommoda, quae Aristoteles contra Platonem adduxerat, ut ex civitate domum, ex domo unus homo efficiatur, atque ea erunt eiusmodi commoda ex hac unione civitati, ut non modo concordiam gignet in civitate, et amicitiam[97]; sed ut propriam quidem civitatis naturam retineat, nam civitas est multitudo quaedam secundum naturam, ut docet Aristoteles in 3 *Politicorum*, et in primo capitolo huius secundi libri satis copiose docuimus[98]. Si dicit unam specie, meminerit etiam ea, quae supra Aristoteles contra Platonem dicit, nam fit ex civitate [†], civitas enim /116v/ est multitudo hominum, quae multitudo specie differat[99]. Quare accusandus est Bessarion, qui non prius responderit obiectis Aristotelis in Platonem, priusquam solveret argumentum Trapezuntii, itaque ego quoque dicere possum (quod pace illius sit dictum) eius rationes nihil infirmare, nec diluere Aristotelis argumenta. Sed levia et frigida admodum esse, quod vero inquit ex illa unione fieri summam in civitate concordiam, ego certe non negarim illam fieri. Sed si fiat, debilem, et admodum examinatam fieri dicerem, nam nati communes non sunt aeque amabiles sicuti proprii, parentes communes non ita amantur et coluntur, ac si essent proprii nesciunt essent suos. Sic etiam de aliis rebus dicimus, ut docuit Aristoteles in superiore lectione, debuit igitur prius respondere his rationibus, nihil enim magis gignit curam et diligentiam in rebus, inquit Aristoteles, quam proprium, et affectio[100]. Quod vero dicit nihil peius esse in civitate quam id quod distrahit, et vano animo ac diversa voluntate multiplicat, ingenerat enim illud meum, et non meum, exitiosum peculiare in Rempublicam sic enim appellat, summamque discordiam facit. Vellem nunc respondere ad argumentum Aristotelis, qui velit ob id quod res propria sint, in civitate concordiam generari, quod quidem sensu ipso /117r/ videmus; lites enim maxime exoriuntur ob hanc causam, quod cives propriis rebus non contenti sunt, sed dum alienos affectant et appetunt, tunc iurgia exoriuntur, et lites fiunt. Praeterea vult omnes simul dicere meum, et non meum. An non videt quae scripsit Aristoteles in ch. 106[101]? Docuit enim omne duplex esse et aequivocum, vel enim dicitur ut unusquisque, vel non ut unusquisque, docuitque alterum posse quidem, sed non esse conducibile. Debuit igitur huic etiam respondere. Docui igitur Bessarionem non apposite retulisse Platonis sententiam. Docui etiam non respondisse Aristotelis argumentis, quae eius et Platonis sui rationes confutabant. Quod autem dicit et si difficile sit hanc unionem

---

96 PLATO, *Resp.* 462a.
97 ARISTOTLE, *Pol.* 1261a17-25.
98 ARISTOTLE, *Pol.* 1274b39-40; 1261a12 ff..
99 ARISTOTLE, *Pol.* 1261a23-30.
100 ARISTOTLE, *Pol.* 1261b33-40.
101 ARISTOTLE, *Pol.* 1261b27-33.

efficere, tamen posse fieri ut communes fiant mulieres, et liberi modo plures illi viri virtutibus praediti sint, et virtus accedat quae efficiat ut idem velint, idem nolint, idem sentiant. Vult ut mihi igitur propter virtutem hanc unionem fieri, at ego dico Aristotelis argumenta non contra virtutes esse facta, sed contra legem, quae causa erat ipsius unionis, quapropter cum nihil dicat ad ea quae dicit Aristoteles in legem, sed dicat virtutem esse unionis huius causam, praemittit firma argumenta /117v/ quae omnia contra legem Platonis, non contra virtutem fecit. Praeterea, si virtus est causa coniunctionis, frustra tulit legem, quae eorum coniungeret res, uxores et liberos. Debuerat enim legem solum ferre qua cogerentur cives assequi ipsam virtutem, qua assecuta eos coniungeret, videtis igitur quam perbelle confutet Aristotelis argumenta, itaque nos etiam peripatetici vere dicere possumus eius argumenta nihil habere momenti in Aristotelis rationes, quemadmodum ipse dicebat de Aristotelis argumentis quod quidem a Bessarione dici tam aperte non potuit. Quod vero affirmat virtutem esse causam huius coniunctionis, ita ut cives si optime instituti sint, et virtutibus ornati, idem velint, idem nolint, idem cogitent, et idem sentiant, hoc falsum est, et fieri nequit. Enimvero ut etiam superius vidimus Plato vult ex multis partibus civitatem constare, ex custodibus qui principes erunt civitatis, ex his qui magistratus gerunt, ex iuvenibus qui sunt auxilio civitati, ex agricolis, ex opificibus, et aliis, ii omnes plurimi sunt, et specie diversi, cum sint diversi specie, eorum etiam virtutes specie different, alia igitur erit imperantium, alia parentium, alia virtus iuvenum, alia agricolarum, et opificum, quod quidem verum esse docuit /118r/ Aristoteles in primo *Politicorum* in extremo, dixit enim imperantium et dominorum virtutes perfectas esse debere tam intellectuales, quam morales, hosque providendi facultatem habere, et consultandi, servos autem hac facultate carere dixit, sed tantummodo eam partem quae caret ratione, obtemperat tamen rationi, habere eos aperte docuit[102]; opifices vero tales et tantas virtutes habere decet, ne propter intemperantiam defficiant ab operibus, et sic de aliis, cum igitur virtutes horum sint diversae, et specie differentes, fieri potest ut idem velint, idem nolint, idem sentiant, efficiet ne ille ut eaedem sint cogitationes servi et domini? Alter enim ut imperet, alter serviat, at parere et imperare sunt admodum diversae operationes, neque efficiet unquam ut idem velint, idem nolint. Ambo enim volunt imperare, neque ambo volunt parere imperio, aliter servus, aliter dominus esse non poterit, sic etiam de aliis dicere licet, accedant enim quantaecumque virtutes opifici possunt, et item agricolae non efficiet ut idem velint, idem nolint, idem sentiant. Iuvenes etiam sint ea summa virtute praediti, qua possunt, senes quoque ea virtute, qua non sit maior, nunquam efficiet, ut idem velint, nolint, sentiant, et cogitent iuvenes et senes, quod si alter alteri ita contrarius est, /118v/ quanto erunt contrarii si omnes coniungantur? Fieri ne unquam ulla ratione poterit ut idem velint, nolint, sentiant? Ut ipse loquitur, probavimus igitur virtutes non efficere ut idem velint et nolint, neque esse causas coniunctionis. Ad illud vero quod dicit, utrumque Aristotelem videlicet et Platonem velle civitatem unam esse, sed alter intensius unam, alter remissius, hoc verum est. Quod vero ait, quo minus sit una eo plura evenire incommoda, et difficultates, cum principium et causa commodi sit, immo hoc falsum est, immo tali eveniunt civitati commoda ex hac unione, ut propriam ipsius amittat

---

102 ARISTOTLE, *Pol.* 1259b32-1260a20.

naturam civitatis, ut docebit Aristoteles in ch. 109, his verbis: αἴτιον δὲ τῷ Σωκράτει τῆς παρακρούσεως χρὴ νομίζειν τὴν ὑπόθεσιν οὐκ οὖσαν ὀρθήν. δεῖ μὲν γὰρ εἶναί πως μίαν καὶ τὴν οἰκίαν καὶ τὴν πόλιν, ἀλλ' οὐ πάντως. ἔστι μὲν γὰρ ὡς οὐκ ἔσται προϊοῦσα πόλις[103]. Quae enim civitas est maxime una, ea est propinquior interitui. Quae est propinquior interitui, illa patitur maiores difficultates et incommoda, quare videmus minime verum esse, ut quae minus sit una, ea maiora incommoda sentiat. Venio nunc ad ipsa principia. Dixit hanc difficultatem ideo evenire, quod Aristoteles in tradendis disciplinis utitur /119r/ principiis sensu propinquioribus, ut phisici officium est. Plato vero utitur principiis quae intellectui propinquiora sunt. Scio unde hanc opinionem sumpserit, sumpsit enim ex proemio Simplicii in Aristotelis *Categorias*, dicit enim in eo loco hanc esse differentiam Arisotelis et Platonis, quod Aristoteles utitur principiis sensu propinquioribus, Plato intellectu. Sed argumenta Aristotelis ab his principiis ducta habere vim cogendi, et esse firmiora[104]. Sed tamen in hac se parum sibi constans videtur Simplicius, enimvero quod argumenta dixit Aristotelis eo loco esse firmiora, et habere vim cogendi, aliter dicit in prohemio *Physicorum*, scilicet infirma esse et minimam vim habere[105]. Hoc idem dicit in 3 *Physicorum*, ch. 103[106], sed relictis huiusmodi expositoribus, ego video Aristotelem modo uti principiis sensui propinquioribus, modo naturae, quod apposite et aperte docet Alexander in expositione primae figurae in primo *Priorum*, in eo enim libro Aristoteles sic describit primam figuram, quando igitur tres, ita inter se, se habuerint termini, ut ultimus in toto medio sit, et medius in toto primo vel sit, vel non sit, extremorum esse rationem perfectam necesse est, quod exponens Alexander inquit: principium vero doctrinae de ratiocinationibus modo /119v/ ab eo quod est in toto, modo ab eo quod est de omni dicitur sumi[107]. Propterea, quod utrumque ex ipsis principium et primum est, in toto esse quantum ad nos spectat primum et principium est, nobis enim quae in toto sunt et subiiciuntur, sunt notiora. De omni vero e contra cum communius sit, et generalius natura primum est, propterea in primo *Posteriorum analyticorum* dividit principia demonstrationis in principia notiora nobis, et secundum naturam, tanquam sit utrisque usurus, non autem altero solum, ut dicit Bessarion, et Simplicius, et in secundo *Posteriorum analyticorum*, in extremo, ubi universe de principiis agit, docet nobis a sensu omnia ingenerari: [*there is a space left for a quotation which has not been inserted*][108]. Quod docet etiam in 3 *de Anima*, quo in loco sunt referenda ea quae dicit Simplicius, itaque de principiis dicimus Aristotelem uti tam principiis nobis notioribus, quam naturae notioribus[109]. Unum est quod extremo dicam: scitis Theodorum Gazam et Bessarion Cardinalem amicissimos fuisse, ut ipsi etiam in suis scriptis saepius ostendunt. Mirum est tamen quod aliquando inter se se dissentiunt, et discrepant. Bessarion /120r/ hoc in loco in capitulo 3, libro 4,

---

103 ARISTOTLE, *Pol.* 1263b 30-32.
104 SIMPLICIUS, *In Aristotelis Categorias*, 8, 7, 30-32 (ed. KALBFLEISCH).
105 SIMPLICIUS, *In Aristotelis Physicorum libros*, 1, prooemium (ed. DIELS).
106 SIMPLICIUS, *In Aristotelis Physicorum libros*, 3, 3 (ed. DIELS).
107 ALEXANDER OF APHRODISIAS, *In Aristotelis Analyticorum Priorum*, 53.20-23 (ed. WALLIES); ARISTOTLE, *APr.* 25b32-36.
108 ARISTOTLE, *APost.* 71b35-72a6; 99b17-100a14.
109 ARISTOTLE, *An.* 432a7-10.

laudat maxime hanc mulierum communionem. Theodorus vero in extremo eius fragmenti, quod mihi superest nondum aediti, in quo tuetur ea quae reprehenduntur in praedicamentis, videtur reprehendere hanc communionem, cum enim responderet Gemisto Platonico philosopho, qui reprehendebat Peripatheticos amantes (ut ita dicam) entis disunitatem, at vos Platonici, inquit Theodorus Gaza, ita entis unitatem, et communionem, ut singulo civi singulam uxorem non vultis esse, verum communes mulieres praebetis omnibus dilaniandas et habendas, nec hoc loco solum, sed etiam aliis in locis, ut in ea re an natura consulto agat, Bessarion, in 6 libro *contra Platonis calumniatorem*, vult consulto agere, cum ita Plato sentiat, Theodorus vero aliter cum Aristoteles ita velit[110]. Reliquum esset afferre Latinorum argumenta, quae in Platonis sententiam dicuntur. Verum cum ita sint levia, ita imbecilla, et vana vix duco digna esse ut referantur.

II.

Letter of Camillo Paleotti to the Assunteria di Studio, June 12, 1588 (ASB, Assunteria di Studio, b. 79, Lettere di diversi all'Assunteria, 1575-1691, np).

Molto Illustrissimi Signori Miei Osservantissimi,

Per essere stato ricercato da gli Illustrissimi Verona [Valier] et Borromeo di mandare all'Illustrissimo Regimento il Dottore Muzoli, essendo lui amato assai da l'uno et l'altro per le molte sue virtù, mi è parso mettere in considerazione alle Signorie Vostre quello che trovandomi io costì fu tra essi discusso, cioè che sendovi più volte ragionato in Regimento di fare opera che si leggesse costì un'opera di Platone, fu detto che tal lettura si havria potuta dare al Papazone, che hora legge in Pavia, et desidera ripatriare, overo dare la medesima lettura al Muzoli, con trasferire poi la lettura sua al Papazone, giudicandosi che così l'uno come l'altro suggetto fusse molto atto a tal lettura. Hora mostrandosi detto Muzoli inclinato a ciò, quando il Regimento fosse di quel pensiero che era all'hora, potriano elle in un tempo istesso satisfare a questi dui soggietti, da quali si potria aspettare per le virtù loro molto frutto; et anco a questi dui//illustrissimi Cardinali. Potranno trattarne et poi darmene aviso. Che Dio Nostro Salvatore le conceda ogni bene, et le baso le mani.

Di Roma li xii Giugno 1588, delle Signorie Vostre molto illustri affettionatissimo servitore Camillo Paleotti

---

110 T. Gaza, *Adversus Plethonem de substantia*, 6 (ed. Mohler, 3, p. 158).

Bibliography

Abbreviations

ASB	Archivio di Stato, Bologna
ASF	Archivio di Stato, Florence
ASPi	Archivio di Stato, Pisa
ASV	Archivio Segreto Vaticano, Vatican City
BAM	Biblioteca Ambrosiana, Milan
BAV	Biblioteca Apostolica Vaticana, Vatican City
BCB	Biblioteca Civica, Belluno
BBV	Biblioteca Bertoliana, Vicenza
BCF	Biblioteca Comunale, Fermo
BML	Biblioteca Medicea Laurenziana, Florence
BMF	Biblioteca Moreniana, Florence
BMV	Biblioteca Marciana, Venice
BSAP	Biblioteca del Seminario Arcivescovile S. Caterina, Pisa
BNCF	Biblioteca Nazionale Centrale, Florence
BNCR	Biblioteca Nazionale Centrale, Rome
BNF	Bibliothèque nationale de France, Paris
BUB	Biblioteca Universitaria, Bologna
BUP	Biblioteca Universitaria, Pisa
PML	Pierpont Morgan Library, New York
UBM	Universitätsbibliothek, Marburg

List of Manuscripts

ASB, Assunteria di Studio, b. 79
ASF, Mediceo del Principato 269
ASPi, Università 1, 1
ASPi, Università 1, 18
ASPi, Università 1, 19
ASPi, Università 1, 20
ASPi, Università 2, G 77
ASV, ABII, MS 69
ASV, ABII, MS 70
ASV, ABII, MS 71

ASV, ABII, MS 89
ASV, ABII, MS 91
ASV, ABII, MS 99
ASV, ABII, MS 100
ASV, ABII, MS 115
ASV, ABII, MS 116
ASV, ABII, MS 128
ASV, ABII, MS 131
ASV, ABII, MS 132
BAM, A48 inf.
BAM, A167 sup.
BAM, B8 inf.
BAM, B221 suss.
BAM, B222 suss.
BAM, B223 suss.
BAM, C9 sup.
BAM, C14 suss.
BAM, D29 sup.
BAM, D381 inf.
BAM, D382 inf.
BAM, D383 inf.
BAM, D447 inf.
BAM, E4 inf.
BAM, E10 sup.
BAM, E40 sup.
BAM, E99 sup.
BAM, F88 sup.
BAM, H18 sup.
BAM, N II 5 inf.
BAM, P267 sup.
BAM, S12 inf.
BAM, S72 inf.
BAM, S87 sup.
BAM, S89 inf.
BAM, S106 sup.
BAM, S107 sup.
BAM, S169 inf.
BAM, S180 inf.
BAM, S181 inf.
BAV, Barb. lat. 344
BAV, Boncompagni K 27
BAV, Vat. lat. 11591
BBV, MS G 3 8 7 (277)
BCB, MS 505

BCF, MS 80 [4 CA 2/80]
BML, Acquisti e doni 706
BMF, Bigazzi 109
BMV, Marcianus gr. 196
BMV, Marcianus gr. 197
BMV, MS lat. IX.52 (=3167)
BNCF, Filze Rinuccini 18
BNCF, Pal. 1025
BNCF, Panc. 126
BNCR, S. Pantaleo 37-38
BNF, lat. 6330
BSAP, MS 124
BUB, Aldrovandi 124-056/2
BUB, MS 56
BUP, MS 384
PML, MS 2841

Primary Sources

Acciaiuoli, D. (1566). *In Aristotelis libros octo Politicorum commentarii*, Venice, apud Vincentium Valgrisium.
Agrippa, H. C. (1534). *De beatissimae Annae monogamia ac unico puerperio propositiones. Defensio propositionum praenarraturum*, s.n. l.
———, (1535). *Orationes X quorum catalogum uersa exhibebit pagella*, Cologne, Ioannes Soter.
———, (s.d.). *Opera in duos tomos concinne digesta*, 2 vols [Lyon, Bering?].
Alexander Aphrodisiensis (1883). *In Aristotelis Priorum Analyticorum*, ed. M. Wallies, Berlin, Reimer.
Ammonius Hermias (1546). *In Praedicamenta Aristotelis Commentarii*, Venice, apud Ioannem Gryphium.
Argelati, F. (1745). *Bibliotheca scriptorum Mediolanensium*, 2 vols, Milan, In aedibus Palatinis.
Atagani, D. (1560). *Lettere di XIII huomini illustri*, Venice, per Francesco Lorenzini da Turino.
Avicenna (1546). *De mahad, idest de dispositione, seu loco ad quem revertitur homo vel anima eius post mortem*, Venice, apud Iuntas.
Bardi, G. (1643). *Medicus politico-catholicus, seu Medicinae sacrae tum cognoscendae, tum faciendae idea [...]*, Genoa, typis Ioannis Mariae Farroni.
———, (1653). *Theatrum naturae iatrochymicae rationalis. Opus dogmaticum theorico-practicum, quo quidquid in universo naturae ambitu medicarum continetur facultatum, ob oculos curiosi, et novitatum amatoris, et melioris medicina studiosi exponitur*, Rome, typis Angeli Bernabò.

Beni, P. (1594). *In Platonis Timaeum sive in naturalem omnem atque divinam Platonis et Aristotelis philosophiam decades tres*, Rome, Ex typographia Gabiana.

———, (1613). *Orationes quinquaginta*, Padua, per Fransciscum Bolzettam.

———, (2000). *Il Cavalcanti overo La difesa dell' Anticrusca di Michelangelo Fonte*, ed. G. Dell'Aquila, Bari, Cacucci.

Bessarion (1927). *In Calumniatorem Platonis Libri IV* in *Kardinal Bessarion als Theologe, Humanist und Staatsmann. II*, , ed. L. Mohler, Paderborn, Schöningh [reprinted Aalen, Scientia Verlag, 1967].

Boccadiferro, L. (1570). *Explanatio libri primi Physicorum Aristotelis*, Venice, apud Hieronymum Scotum.

———, (1571). *In duos libros Aristotelis de generatione et corruptione doctissima commentaria*, Venice, apud Franciscum de Franciscis Senensem.

———, (1590). *Lectiones super primum librum Meteorologicorum*, Venice, apud haeredem Hieronymi Scoti.

Botero, G. (1614). *Detti memorabili di personaggi illustri*, Turin, per Gio. Domenico Tarino.

Breventano, S. (1570). *Istoria della antichità, nobiltà, et delle cose notabili della città di Pavia*, Pavia, appresso Hieronimo Bartholi.

Calonymos, C. (1527). *Liber de mundi creatione physicis rationibus probata*, Venice, per Bernardinum de Vitalibus.

Camozzi, G. B. (1545). *Oratio in funere Ludouici Buccaferreae clarissimi philosophi Bononiensis*, Bologna, in officina Bartholomaei Bonardi et Marci Antonij Groscij.

Camuzio, A. (1541). *In sacrarum literarum cum Aristotele & Platone concordiam, praefatio*, Pavia, Io. Maria Simoneta.

Cattani da Diacceto, F. (1563). *Opera omnia*, Basel, per Henrichum Petri et Petrum Pernam [reprinted Enghien-les-Bains, Editions du Miraval, 2009].

———, (1986). *De pulchro libri III, accedunt opuscula inedita et dispersa necnon testimonia quaedam ad eumdem pertinentia*, ed. S. Matton, Pisa, Scuola Normale Superiore.

Champier, S. (1519). *Duellum epistolare Galliae et Italiae antiquitates complectens*, [Lyon], Impressum per Ioannem Phiroben & Ioannem Diuineur sumptibus Iacobi Francisci De Ionta.

Charpentier, J. (1573). *Platonis cum Aristotele in universa philosophia comparatio, quae hoc commentario in Alcinoi institutionem ad eiusdem Platonis doctrinam explicatur*, Paris, ex officina Iacobi du Puys.

Ciceri, F. (1782). *Epistolarum libri*, 2 vols, Milan, S. Ambrogio.

(1723). *Decreta Ill. mi Collegii DD. J. PP. Mediolani Judicum, Comitum Et Equitum*, Milan, ex typographia Petri Francisci Navae.

Donato, B. (1540). *De Platonicae atque Aristotelicae philosophiae differentia*, Venice, apud Hieronymum Scotum.

Fantuzzi, G. (1781). *Notizie degli scrittori bolognesi*, Bologna, San Tommaso d'Aquino.

Ferrari, O. (1560). *De disciplina encyclio*, Venice, apud Paulum Manutium.

———, (1575). *De sermonibus exotericis*, Venice, apud Aldum.

Ficino, M. (1576). *Opera*, 2 vols, Basel, ex officina Henricpetrina.

———, (2008). *Commentaries on Plato, I. Phaedrus and Ion*, ed. and transl. by M.J.B. Allen, Cambridge, MA-London, Harvard University Press.

———, (2011). *Teologia Platonica*, ed. E. Vitale, Milan, Bompiani.

Fornari, C. (1541). *Expositione di Ageo propheta*, Pavia, Io. Maria Simoneta.

Fornari, G. (1519). *De anime humane immortalitate examen perspicacissimum totius disceptationis inter Augustinum Suessanum et Petrum Pomponatium Mantuanum vertentis circa anime immortalitatem*, Bologna, per Iustinianum Ruber.

Fuligatti, G. (1624). *Vita del cardinale Roberto Bellarmino della Compagnia di Giesù*, Rome, Herede di Bartolomeo Zannetti.

Galilei, G. (1890-1909). *Le opere di Galileo Galilei, Edizione Nazionale*, ed. A. Favaro, 20 vols, Florence, Barbera.

Gaza, T. (1942), *Adversus Plethonem de substantia*, in *Kardinal Bessarion als Theologe, Humanist und Staatsmann: Funde und Forschungen. III Aus Bessarionis Gelehrtenkreis: Abhandlungen, Reden, Briefe*, ed. L. Mohler, Paderborn, Schoningh, pp. 151-158 [reprinted Aalen, Scientia Verlag, 1967].

Gessner, K. (1545). *Bibliotheca Universalis, sive Catalogus omnium scriptorum locupletissimus*, Zurich, apud Christophorum Froschoverum.

Hermes Trismegistus (1554). *Poemander*, Paris, apud Adrianum Turnebum.

Javelli, C. (1536). *Moralis philosophie platonice dispositio*, Venice, in officina Aurelij Pincij Veneti.

———, (1568). *In universam moralem Aristotelis, Platonis et christianam philosophiam epitomes in certas partes distinctae*, Lyon, apud haeredes Jacobi Juntae.

Leonico Tomeo, N. (1525). *Opuscula nuper in lucem aedita quorum nomina proxima*, Venice, Bernardinus Vitalis.

(1575). *Letture instituite dal Sig. Paolo Canobio, gentil'huomo milanese*, Milan, appresso Pacifico Pontio.

Liceti, F. (1640). *De Quaesitis per epistolas a claris viris responsa*, Bologna, typis Nicolai Tebaldini.

Mazzoni, J. (2010). *In universam Platonis et Aristotelis philosophiam Praeludia, sive de Comparatione Platonis et Aristotelis*, ed. S. Matteoli, introduction by A. De Pace, Naples, D'Auria.

Mazzucchelli, G. M. (1753). *Gli scrittori d'Italia*, Brescia, presso a Giambattista Bossini.

Michael Ephesius (1552). *Scholia in Aristotelem opuscula aliquot*, Venice, apud Hieronymum Scotum.

Muret, M. A. (1580). *Epistolae*, Paris, Michel Clopeiau and Robert Coulombel.

———, (1590). *Orationum volumen secundum*, Verona, apud Hierony. Discipulum.

———, (1602). *Commentarii in Aristotelis X. Libros Ethicorum ad Nicomachum, [et] in Oeconomica. Aristotelis Topicorum Libri Septimi, et in eundem Alexandri Aphrodisiensis commentarii interpretatio. Commentarius In Lib. I. Et II. Platonis De Republica. Notae in Cyropaediam et Ἀνάβασις Xenophontis*, Ingolstadt, excudebat Adam Sartorius.

———, (1789). *Opera omnia, ex mss aucta et emendata cum brevi annotatione*, 4 vols, ed. D. Ruhnken, Leiden, apud Samuel et Johannes Luchtmans, 1789.

Musso, C. (1556). *Prediche*, Venice, appresso Gabriel Giolito de' Ferrari.

———, (1590). *Prediche sopra il Simbolo degli Apostoli*, Venice, nella stamperia de' Giunti.

Muzzoli, G. P. (1593). *Sermo habitus in ingressu suarum scholarum*, Pavia, apud haeredes Hieronymi Bartoli.

———, (1594), *Sermo habitus in egressu scholarum*, Pavia, apud haeredes Hieronymi Bartoli.

Niavis, P. (1490a). *Liber de philosophia Platonis*, Leipzig, Moritz Brandis.

———, (1490b). *Platonis epistolae*, Leipzig, Conrad Kachelofen.

Piccolomini, F. (1583). *Universa philosophia de moribus*, Venice, apud Franciscum de Franciscis Senensem.

Plato (1548). *Omnia opera translatione Marsilii Ficini, emendatione et ad Graecum codicem collatione Simonis Grynaei, summa diligentia repurgata*, Lyon, apud Antonium Vincentium.

Portenari, A. (1623). *Della felicità di Padova*, Padua, per Pietro Paolo Tozzi.

Olympiodorus (1913). *In Platonis Phaedonem commentaria*, ed. W. Norvin, Leipzig, Teubner.

———, (1956). *Commentary on the First Alcibiades of* Plato, ed. L.G. Westerink, Amsterdam, North-Holland Publishing Company.

———, (2015). *Life of Plato and On Plato First Alcibiades 1-9*, ed. M. Griffin, London, Bloomsbury.

———, (2016). *On Plato First Alcibiades 10-28*, ed. M. Griffin, London, Bloomsbury.

Proclus (1560). *In primum Euclidis Elementorum librum commentariorum*, Padua, Gratiosus Perchacinus.

———, (1906). *In Timaeum*, ed. E. Diehl, Leipzig, Teubner.

Riccobono, A. (1598). *De gymnasio patavino*, Padua, Francesco Bolzeta.

Selvatico, G. B. (1607). *Collegii Mediolanensium medicorum origo, antiquitas, necessitas, utilitas, dignitates, honores, privilegia, et viri illustres*, Milan, apud Hieronymum Bordonum, Petrum Martyrem Locarnum, & Bernardinum Lantonum.

Simplicius (1882). *In Aristotelis Physicorum libros quattuor priores commentaria*, ed. H. Diels, Berlin, Reimer.

———, (1909). *In Aristotelis Categorias commentarium*, ed. C. Kalbfleisch, Berlin, Reimer.

Taegio, B. (1572). *Il Liceo, dove si ragiona dell'ordine delle accademie*, Milan, appresso Girardo di Comaschi.

Tiepolo, S. (1576). *Academicarum contemplationum libri decem*, Venice, apud Petrum Dehuchinum.

Tomasini, G. F. (1644). *Elogia virorum literis et sapientia illustrium ad vivum expressis imaginibus exornata*, Padua, ex Typographia Sebastiani Sardi.

Valier, A. (2015). *Instituzione d'ogni stato lodevole delle donne cristiane*, Cambridge, Modern Humanities Research Association.

de' Vieri, F. (1576). *Compendio della dottrina di Platone in quello che ella e conforme con la fede nostra*, Florence, appresso Giorgio Marescotti.

———, (1586). *Liber in quo a calumniis detractorum philosophia defenditur, & eius praestantia demonstratur*, Rome, apud Ioannem Angelum Ruffinellum.

———, (1589). *Vere conclusioni di Platone conformi alla dottrina Christiana et a quella di Aristotele*, Florence, appresso Georgio Marescotti.

———, (s.d.). *Delle stelle lezzioni due*, Padua, appresso il Bolzetta.

Zimara, T. (1584). *In tres Aristotelis libros De anima*, Venice, Giunta.

Secondary Sources

Allen, M. J. B. (1998). *Synoptic Art: Marsilio Ficino on the History of Platonic Interpretation*, Florence, Olschki.

Angelini, A. (2003). *Simboli e questioni: l'eterodossia culturale di Achille Bocchi e dell'Hermathena*, Bologna, Pendragon.

Baldini, A. E. (1980a). "La politica 'etica' di Francesco Piccolomini", in *Il pensiero politico*, 13, pp. 161-185.

———, (1980b). "Per la biografia di Francesco Piccolomini", in *Rinascimento*, 20, 2nd s., pp. 389-420.

———, (1992). "Botero e la Francia", in A. E. Baldini (ed.), *Botero e la "ragion di stato"*. Atti del convegno in memoria di Luigi Firpo (Torino 8-10 marzo 1990), Florence, Olschki, pp. 335-359.

———, (1995). "Aristotelismo e platonismo nelle dispute romane sulla ragion di stato di fine Cinquecento", in A. E. Baldini (ed.), *Aristotelismo politico e ragion di stato*. Atti del convegno internazionale di Torino (11-13 febbraio 1993), Florence, Olschki, pp. 201-226.

———, (2008). "Ragion di stato e platonismo nel dibattito politico italiano di fine Cinquecento", in F. B. Nalis (ed.), *Studi in memoria di Enzo Sciacca*, 2 vols, Milan, A. Giuffrè.

Barsanti, D. (1993). "I docenti e le cattedre dal 1543 al 1737", in *Storia dell'Università di Pisa 1343-1737*, pp. 505-567.

Bartocci, B. (2011). "Il Platonismo di Paolo Beni da Gubbio e la critica della tradizione neoplatonica", in *Accademia*, 13, pp. 75-108.

———, (2013). "L'*In Platonis Timaeum* e le altre opere inedite di Paolo Beni da Gubbio", in *Recherches de Théologie et Philosophie médiévales*, 80, pp. 165-219.

———, (2014). "Paolo Beni and His Friendly Criticism of Patrizi", in T. Nejeschleba and P. R. Blum (eds), *Francesco Patrizi Philosopher of the Renaissance*, Olomouc, Univerzita Palackeho, pp. 261-295.

———, (2016). "Paolo Beni and Galileo Galilei: The Classical Tradition and the Reception of the Astronomical Revolution", in *Rivista di Storia della Filosofia*, 71, pp. 423-452.

Bernard-Pradelle, L., C. De Buzon, J.-E. Girot and R. Mouren, eds (2020). *Marc Antoine Muret, un humaniste français en Italie*, Geneva, Droz.

Beuchot, M. (1994). "Chrysostom Javellus (b. 1472; d. 1538) and Francis Sylvester Ferrara (b. 1474; d. 1526)", in J. J. E. Gracia (ed.), *Individuation in Scholasticism: The Later Middle Ages and the Counter-Reformation, 1150-1650*, Albany, NY, State University of New York Press, pp. 457-472.

Bianchi, L. (1995). "Una caduta senza declino? Considerazioni sulla crisi dell'aristotelismo fra rinascimento ed età moderna", in F. Dominguez, R. Imbach, T. Pindl and P. Walter (eds), *Aristotelica et Lulliana magistro doctissimo Charles H. Lohr septuagesimum annum feliciter agenti dedicata*, Turnhout, Brepols, pp. 181-222.

———, (1997). "L'acculturazione filosofica dell'Occidente", in L. Bianchi (ed.), *La filosofia delle università. Secoli XIII-XIV*, Florence, La nuova Italia, pp. 17-21.

———, (2000). "From Lefèvre d'Étaples to Giulio Landi: Uses of the Dialogue in Renaissance Aristotelianism", in J. Kraye and M.W.F. Stone (eds), *Humanism and Early Modern Philosophy*, London and New York, Routledge, pp. 41-58.

———, (2002). "Interpréter Aristote par Aristote. Parcours de l'herméneutique philosophique à la Renaissance", in *Methodos*, 2 (2002) [https://journals.openedition.org/methodos/98?lang=fr, last accessed December 7, 2021].

———, (2003). *Studi sull'Aristotelismo del Rinascimento*, Padua, Il Poligrafo.

———, (2004). "Fra Ermolao Barbaro e Ludovico Boccadiferro: qualche considerazione sulle trasformazioni della 'fisica medievale' nel Rinascimento italiano", in *Medioevo*, 29, pp. 341-378.

———, (2008). *Pour une histoire de la "double vérité"*, Paris, Vrin.

———, ed. (2011). *Christian Readings of Aristotle from the Middle Ages to the Renaissance*, Turnhout, Brepols.

Blackwell, C. (2011). "Neo-Platonic Modes of Concordism Versus Definitions of Difference", in S. Clucas, P. J. Forshaw, V. Rees (eds), *Laus Platonici Philosophi*, Leiden, Brill, pp. 321-432.

Bossi, P. (2008). "Le Scuole Cannobiane 'celebrius inter alia publica gymnasia', nel panorama delle scuole pubbliche milanesi in età moderna", in B. Azzaro (ed.), *L'università di Roma La Sapienza e le università italiane*, Rome, Gangemi, pp. 133-146.

Bruzzone, G. L. (2004). *Girolamo Bardi (1603-1675) tra filosofia e medicina*, Genoa, Accademia Ligure di Scienze e Lettere.

Buzzetti, D. (1997). "La Faculté des arts dans les universités de l'Europe méridionale. Quelques problèmes de recherches", in O. Weijers and L. Holtz (eds), *L'enseignement des disciplines à la Faculté des arts (Paris et Oxford, XIIIe-XVe siècles)*, Turnhout, Brepols, pp. 457-466.

Camerota, M. (1997). "Flaminio Papazzoni: un aristotelico bolognese maestro di Federico Borromeo e corrispondente di Galileo", in Di Liscia D. A., E. Kessler and C. Methuen (eds), *Method and Order in Renaissance Philosophy of Nature: The Aristotle Commentary Tradition*, Aldershot, Ashgate, pp. 271-300.

Cagnetti, F. (1964). "Girolamo Bardi", in *Dizionario Biografico degli Italiani*, 6, permanent link http://www.treccani.it/enciclopedia/girolamo-bardi_(Dizionario-Biografico)/ [last accessed December 13, 2021].

Caroti S., and V. Perrone Compagni, eds (2012), *Nuovi maestri e antichi testi. Umanesimo e Rinascimento alle origini del pensiero moderno. Atti del convegno internazionale di studi di Mantova, 1-3 dicembre 2010, in onore di Cesare Vasoli*, Florence, Olschki.

Carugo, A. (1984). "L'insegnamento della matematica all'Università di Padova prima e dopo Galileo", in *Storia della cultura veneta. Dalla Controriforma alla fine della Repubblica IV.2*, Vicenza, Neri Pozza, pp. 151-199.

Catana, L. (2008). *The Historiographical Concept 'System of Philosophy'. Its Origin, Nature, Influence*, Leiden, Brill.

———, (2019). *Late Ancient Platonism in Eighteenth-Century German Thought*, Cham, Springer.

Chenu, M.-D. (1932). "Note pour l'histoire de la notion de philosophie chrétienne", in *Revue des Sciences philosophiques et théologiques*, 21, pp. 231-235.

Chiellini, S. (1991). "Contributo per la storia degli insegnamenti umanistici", in P. Castelli (ed.), *La rinascita del sapere. Libri e maestri dello Studio ferrarese*, Ferrara, Marsilio, pp. 210-245.

Cipriani, G. (2009). *La mente di un inquisitore. Agostino Valier e l'Opusculum* De cautione adhibenda in edendis libris *(1589-1604)*, Florence, Nicomp.

Conte, E. (1991). *I maestri della Sapienza di Roma dal 1514 al 1787: i rotuli e altre fonti*, Rome, Istituto storico italiano per il Medioevo.

Copenhaver, B. P. (1978). *Symphorien Champier and the Reception of the Occultist Tradition in Renaissance France*, The Hague-Paris-New York, Mouton.

Corradi, A. (1878). *Memorie e documenti per la storia dell'Università di Pavia. Vol. I*, Pavia, Bizzoni.

Corrias, A. and E. Del Soldato, eds (2022). *Harmony and Contrast: Plato and Aristotle in the Early Modern Period*, Oxford, Oxford University Press.

Costa, E. (1907). *Ulisse Aldrovandi e lo Studio bolognese nella seconda metà del secolo XVI*, Bologna, Stabilimento Poligrafico Emiliano.

Couzinet, M.-D. (2015), *Pierre Ramus et la critique du pédantisme: philosophie, humanisme et culture scolaire au XVIe siècle*, Paris, Champion.

Croll, M. W. (1924). "Muret and the History of 'Attic' Prose", in *Proceedings of the Modern Languages Association*, 39, pp. 254-309.

Dallari, U. (1888). *I Rotuli dei lettori legisti e artisti dello Studio bolognese dal 1384 al 1799. Vol. II*, Bologna, Merlani.

Dalmas, D. (2008). "Jacopo Mazzoni", in *Dizionario Biografico degli Italiani*, 72, permanent link at http://www.treccani.it/enciclopedia/jacopo-mazzoni_(Dizionario-Biografico)/ [last accessed December 13, 2021]

Davies, J. (2009). *Culture and Power. Tuscany and Its Universities 1537-1609*, Leiden, Brill.

Del Fante, A. (1980). "Lo studio di Pisa in un manoscritto inedito di Francesco Verino secondo", in *Nuova Rivista Storica*, 64, pp. 396-420.

Del Gratta, R. (1993). "L'età della dominazione fiorentina (1406-1543)", in *Storia dell'Università di Pisa 1343-1737. I*, pp. 33-78.

Del Soldato, E. (2010). "Sulle tracce di Bessarione: la fortuna cinquecentesca dell'*In calumniatorem Platonis*", in *Rinascimento*, 50, 2nd s., pp. 321-342.

———, (2017). Del Soldato, "Saving the Philosopher's Soul: The *De pietate Aristotelis* by Fortunio Liceti", in *Journal of the History of the Ideas*, 78, pp. 531-547.

———, (2020). *Early Modern Aristotle. On the Making and Unmaking of Authority*, Philadelphia, University of Pennsylvania Press.

———, (2021). "Bessarion as an Aristotelian, Bessarion among the Aristotelians", in S. Mariev (ed.), *Bessarion's Treasure. Editing, Translating and Interpreting Bessarion's Literary Heritage*, Berlin-Boston, De Gruyter, pp. 169-184.

———, (2022). "Between Past and Present: Paganino Gaudenzi (1595-1649) and the *comparatio* Tradition", in Corrias, A. and E. Del Soldato (2022), pp. 172-188.

Diffley, P. B. (1988). *Paolo Beni. A Biographical and Critical Study*, Oxford, Clarendon Press.

Di Liscia, D. A., E. Kessler and C. Methuen, eds (1997). *Method and Order in Renaissance Philosophy of Nature: The Aristotle Commentary Tradition*, Aldershot, Ashgate.

Dillon, J. M. and A. A. Long, eds (1988). *The Question of "Eclecticism". Studies in Later Greek Philosophy*, Berkeley-Los Angeles-London, University of California Press.

Donahue, W. H. (1981). *The Dissolution of the Celestial Spheres 1595-1650*, New York, Arno.

Dutton, P. E. (1996). "Material Remains of the Study of the *Timaeus* in the later Middle Ages", in C. Lafleur (ed.), *L'enseignement de la philosophie au XIIIe siècle*, Turnhout, Brepols, pp. 203-230.

———, (2003). "Medieval Approaches to Calcidius", in G. Reydams-Schils (ed.), *Plato's Timaeus as Cultural Icon*, Notre Dame, University of Notre Dame Press, pp. 183-295.

Facca, D. (2020). *Early Modern Aristotelianism and the Making of Philosophical Disciplines*, Bloomsbury, London.

Fazzo, S. (1999a). "Girolamo Cardano e lo Studio di Pavia", in M. Baldi and G. Canziani (eds), *Girolamo Cardano: le opere, le fonti, la vita*, Milan, Franco Angeli, pp. 521-574.

———, (1999b). "Philology and Philosophy in the Margins of Early Printed Editions of the Ancient Greek Commentators on Aristotle, with Special Reference to Copies Held at the Biblioteca Nazionale Braidense, Milan", in C. Blackwell and S. Kusukawa (eds), *Philosophy in the Sixteenth and Seventeenth Centuries. Conversations with Aristotle*, London, Routledge, pp. 48-75.

Fellina, S. (2012). "Cristoforo Landino e le ragioni della poesia: il dissenso con Marsilio Ficino sull'origine della *pia philosophia*", in Caroti, S. and Perrone Compagni V. (eds), *Nuovi maestri e antichi testi. Umanesimo e Rinascimento alle origini del pensiero moderno. Atti del convegno internazionale di studi in onore di Cesare Vasoli, 1-3 dicembre 2010*, Florence, Olschki, pp. 191-222.

———, (2015a). "Platone a scuola: l'insegnamento di Francesco de' Vieri detto il Verino secondo", in *Noctua*, 2/1-2, pp. 97-181.

———, (2015b). *Alla scuola di Marsilio Ficino: il pensiero filosofico di Francesco Cattani da Diacceto*, Pisa, Edizioni della Normale - Istituto Nazionale di Studi sul Rinascimento.

———, (2019). *Platone allo Studium Fiorentino-Pisano (1576-1635): l'insegnamento di Francesco de'Vieri, Jacopo Mazzoni, Carlo Tomasi, Cosimo Boscagli, Girolamo Bardi*, Verona, Scripta.

———, (2019b). "Platone a Ferrara: il *De providentia ad sententiam Platonis et Platonicorum liber unus* di Tommaso Giannini", in *Noctua*, 5, pp. 466-553.

———, (2022) "Le fonti platoniche di Federico Pendasio: note sulla diffusione nel '500 degli scholia al *Fedro* di Ermia Alessandrino e dei commenti al *Fedone* e al *Filebo* di Olimpiodoro e Damascio", in *Noctua*, 9, pp. 188-221.

Festugière, A.-J. (1969). "L'ordre de lecture des dialogues de Platon aux ve/vi^e siècles", in *Museum Helveticum*, 26, 1969, pp. 281-296.

Franceschini, A. (1970). *Nuovi documenti relativi ai docenti dello Studio di Ferrara nel sec. XVI*, Ferrara, SATE.

Frati, L. with A. Chigi and A. Sorbelli, (1907). *Catalogo dei manoscritti di Ulisse Aldrovandi*, Bologna, Zanichelli.

de Gandillac, M. and J.-C. Margolin, eds (1976). *Platon et Aristote à la Renaissance.* XVIe colloque international de Tours, Paris, Vrin.

Garin, E. (1957). "Note and notizie", in *Giornale critico della filosofia italiana* 11, 3rd s., pp. 406-412.

―――, (1994). *L'umanesimo italiano. Filosofia e vita civile nel Rinascimento*, Rome-Bari, Laterza.

Gentile, S. (1990). "Sulle prime traduzioni dal greco di Marsilio Ficino", in *Rinascimento*, 30, 2nd s., pp. 57-104.

―――, (2012). "Considerazioni attorno al Ficino e alla *prisca theologia*", in S. Caroti and V. Perrone Compagni (eds), *Nuovi maestri e antichi testi. Umanesimo e Rinascimento alle origini del pensiero moderno. Atti del convegno internazionale di studi in onore di Cesare Vasoli, Mantova, 1-3 dicembre 2010*, Florence, Olschki, pp. 57-72.

Gersh, S. (1986). *Middle Platonism and Neoplatonism: The Latin Tradition*, 2 vols, Notre Dame, Notre Dame University Press.

Gibson, M. (1969). "The Study of the *Timaeus* in the Eleventh and Twelfth Centuries", in *Pensamiento*, 25, pp. 183-194.

Gilly, C. (2012). *Theodor Zwinger e la crisi culturale della seconda metà del Cinquecento*, http://www.saavedrafajardo.org/Archivos/LIBROS/Libro0844.pdf. [last accessed, December 13, 2021].

Giovannozzi, D. (2015). "*Amoris fulgoribus ego accensus, amorem vobis praedico. L'Oratio in Convivium Platonis* di Cornelio Agrippa", in *Bruniana & Campanelliana*, 21, pp. 347-361.

Girot, J.-E. (2012). *Marc Antoine Muret. Des Isles Fortunées au rivage romain*, Geneva, Droz.

Giustiniani, M. (1667). *Gli scrittori liguri*, Rome, appresso di Nicol'Angelo Tinassi.

Granada, M. A. (2002). *Sfere solide e cielo fluido: Momenti del dibattito cosmologico nella seconda metà del Cinquecento*, Milan, Guerini.

Gregory, T. (1958). *Platonismo medievale. Studi e ricerche*, Rome, Istituto storico italiano per il Medio Evo.

Grendler, P. F. (2002). *The Universities of the Italian Renaissance*, Baltimore and London, Johns Hopkins University Press.

―――, (2017). *The Jesuits and Italian Universities*, Washington, D.C., Catholic University of America Press.

Gualdo Rosa, L. (2020). "L'insegnamento romano di Muret e il suo contributo di oratore e filologo alla controffensiva europea della Riforma cattolica", in Bernard-Pradelle, L., C. De Buzon, J.-E. Girot and R. Mouren (eds), *Marc Antoine Muret, un humaniste français en Italie*, Geneva, Droz, pp. 281-294.

Guerlac, H. (1978). "Amicus Plato and Other Friends", in *Journal of the History of Ideas*, 39, pp. 627-633.

Hadot, I. (1990). "Du bon et mauvais usage du terme 'éclectisme' dans l'histoire de la philosophie antique", in R. Brague and J.-F. Courtine (eds), *Herméneutique et ontologie. Mélanges en hommage à P. Aubenque*, Paris, Presses universitaires de France, pp. 147-162.

—, (1991). "The Role of the Commentaries on Aristotle in the Teaching of Philosophy According to the Prefaces of the Neoplatonic Commentaries on the *Categories*", in H. Blumenthal and H. Robinson (eds), *Aristotle and the Later Tradition*, Oxford, Oxford University Press, 1991, pp. 175-189.

—, (1992). "Aristote dans l'enseignement philosophique néoplatonicien. Les préfaces des commentaires sur les *Catégories*", in *Revue de Théologie et de Philosophie*, 124, pp. 407-425.

Hankins, J. (1990). *Plato in the Italian Renaissance*, 2 vols, Leiden, Brill.

—, (1996). "Antiplatonism in the Renaissance and the Middle Ages", in *Classica et mediaevalia*, 47, pp. 359-376.

—, (1999). "The Study of the *Timaeus* in Early Renaissance Italy", in A. Grafton and N. Siraisi (eds), *Natural Particulars: Nature and the Disciplines in Renaissance Europe*, Cambridge, MA, MIT University Press, pp. 77-119.

—, (2005). "Plato's Psychogony in the Later Renaissance: Changing Attitudes to the Christianization of Pagan Philosophy", in T. Leinkauf and C. Steel (eds), *Plato's Timaeus and the Foundations of Cosmology in Late Antiquity, the Middle Ages & the Renaissance*, Leuven, Leuven University Press, pp. 387-406.

Hoffmann, P. (1998). "La fonction des prologues exégétiques dans la pensée pédagogique néoplatonicienne", in B. Roussel and J.-D. Dubois (eds), *Entrer en matière*, Paris, Cerf, pp. 209-245.

—, (2006). "What was Commentary in Late Antiquity? The Example of the Neoplatonic Commentators", in M.L. Gill and P. Pellegrin (eds), *A Companion to Ancient Philosophy*, Oxford, Blackwell, pp. 597-622.

Jardine, N. (1997). "Keeping Order in the School of Padua: Jacopo Zabarella and Francesco Piccolomini on the Offices of Philosophy", in Di Liscia, D.A., E. Kessler and C. Methuen (eds), *Method and Order in Renaissance Philosophy of Nature. The Aristotle Commentary Tradition*, Aldershot, Ashgate, pp. 183-209.

Jeauneau, É. (1973). *'Lectio philosophorum': Recherches sur l'École de Chartres*, Amsterdam, A. M. Hakkert.

—, (1977). "Extraits des *Glosae super Platonem* de Guillaume de Conches dans un manuscrit de Londres", in *Journal of the Warburg and Courtauld Institutes*, 60, pp. 212-222.

Jost, L. (2014). "The *Eudemian Ethics* and Its Controversial Relationship to the *Nicomachean Ethics*", in R. Polonsky (ed.), *The Cambridge Companion to Aristotle's Nicomachean Ethics*, Cambridge, Cambridge University Press, pp. 410-427.

Klibansky, R. (1939). *The Continuity of the Platonic Tradition*, London, The Warburg Institute.

Klutstein, I. (1987). *Marsilio Ficino et la théologie ancienne*, Florence, Olschki.

Kraye, J. (1995). "Like Father, Like Son: Aristotle, Nicomachus and the *Nicomachean Ethics*", in R. Imbach, F. Dominguez, T. Pindl-Büchel, P. Walter (eds), *Aristotelica et Lulliana magistro doctissimo Charles H. Lohr septuagesimum annum feliciter agenti dedicata*, Turnhout, Brepols, 1995, pp. 155-180.

———, (2002). "Eclectic Aristotelianism in the Moral Philosophy of Francesco Piccolomini", in G. Piaia (ed.), *La presenza dell'aristotelismo padovano nella filosofia della prima modernità. Atti del colloquio internazionale in memoria di Charles B. Schmitt* (Padova, 4-6 settembre 2000), Rome-Padua, Antenore, pp. 57-82.

———, (2005). "Marc Antoine Muret as Editor of Seneca and Commentator on Aristotle", in J. Kraye and R. Saarinen (eds), *Moral Philosophy on the Threshold of Modernity*, Dordrecht, Kluwer, pp. 307-330.

Kristeller, P. O. (1937). *Supplementum Ficinianum Marsilii Ficini Florentini Philosophi platonici opuscula inedita et dispersa*, 2 vols, Florence, Olschki.

———, (1956). "Francesco da Diacceto and Florentine Platonism in the Sixteenth Century", in *Id., Studies in Renaissance Thought and Letters*, I, Rome, Edizioni di Storia e Letteratura, pp. 287-336.

———, (1987). *Marsilio Ficino and His Work After Five Hundred Years*, Florence, Olschki.

———, (1990). *Iter Italicum: A Finding List of Uncatalogued or Incompletely Catalogued Humanistic Manuscripts of the Renaissance in Italian and Other Libraries*, 5 vols, London, The Warburg Institute.

———, (1993). "The European Significance of Florentine Platonism", in *Id., Studies in Renaissance Thought and Letters*, III, Rome, Edizioni di Storia e Letteratura, pp. 49-68.

———, (1996). "Marsilio Ficino e Venezia", in *Id., Studies in Renaissance Thought and Letters*, IV, Rome, Edizioni di Storia e Letteratura, pp. 245-263.

Lafleur, C. and J. Carrier (2004). "L'enseignement philosophique à la Faculté des arts de l'Université de Paris en la première moitié du XIIIe siècle dans le miroir des textes didascaliques", in *Laval philosophique et théologique*, 60, pp. 409-448.

Lepori, F. (1980). "La scuola di Rialto dalla fondazione alla metà del Cinquecento", in G. Aladi and M. Pastore Stocchi (eds), *Storia della cultura veneta. III/2. Dal primo Quattrocento al Concilio di Trento*, Vicenza, Neri Pozza, pp. 539-605.

Lines, D. A. (2001). "Natural Philosophy in Renaissance Italy: The University of Bologna and the Beginnings of Specialization" in *Science and Universities of Early Modern Europe: Teaching, Specialization, Professionalization*, special issue of *Early Science and Medicine*, 6, pp. 267-323.

———, (2002). *Aristotle's Ethics in the Italian Renaissance (ca. 1300-1600): The Universities and the Problem of Moral Education*, Leiden, Brill.

———, and S. Ebbersmeyer, eds (2013). *Rethinking Virtue, Reforming Society. New Directions in Renaissance Ethics, c. 1350-c. 1650*, Turnhout, Brepols.

———, (2014). "Latin and the Vernacular in Francesco Piccolomini's Moral Philosophy", in D. A. Lines and E. Refini (eds), *'Aristotele fatto volgare'. Tradizione aristotelica e cultura volgare nel Rinascimento*, Pisa, ETS, pp. 169-199.

Lohr, C. H. (1988). *Latin Aristotle Commentaries. II. Renaissance Authors*, Florence, Olschki.

Loverci, F. (2000). "Gli studi umanistici del Rinascimento alla Controriforma", in L. Capo and M.R. Di Simone (eds), *Storia della facoltà di lettere e filosofia de 'La Sapienza'*, Rome, Viella, pp. 199-243.

Maiocchi, R. and A. Moiraghi (1916). *L'almo Collegio Borromeo. Federico Borromeo studente e gli inizi del Collegio*, Pavia, Scuola tipografica Artigianelli.

Marcora, C. (1960). "La chiesa milanese nel decennio 1550-1560", in *Memorie Storiche della Diocesi di Milano*, 7, pp. 254-501.

———, ed. (1988). *Catalogo dei manoscritti del card. Federico Borromeo nella biblioteca Ambrosiana*, Milan, Biblioteca Ambrosiana.

Marongiu, A. (1974). "L'Università di Macerata nel periodo delle origini", in *Id., Stato e scuola. Esperienze della scuola occidentale*, Milan, A. Giuffrè.

Martin, C. (2011). *Renaissance Meteorology. Pomponazzi to Descartes*, Baltimore, The Johns Hopkins University Press.

———, (2022). "Interpreting Plato's Geometrical Elements in Renaissance Aristotle Commentaries", in Corrias, A. and E. Del Soldato (eds), *Harmony and Contrast: Plato and Aristotle in the Early Modern Period*, Oxford, Oxford University Press, pp. 149-171.

Martinelli Tempesta, S. (2000). "La versione latina di Pier Vettori del *Liside* platonico", in *Atti e memorie dell'Academia Toscana di scienze e lettere La Colombaria*, 65 [51 n.s.], pp. 112-171.

Matton, S. (1986). "Le face à face Charpentier-La Ramée. À propos d'Aristote", *Revue des sciences philosophiques et théologiques*, 70, pp. 67-86.

McDonald, G. (2008). "Cornelius Agrippa's School of Love: Teaching Plato's *Symposium* in the Renaissance", in P. Sherlock and M. Cassidy-Welch (eds), *Practices of Gender in Late-Medieval and Early Modern Europe*, Turnhout, Brepols, pp. 151-175.

———, (2022). *Marsilio Ficino in Germany from Renaissance to Enlightenment. A Reception History*, Geneva, Droz.

(1878). *Memorie e documenti per la storia dell'Università di Pavia, e degli uomini più illustri che v'insegnarono*, Pavia, Successori Bizzoni.

Monfasani, J. (1983). "The Byzantine Rhetorical Tradition and the Renaissance", in J. J. Murphy (ed.), *Renaissance Eloquence. Studies in the Theory and Practice of Renaissance Rhetoric*, Berkeley, University of California Press, pp. 174-187.

———, (1990). "L'insegnamento universitario e la cultura bizantina in Italia nel Quattrocento", in L. Avellini (ed.), *Sapere e/è potere. Discipline, Dispute e Professioni nell'Università Medievale e Moderna: il caso bolognese a confronto*, 3 vols, Bologna, Istituto per la Storia di Bologna, I, pp. 43-65.

Morley, H. (1856). *Cornelius Agrippa. The Life of Henry Cornelius Agrippa von Nettesheim, Doctor and Knight, Commonly Known as a Magician*, 2 vols, London, Chapman and Hall.

Motta, U. (1997). *Antonio Quarenghi (1546-1633): un letterato padovano nella Roma del tardo Rinascimento*, Milan, Vita e Pensiero.

Muccillo, M. (1992). "Il platonismo all'Università di Roma: Francesco Patrizi", in P. Cherubini (ed.), *Roma e lo Studium Urbis. Spazio urbano e cultura dal Quattro al Seicento. Atti del convegno (Roma, 7-10 giugno 1989)*, Rome, Ministero per i beni culturali e ambientali, pp. 200-247.

———, (1996). *Platonismo, ermetismo e 'prisca theologia'. Ricerche di storiografia filosofica rinascimentale*, Florence, Olschki.

———, (2006). "Le *cautiones* antificiniane di Giovanni Battista Crispo", in S. Gentile and S. Toussaint (eds), *Marsilio Ficino: fonti, testi, fortuna*. Atti del convegno internazionale di Firenze, 1-3 ottobre 1999, Rome, Edizioni di Storia e letteratura, pp. 339-380.

Nardi, B. (1958). *Saggi sull'aristotelismo padovano dal secolo XIV al XVI*, Florence, Sansoni.

———, (1963). "La scuola di Rialto e l'umanesimo veneziano", in V. Branca (ed.), *Umanesimo europeo e umanesimo veneziano*, Florence, Sansoni, pp. 93-139.

Negruzzo, S. (2015). "Le Cardinal Auguste Valier, un humaniste au service de la Contre-Réforme", in *Seizième siècle*, 11, pp. 259-273.

Nolhac, P. de (1883). "La bibliothèque d'un humaniste au XVIe siècle. Catalogue des livres annotés par Muret", in *Mélanges de l'école française de Rome*, 3, pp. 202-238.

Nutton, V. (1988). "*De Placitis Hippocratis et Platonis* in the Renaissance", in P. Manuli and M. Vegetti (eds), *Le opere psicologiche di Galeno*. Atti del terzo colloquio galenico internazionale di Pavia, 10-12 settembre 1986, Naples, Bibliopolis, pp. 281-309.

Oosterhoff, R. (2018). *Making Mathematical Culture: University and Print in the Circle of Lefèvre d'Étaples*, Oxford, Oxford University Press.

Pantin, I. (2020). "Le commentaire de Muret à l'*Éthique à Nicomaque*", in Bernard-Pradelle, L., C. De Buzon, J.-E. Girot and R. Mouren (eds), *Marc Antoine Muret, un humaniste français en Italie*, Geneva, Droz, pp. 319-336.

Pasini, C. (2004). "Giovanni Donato Ferrari e i manoscritti greci dell'Ambrosiana", in *Νέα ‘ Ρώμη. Rivista di ricerche bizantinistiche*, 1, pp. 351-386.

Piana, C. (1969). "La Facoltà teologica dell'Università di Bologna nella prima metà del Cinquecento", in *Archivum historicum franciscanum*, 62, pp. 196-266.

Piergentili, P. P. (2003). *L'Archivio dei conti Beni di Gubbio. Note storiche e inventario*, Vatican City, Archivio Segreto Vaticano.

Pintaudi, R. (1976). "Il Platone di Francesco Verino secondo", in *Rinascimento*, 16, 2nd s., pp. 241-249.

Pissavino, P. (1995). "Politica e accademie nella Lombardia spagnola", in D.S. Chambers and F. Quiviger (eds), *Italian Academies of the Sixteenth Century*, London, Warburg Institute, pp. 91-103.

———, (2000). "Il capitano neoplatonico", in M. Rizzo and G. Mazzocchi (eds), *La espada y la pluma. Il mondo militare nella Lombardia spagnola cinquecentesca*, Viareggio, Baroni, pp. 131-149.

———, (2013). "Università e Accademie", in D. Mantovani (ed.), *Almum Studium Papiense I.2*, Pavia, Cisalpino, pp. 1223-1258.

Plaisance, M. (2004). *L'Accademia e il suo principe. Cultura e politica a Firenze al tempo di Cosimo I e di Francesco de' Medici*, Rome, Vecchiarelli Editore.

Plastina, S. (2002). "*Concordia discors*: Aristotelismus und Platonismus in der Philosophie des Francesco Piccolomini", in M. Mulsow (ed.), *Das Ende des Hermetismus: Historische Kritik und neue Naturphilosophie in der Spätrenaissance*, Tübingen, Mohr Siebeck, pp. 213-234.

Poppi, A. (1976). "Il problema della filosofia morale nella scuola padovana del Rinascimento: Platonismo e Aristotelismo nella definizione del metodo dell'etica", in de Gandillac, M. and J.-C. Margolin (eds), *Platon et Aristote à la Renaissance*, Paris, Vrin, pp. 105-146.

———, (2013). "Happiness", in Lines, D.A. and Ebbersmeyer, S. (eds), *Rethinking Virtue, Reforming Society: New Directions in Renaissance Ethics, c. 1350 - c. 1650*, Turnhout, Brepols, pp. 243-275.

Prete, S. (1960). *I codici della Biblioteca comunale di Fermo. Catalogo*, Florence, Olschki.

Prodi, P. (1971). "Borromeo, Federico", in *Dizionario Biografico degli Italiani*, 13, permanent link at https://www.treccani.it/enciclopedia/federico-borromeo_(Dizionario-Biografico), [last accessed December 13, 2021].

Prost, A. (1881-1882). *Les sciences et les arts occultes au XVIe siècle. Corneille Agrippa: Sa vie et ses oeuvres*, 2 vols, Paris, Champion.

Puliafito, A. L. (1990). "Filosofia aristotelica e modi dell'apprendimento. Un intervento di Agostino Valier su *Qua ratione versandum sit in Aristotele*", in *Rinascimento*, 30, 2nd s., pp. 153-172.

Purnell Jr., F. (1971). *Jacopo Mazzoni and His Comparison of Plato and Aristotle*, Ph.D. dissertation, Columbia University.

———, (1974). "Iacopo Mazzoni as a Student of Philosophy at Padua", in *Quaderni per la storia dell'Università di Padova*, 7, pp. 17-26.

Rambaldi, P. L. and A. Saitta Revignas, eds (1950). *I manoscritti palatini*, Rome, La libreria dello Stato.

Raspadori, F. (1991). *I maestri di medicina ed arti dell'Università di Ferrara (1391-1950)*, Florence, Olschki.

Renaud, F. (2008). "Le commentaire philosophique dans l'Antiquité et ses prolongements: méthodes exégétiques (I): Tradition et critiques: lecture jumelée de Platon et Aristote chez Olympiodore", in *Laval théologique et philosophique*, 64, pp. 89-104.

———, and H. Tarrant, (2015). *The Platonic Alcibiades I. The Dialogue and Its Ancient Reception*, Cambridge, Cambridge University Press.

Renzi, P. (1993). *I libri del mestiere: la Bibliotheca Mureti del Collegio romano*, Siena, Università degli studi di Siena.

Ribas, M.-N. (2018). "S'affilier. Le Platon de Leibniz", in D. Antoine-Mahut and S. Lézé (eds), *Les classiques à l'épreuve: Actualité de l'histoire de la philosophie*, Paris, Editions des archives contemporaines, pp. 23-34.

Rolet, A. (2008). "L'*Hermathena Bocchiana* ou l'idée de la parfaite académie", in Deramaix, M., P. Galan-Hallyn and G. Vagenheim (eds), *Les Académies dans l'Europe humaniste: idéaux et pratiques*, Geneva, Droz, pp. 295-323.

Ross, J. B. (1976). "Venetian Schools and Teachers, Fourteenth to Early Sixteenth Century: A Survey and a Study of Giovanni Battista Egnazio", in *Renaissance Quarterly*, 29, pp. 521-566.

Rossi, G. (2020). "Filologia e giurisprudenza nell'insegnamento romano di Marc Antoine Muret: alla ricerca di un nuovo metodo", in Bernard-Pradelle, L., C. De Buzon, J.-E. Girot and R. Mouren (eds), *Marc Antoine Muret, un humaniste français en Italie*, Geneva, Droz, pp. 295-318.

Rotondò, A. (1962). "Per la storia dell'eresia a Bologna del secolo XVI", in *Rinascimento*, 2, 2nd s., pp. 107-154.

———, (1982). "Cultura umanistica e difficoltà di censori. Censura ecclesiastica e discussioni cinquecentesche sul platonismo", in *Le pouvoir et la plume: incitation, contrôle et répression dans l'Italie du XVIe siècle*. Actes du Colloque international d'Aix-en-Provence-Marseille, 14-16 mai 1981, organisé par le Centre Interuniversitaire de Recherche sur la Renaissance italienne et l'Institut Culturel Italien de Marseille, Paris, Université de la Sorbonne Nouvelle, pp. 33-50.

Rozzo, U. and R. Ferrari (1984). "Un filosofo e bibliofilo milanese del '500: Cesare Rovida", in *Stasimon*, 3, pp. 81-115

Rurale, F. (1992). *I Gesuiti a Milano. Religione e politica nel secondo Cinquecento*, Rome, Bulzoni.

Ruysschaert, J. (1959). *Codices Vaticani Latini 11414-11709*, Vatican City, Biblioteca Vaticana.

Saarinen, R. (2013). "Renaissance Ethics and the European Reformations", in Lines, D.A. and S. Ebbersmeyer (eds), *Rethinking Virtue, Reforming Society: New Directions in Renaissance Ethics, c. 1350 - c. 1650*, Turnhout, Brepols, pp. 81-106.

Santinello, G. (1983) "Politica e filosofia alla Scuola di Rialto: Agostino Valier (1531-1606)", in *Quaderni del Centro tedesco di studi veneziani*, 24, pp. 1-24 [reprinted in his *Traduzione e dissenso nella filosofia veneta*, Padua, Antenore, 1991, pp. 116-139].

Scalvanti, O. (1898). *Inventario-regesto dell'Archivio Universitario di Perugia*, Perugia, Unione Tipografica Cooperativa.

Schmitt, C. B. (1965). "Aristotle as a Cuttlefish: The Origin and Development of a Renaissance Image", in *Studies in the Renaissance*, 12, pp. 60-72.

———, (1971). "Olympiodorus Alexandrinus philosophus", in P. O. Kristeller et al. (eds), *Catalogus translationum et commentariorum*, Washington, Catholic University of America, vol. II, pp. 199-204.

———, (1976). "Platon et Aristote dans les universités et les collèges du XVIe siècle. L'introduction de la philosophie platonicienne dans l'enseignement des universités à la Renaissance", in de Gandillac, M. and J.-C. Margolin (eds), *Platon et Aristote à la Renaissance*, Paris, Vrin, pp. 93-104.

———, (1982). "Andreas Camutius on the Concord of Plato and Aristotle with Scripture", in D.J. O'Meara (ed.), *Neoplatonism and Christian Thought*, Norfolk, SUNY Press, pp. 178-184.

———, (1983). *Aristotle and the Renaissance*, Cambridge, MA, Harvard University Press.

———, (1988). "The Rise of the Philosophical Textbook", in C.B. Schmitt and Q. Skinner (eds), *The Cambridge History of Renaissance Philosophy*, Cambridge, Cambridge University Press, pp. 792-804.

Schreiner, P. (1974). "Camozzi, Giovanni Battista", in *Dizionario Biografico degli Italiani*, 17, permanent link at https://www.treccani.it/enciclopedia/giovanni-battista-camozzi_%28Dizionario-Biografico%29/, [last accessed December 3, 2023].

Secchi, S. O. (1988). "Laici ed ecclesiastici fra sogno e ragione in un'accademia padovana del '500: gli Animosi", in *Archivio Veneto*, 130, pp. 5-30.

Sedley, D. (1999). "The Ideal of Godlikeness", in G. Fine (ed.), *Plato 2: Ethics, Politics, Religion, and the Soul*, Oxford, Oxford University Press, pp. 309-328.

Seidel Menchi, S. (1987). *Erasmo in Italia 1520-1580*, Turin, Bollati Boringhieri.

Serangeli, S. (1999). *Atti dello Studium Generale Maceratense dal 1551 al 1579*, Turin, Giappichelli.

Serassi, P. (1790). *Vita di Jacopo Mazzoni patrizio cesenate*, Rome, nella stamperia Pagliarini.

Sharratt, P. (1975). "Nicolaus Nancelius 'Petri Rami Vita.' Edited with an English Translation", in *Humanistica Lovaniensia*, 24, pp. 161-277.

Siraisi, N. (1987). *Avicenna in Renaissance Italy: The Canon and Medical Teaching in Italian in Universities After 1500*, Princeton, Princeton University Press.

Somfai, A. (2002). "The Eleventh-Century Shift in the Reception of Plato's *Timaeus* and Calcidius' *Commentary*", in *Journal of the Warburg and Courtauld Institutes*, 65, pp. 1-21.

Steenbeek, A. W. (1996). "The Christologies of Erasmus and Lefèvre", in Erasmus, *Opera omnia*. vol. IX/3. *Apologia ad Iacobum Fabrum Stapulensem*, Amsterdam, Elsevier, pp. 22-45.

(1993). *Storia dell'Università di Pisa 1343-1737. I*, Pisa, Pacini Editore.

Sturlese, L. and M. R. Pagnoni Sturlese. (1980). *Catalogo di manoscritti filosofici nelle biblioteche italiane*, Florence, Olschki.

Tarán, L. (1984). "*Amicus Plato sed magis amica veritas*: From Plato and Aristotle to Cervantes", in *Antike und Abendland*, 30, pp. 93-124.

Tavuzzi, M. (1990). "Chrysostomus Javelli O.P. (ca. 1470-1538). A Biobibliographical Essay. Part I: Biography", in *Angelicum*, 67, pp. 457-482.

———, (1991). "Chrysostomus Javelli O.P. (ca. 1470-1538). A Biobibliographical Essay. Part II: Bibliography", in *Angelicum*, 68, pp. 109-121.

———, (2007). *Renaissance Inquisitors: Dominican Inquisitors and Inquisitorial Districts in Northern Italy, 1474-1527*, Leiden-Boston, Brill.

———, "Chrysostomus Javelli OP (c. 1470–1540): A Biographical Introduction", in T. De Robertis and L. Burzelli (eds), *Chrysostomus Javelli. Pagan Philosophy and Christian Thought in the Renaissance*, Cham, Springer, 2023, pp. 3-28.

Tigerstedt, E. N. (1974). *The Decline and Fall of the Neoplatonic Interpretation of Plato: An Outline and Some Observations*, Helsinki, Societas Scientiarum Fennica.

Tracy, J. D. (1996). *Erasmus of the Low Countries*, Berkeley, University of California Press.

Van Der Poel, M. (1997). *Cornelius Agrippa, the Humanist Theologian and His Declamations*, Leiden, Brill.

Vanhaelen, M. (2010). "L'entreprise de traduction et d'exégèse de Ficin dans les années 1486-89: Démons et prophétie à l'aube de l'ère savonarolienne", in *Humanistica*, 4, pp. 125-136.

———, (2016). "What Is the Best Method to Study Philosophy? Sebastiano Erizzo and the 'Revival' of Plato in Sixteenth-Century Venice", in *Italian Studies*, 71, pp. 311-334.

———, (2021). "Éclectisme, aristotélisme et platonisme dans la pensée italienne du XVIe siècle", in D. Dumouchel et C. Leduc (eds), *Les -ismes et catégories historiographiques: Formation et usage à l'époque moderne*, Quebec City, Les Presses de l'Université Laval, pp. 95-112.

———, (2023)."Chrysostomus Javelli's Commentaries on Plato's Moral Philosophy", in T. De Robertis and L. Burzelli (eds), *Chrysostomus Javelli*, Cham, Springer, pp. 171-193.

Vasoli, C. (2001). "Platone allo Studio Fiorentino-Pisano", in *Rinascimento*, 41, 2nd s., pp. 39-69.

Venier, M. (2008). "Note su due traduzioni umanistiche del *Gorgia*", in C. Griggio and F. Vendruscolo (eds), *Suave mari magno... Studi offerti dai colleghi udinesi a Ernesto Berti*, Udine, Forum, pp. 232-236.

Verde, A. F. (1973). *Lo studio fiorentino (1473-1503). Ricerche e documenti. Vol. II. Docenti-dottorati*, Florence, Istituto Nazionale di Studi sul Rinascimento.

———, (1983). "Il 'Parere' del 1587 di Francesco Verino sullo Studio pisano", in *Firenze e la Toscana dei Medici nell'Europa del '500*. Atti del colloquio internazionale di Firenze, 9-14 giugno 1980, 2 vols, Florence, Olschki, I, pp. 72-94.

Vieillard-Baron, J.-L. (1979). *Platon et l'idéalisme allemand (1770-1830)*, Paris, Beauchesne.

Von Wille, D. (2004). "Javelli, Giovanni Crisostomo", in *Dizionario Biografico degli Italiani*, 62, permanent link at https://www.treccani.it/enciclopedia/giovanni-crisostomo-javelli_(Dizionario-Biografico), [last accessed December 3, 2023].

Watson, E. S. (1993). *Achille Bocchi and the Emblem Book as Symbolic Form*, Cambridge and New York, Cambridge University Press.

Westerink, L. G. (1968). "Ficino's Marginal Notes on Olympiodorus in Riccardi Greek MS 37", in *Traditio*, 24, pp. 351-378.

Index

Since the names of Plato and Aristotle appear almost on every page, the index only includes mentions of their works.

A
Acciaiuoli, Donato 133, 135
Acquaviva, Claudio 95
Agrippa, Henricus Cornelius 119-120, 140-141
Albuzio, Pietro 140
Alcinous 61
Aldobrandini, Cinzio 75, 92, 95
Aldobrandini, Pietro 75
Alemanni, Sforza 140
Alexander of Aphrodisias 32, 64, 93, 126, 147
Ammonius 66
Aristotle *Eudemian Ethics* 132-133; *Generation and Corruption* 46, 96; *On the Generation of the Animals* 65; *Metaphysics* 33, 132; *Meteorology* 31-32, 44, 46-47, 96; *Nicomachean Ethics* 22-24, 50, 52-54, 62, 70, 92-94, 98, 130-133, 139; *On the Heavens* 78, 96, 125; *On the Soul* 70, 78, 81, 96, 125, 134, 147; *Physics* 48, 78, 96; *Poetics* 98, 139; *Politics*, 17, 51, 98, 106, 130-131, 133-134, 139, 143-148; *Posterior Analytics* 133-134, 147; *Prior Analytics* 147; *Rhetoric* 32-33, 52, 94-95, 98, 139
Aquila, Sebastiano 16, 21-22
Aquinas, Thomas 29, 65-66, 71-72, 77, 81, 85, 93, 104
Argelati, Filippo 125
Aristarchus of Samos 25

Augustine of Hippo 36, 54, 71, 81-82, 94, 104
Augustis, Nicolaus de 121
Averroes (Ibn Rushd) 22, 26, 93, 122
Avicenna (Ibn Sina) 68, 121

B
Baldini, Artemio E. 117
Barbaro, Ermolao 65
Bardi, Girolamo 14, 82-85, 89
Bartocci, Barbara 14
Bellarmino, Roberto 19, 75
Benci, Francesco 49
Beni, Paolo 14, 18, 80, 86, 91-117, 123, 135
Bernardi, Antonio 43
Bessarion, Basil 12-13, 27, 34, 47, 71, 133-135, 137, 143-148
Bianchi, Luca 9, 12, 44
Boccadiferro, Ludovico 18, 31-32, 43-47
Bocchi, Achille 32, 44
Boethius, 24
Bonaventura of Bagnoregio 72
Boncompagni, Filippo 33
Borromeo, Carlo 136
Borromeo, Federico 18, 136, 138-139, 148
Boscagli, Cosimo 78-82, 85-86, 88
Botero, Giovanni 122
Bracciolini, Poggio 62
Brahe, Tycho 111
Brucker, Johann Jakob 18

INDEX

Bruni, Leonardo 41, 62
Bruno, Giordano 99
Buonamico, Lazzaro 131
Buratelli, Gabriele 86

C

Cajetanus, Thomas 72, 77
Calcidius, 24, 47, 68, 127
Calonymus, Calo 67
Camozzi, Giovan Battista 18, 31-37, 43-44, 50, 55
Campanella, Tommaso 99
Camuzio, Andrea 18, 122-124, 128, 140-141
Cannobio, Paolo da 129-131, 133
Capra, Bartolomeo 126
Cardano, Girolamo 122, 140
Carneades 51
Castiglioni, Filippo 122-123
Cato the Censor 144
Cattani da Diacceto, Francesco 13, 22, 30, 59-60, 76, 85
Cephalus 54
Champier, Symphorien 120-121, 123
Charpentier, Jacques 62, 71, 81-82, 129
Ciampoli, 139
Cicero 9, 32, 42, 46-47, 50-54, 56-57, 79, 82, 98, 111
Clement VIII (pope) 16, 19, 75, 95-96
Copernicus, Nicolaus 112
Cremonini, Cesare 141
Crispo, Giovanni Battista 74

D

Damascius, 10, 31, 35, 37
Del Soldato, Eva 7, 15
Deucalion 80
Dillon, John 11
Dionysius the Areopagite 66, 73
Donato, Bernardino 123-124
Duchesne, Léger 128

E

Equicola, Mario 120
Erizzo, Sebastiano 33-35, 86
Eusebius of Caesarea 75
Eustratius of Nicaea 130, 132

F

Farnese, Alessandro 44
Farra, Alessandro 140
Fellina, Simone 13
Ferrari, Giulio 121
Ferrari, Ottaviano 15, 126-135, 139, 141, 143-148
Ficino, Marsilio 7, 10, 12-14, 22-23, 27, 30-31, 34, 36, 38, 40, 44, 47, 51, 53, 55, 57, 59, 63, 65, 67-70, 72-73, 75-76, 80, 82, 84-86, 89, 102, 120, 122, 135, 137
Filalteo, Lucilio 131
Fornari, Callisto 124
Fornari, Girolamo 121
Fox Morcillo, Sebastián 65, 71, 81
Fracastoro, Girolamo 47
Frigillanus, Matthaeus 65

G

Gaffarel, Jacques 84
Galen 44, 47, 64, 78, 123, 140
Galilei, Galileo 83-84, 98, 111, 139
Galland, Pierre 128
Gaza, Theodore 16, 21, 135, 147-148
Gellius, Aulus 79, 82
George of Trebizond (*Trapezuntius*) 143-144
Gessner, Konrad 123
Giannini, Tommaso 16-17
Giles of Viterbo 27, 72
Giovanni d'Arcolo 121
Giustiniani, Benedetto 95
Gonzaga, Ercole 48
Gonzaga, Scipione 49
Gregory XIII (pope) 33

H
Habsburg-Gonzaga, Eleonora 140
Hankins, James 11
Hasdai ibn Shaprut 67
Henry of Ghent 77
Hermes Trismegistus 59, 72, 76, 109
Hippocrates of Kos 36
Homer 25, 53, 57
Horace 54, 79, 82

I
Iactilia Ben Joseph 84
Iamblichus 36, 47, 59, 73, 82, 125
Isaiah 84
Isocrates 37

J
Javelli, Chrysostomus 12, 14, 28-31, 86, 108, 114
Justin Martyr 73

K
Kepler, Johannes 111
Kristeller, Paul Oskar 21

L
Lactantius 82
Laertius, Diogenes 10, 82
Lefèvre d'Étaples, Jacques 121, 125
Leibniz, Gottfried 18
Leonico Tomeo, Niccolò 22, 65
Libri, Giulio 140
Liceti, Fortunio 84
Lipsius, Justus 80
Livy 53
Lollino, Luigi 38
Luther, Martin 26

M
Machiavelli, Niccolò 106, 116
Madruzzo, Cristoforo 18, 123
Manutius, Aldus 133
Marcello, Cristoforo 76, 92

Maurizi, Leone 140-141
Mazzoni, Jacopo 13, 61, 74-79, 81-82, 85-87, 140
Medici, Francesco I de' (Grand Duke) 22, 140
Medici, Giuliano de' 82
Michael of Ephesus 66
Montecatini, Antonio 17
Muret, Marc Antoine 18, 25, 32, 49-57, 94
Musso, Cornelio 121-122, 128, 141
Muzzoli, Giovan Paolo 138, 148

N
Nani, Agostino 40
Naudé, Gabriel 83
Niavis, Paulus 21, 41
Nicomachus 132
Nizolio, Mario 132
Nogarola, Lodovico 45, 47

O
Olympiodorus 9-10, 12, 31, 33-37, 55

P
Paleotti, Camillo 138, 148
Papazzoni, Flaminio 15, 18, 135-139, 141, 148
Patrizi, Francesco 7, 14, 16, 18-19, 22, 74, 76, 94-96, 99, 116-117, 138-139, 141
Pellegrini, Lelio 95
Pellegrini, Tommaso 39
Pendasio, Federico 48-49, 56-57, 137
Pereira, Benedict 77, 80
Philoponus, John 65, 67
Piccolomini, Ascanio 82
Piccolomini, Francesco 12, 37-39, 71, 81-82, 89
Pico della Mirandola, Giovanni 76, 122
Pinelli, Gian Vincenzo 48, 92, 95, 98, 126-127
Pinzi, Aurelio 29
Pius IV (pope) 32

Plato: *Axiochus* 103; *Apology* 40-42, 55; *Charmides* 79, 84, 100; *Clitophon* 84; *Cratylus* 100, 127; *Crito* 100; *Epinomis* 17; *Euthydemus* 84; *Euthyphro* 103, 116; *First Alcibiades* 31, 33-37, 50, 55, 76, 127; *Gorgias* 16, 21, 33, 40-42, 51, 55, 84, 100; *Hipparchus* 61-63, 70-71, 73, 87; *Laches* 79, 100; *Laws* 17, 44, 84, 100; *Letters* 21; *Lovers* 21, 70; *Lysis* 22, 100; *Meno* 78, 84, 100; *Parmenides* 87, 100; *Phaedo* 34, 78-79, 81-82; *Phaedrus* 84, 94, 100; *Philebus* 87; *Protagoras* 71, 82; *Republic*, 12, 17, 49-55, 76, 78-79, 82, 84, 94, 98, 100, 130, 133, 134, 139, 143, 145; *Second Alcibiades* 84; *Statesman* 78, 84; *Symposium* 84, 87, 120, 139; *Timaeus*, 11, 14, 16, 22, 24, 43-49, 55-56, 61, 63-70, 72, 78-80, 83, 87, 95, 97, 100-101, 103, 107-110, 116, 125, 127, 139-140

Pletho, Georgius (Gemistus) 124, 148
Plotinus 9, 30, 36, 47, 59, 67, 72-73, 76, 82, 137
Plutarch 50, 127, 144
Pomponazzi, Pietro 12, 27, 121
Porphyry 47, 59, 82
Proclus 12, 22, 30-31, 35-37, 47, 53-55, 59, 67, 69, 76, 82, 125, 127, 137

Q
Querenghi, Antonio 92, 95, 98

R
Ramus, Petrus 128-129
Rovere, Francesco Maria II della (Duke) 92
Rovida, Cesare 124-129, 131
Rustico, Pietro Antonio 121

S
Sartorius, Adam 49
Schmitt, Charles B. 21, 111, 117
Scutellius, Nicolaus 71
Selvatico, Giovan Battista 125
Seneca 50-51
Serres, Jean de 14, 86
Servius Sulpicius 53
Simplicius 23, 38, 64, 125, 127, 134, 147
Sixtus V (pope) 74
Socrates 35, 37, 42, 51, 54, 73, 80, 82, 132
Sommaia, Girolamo da 79
Syrianus 76, 125

T
Tacitus 50-51, 79, 82
Taegio, Bartolomeo 130
Tasso, Torquato 92, 95
Telesio, Bernardino 99
Themistius 64-65, 125
Theodoretus of Cyrus 75
Theophrastus 33
Thrasymachus 82
Tiepolo, Stefano 37-39, 82
Tomasi, Carlo 78
Tomasini, Giacomo Filippo 38, 44
Tomitano, Bernardino 92
Trivulzio, Catalano 29
Turnèbe, Adrien 128

U
Usimbardi, Piero 63

V
Valier, Agostino 16, 18, 25, 40-42, 50, 56, 94, 131, 138, 148
Valori, Baccio 60-63, 72
Vanhaelen, Maude 7, 11, 122
Vettori, Pier 22
Vieri de', Francesco (Verino Primo) 89
Vieri de', Francesco (Verino Secondo) 7-8, 13-14, 22, 60-74, 79, 85-89, 139-140

Vimercato, Francesco 15, 80, 127-129, 131, 139, 141
Virgil 54, 57
Vives, Juan Luis 81

X
Xenophon 49-50, 144

Z
Zeller, Eduard 25
Zabarella, Jacopo 93
Zimara, Marcantonio 8, 93
Zimara, Teofilo 8
Zoroaster 59, 72, 76
Zwinger, Theodor 86-87